The Customer
Comes Second

The Customer
Comes Second

**Put Your People First and
Watch 'em Kick Butt**

Hal F. Rosenbluth
AND
Diane McFerrin Peters

HarperBusiness
An Imprint of HarperCollins*Publishers*

HarperCollins books may be purchased for educational, business, or sales
promotional use. For information, please write to:
Special Markets Department, HarperCollins Publishers Inc.,
10 East 53rd Street, New York, New York 10022.

Designed by Joy O'Meara

Library of Congress Cataloging-In-Publication has been applied for.

ISBN 0-06-052656-4

02   03   04   05   06   RRD   10   9   8   7   6   5   4   3   2

In dedication to the associates of Rosenbluth International and our clients who inspire us to provide service from our hearts.

Contents

Prologue ▌ ix

Part One: The Power of People

1   How It All Begins ▌ 3

2   Happiness in the Workplace ▌ 7

3   Finding the Right People ▌ 28

4   Perpetual Learning: A Secret Weapon ▌ 53

5   Service Is an Attitude, an Art, and a Process ▌ 73

6   The Creation of a Culture ▌ 97

7   The Birth and Nurturing of Ideas ▌ 115

8   The Gardening Process ▌ 128

Part Two: Inventing the Future

9   Inventing the Future ▌ 147

10   Technology as a Tool ▌ 157

11   Look Around You ▌ 184

12   Open Partnerships ▌ 194

13   Blazing New Trails ▌ 209

Afterword: A Lot to Digest ▌ 221

Epilogue: A Changed World ▌ 225

Notes ▌ 265

Bibliography ▌ 267

Index ▌ 269

Prologue

If today's business world doesn't have you simultaneously feeling exhilarated, exhausted, excited, dizzy, dazzled, scared, and confident then you're probably living in some other world, and God only knows how you got your hands on a copy of this book.

I've now been working for more than twenty-five years, and each year it gets more challenging. Lately, however, the pace of change and the constant velocity in which business models must be altered to remain successful has exceeded even my wildest prognostications. It is with this background in mind that I have reluctantly decided to update a book that my co-author Diane McFerrin Peters and I wrote nearly a decade ago.

Interestingly enough, what worked then still works today. In fact, the premise on which this book is written is perhaps the single most important ingredient for success in today's wild-ass business environment. It is, by far, the only element that can lead you to that elusive *sustainable competitive advantage.*

In 1992 we were presented with an opportunity to retrace the steps of our inadvertent journey when we wrote the first version of *The Customer Comes Second.* Now, a decade later, much has changed, and we have received requests from every corner of the world to share the next generation of ideas outlined in the original version and reveal our latest practices. This new version of the book blends the best of our original ideas together with our newest approaches, uncovering lessons learned along the way.

A lot of great articles and books have been written about business since *The Customer Comes Second* first appeared in 1992, and I've probably read most of them. In the last few years everything seems to be about e-this or e-that. For the most part, their theoretical shelf life seems to be about nine to twelve months—that's how quickly things change. What hasn't changed, and appears to have outlasted every trend for the last decade, has been the need for business to attract, retain, and develop astonishingly great people. It is with this in mind that we have updated and re-released this book.

I hope that you enjoy its contents and that it motivates you to cleanse your company of what is wrong and replace it with what is right, humanistic, and competitively essential. You owe it to yourself, your people, your company, and your stakeholders.

CULTURAL METAMORPHOSIS

Just a couple of decades ago, we were like most companies. Back then, if someone had described our company to me as it is today, I would have thought he or she were crazy. I also would have given just about anything for it to be true.

A lot has happened; much of it by accident, some by design. But the transformations our company has gone through are being studied and written about everywhere. We didn't solicit the curiosity and attention, but we found ourselves in the middle of it.

Over the past twenty-five years, our revenues have jumped from $20 million to $6.2 billion, while maintaining profitability above industry standards. Because of that growth and our unorthodox style, we have been inundated continually with questions about the "secret" to success. Our secret is controversial. It centers around our basic belief that *companies must put their people—not their customers—first.*

You might wonder how our clients feel about this. For our people, the clients are priority number one. Our company has built a solid reputation in the field of customer service (in fact, our client retention rate is 98 percent—unheard of in our industry), but we have actually done it by focusing inside, on our own people.

Companies have profound and far-reaching effects on the lives of the people who work for them, so it becomes the obligation of companies to make the effects positive. All too often companies bring stress, fear, and frustration to their people—feelings they bring home with them each night. This creates problems at home that people bring back to work in the morning. The cycle is both terrible and typical, but not what most companies would want as their legacy. It's certainly not what our company wants: especially when there are so many things we can all do to enrich the lives of our people.

If this all sounds simple, it's not. Let's take a look at where we came from, where we are today, and just how we got there. Here begins the charting of a road map for change.

LONG, LONG AGO . . .

Our company began more than a century ago as a forerunner to travel agencies as we know them today. My great-grandfather, Marcus Rosenbluth, founded the company in 1892 to provide transportation for immigrants from Europe to the United States via steamship.

It was a full-service business. The company acted as a bank to help families save for the fifty-dollar ticket. Because he spoke nine languages, Marcus was able to help sort out the immigration paperwork and facilitate the process of reuniting families. Through the network he built, he even helped immigrants find work in their new country.

THE SEEDS OF CHANGE

The company survived the astronomical changes in the world around it and thrived. Some eighty-two years after its founding, Rosenbluth was firmly entrenched as the largest and strongest travel agency in the Philadelphia area. The firm's success was indisputable. Then I joined the firm.

I didn't start out to change our company from sixty disparate and somewhat nasty personalities, to six thousand friends with a common desire to help one another. I just didn't have the schooling or experience to know much better.

When I joined our company in 1974, I found an organization focused almost solely on clients and fractionally on its people. It wasn't by design that our people came second. I just think that the company's management was so overwhelmingly consumed by our customers that they lost track of the fact that somebody had to serve them.

What I noticed from the start was that hardly anyone in the company liked one another, and for good reason. Most weren't inherently nice people. In my mind, not a great formula for inspirational customer service, let alone associate morale and profitability. The only sustainable variable was stress. In the long run, unhappy people will produce unhappy service and deteriorating profitability.

My dilemma, of course, was that I was twenty-two, just out of college, and any suggestions I made were surely going to be dismissed as immature and brash. So I did what any aspiring young turk might do: I did nothing. Well almost nothing. Actually, I just wandered around the company working for one lousy manager after another. Each added to a growing list of negative role models I had come in contact with over the years.

There was my junior high baseball coach who berated me in front of my teammates, family, and friends after I misjudged a line drive in center field and we lost the championship game. There was my high school disciplinarian who took it upon himself to invite my mother into his office to show her my bloodied shirt that had resulted from a fight in the men's room an hour earlier. And my favorite, my English teacher who tossed me from her class claiming that I was undermining her authority and was about to undertake a campus coup. What actually happened was that she was stupid enough to challenge the class with the old, "If anyone thinks they can teach this class better than me, just raise your hand." Mine went up and the rest is legend at good old Cheltenham High, just outside of Philadelphia.

Fortunately, I learned a lot from all these negative role models. First, never be one myself. Second, in each case it was my friends who came to my aid and stuck by me, and for that I'll be eternally grateful.

Some say your life is molded at an early age; in my case they were right. I learned the most valuable business lesson before I was seventeen: Friends never let friends down.

I was determined to eventually build a company of friends. Not that I would set out to hire friends. In fact, I don't think I ever have. I would just live by two basic musts. First, create and sustain a climate that breeds friendships, and second, only hire nice people. This formula has worked for more than two decades now, and it has become our sustainable competitive advantage. There is nothing we can't accomplish when we set out to do the right thing. None of us would have it any other way.

I admit, I didn't want to join the family business in the first place, which probably made me look at it with an unusually harsh eye. What I saw was a flourishing business held back by politics; powerful individual efforts thwarted by a lack of teamwork. This was an environment I didn't relish working in, so it was likely many of my colleagues didn't like it much either.

Change has to start somewhere, and here it began with a group of mavericks who pioneered our corporate travel department, at the time a low-profile start-up unit. Today it makes up more than 90 percent of our company's operations.

Prior to airline deregulation there was not much of a market for corporate travel services. But when fares and schedules began to change by the minute in the new deregulated environment, corporations saw the impact business travel could have on their lives and their bottom lines. That's when corporate travel management skyrocketed for us.

This budding operation wasn't a place for creatures of habit, lovers of the status quo. Every day meant change, a whirlwind of activity, a future unfolding by the minute. The nine-to-five routine became more like five (A.M.) to nine (P.M.) in this uncharted territory.

I was drawn to it instinctively, as though I were coming home. This was the perfect place for the transformation of our company to begin. I had no specific plan for the change but I wanted to capture the spirit I had found in this unsung department, a spirit of cooperation, friendship, fierce dedication, and hard work. I knew we had to concentrate, above all, on the people *providing* the service. From there, everything else would fall into place.

THE TURNING POINT

The changes began in our little corner of the company, and the turning point came when we put our people first. It didn't happen overnight. A sweeping change like that takes commitment, persistence, and time. People have to change and so do the infrastructure and systems that support them.

Such change can start as a grassroots movement. It can be embraced by top leadership and filter throughout an organization. Or, as in our case, it can take hold in one segment of a company and spread laterally. The only important thing is for it to start.

We're talking about a change that puts the people in organizations above everything else. They are cared for, valued, empowered, and motivated to care for their clients. When a company puts its people first, the results are spectacular. Their people are inspired to provide a level of service that truly comes from the heart. It can't be faked. The only way to emulate it is to create it from scratch.

When something this positive is set in motion, it gets noticed. It spreads. It's natural—compatible with the way we are supposed to live as human beings. No longer must we each be one person at home and another at work.

At Rosenbluth, these changes produced very tangible results in our underdog department, and company leaders took note. Everyone around us wanted to work in an environment like ours. Our people were happy, fulfilled, and excelling, and it showed. Clients enjoyed working with our people and they let us know it.

It was just a matter of time before, department by department, our entire organization was completely transformed. Today, people-first behavior permeates our company and impacts everything we do.

We begin by hiring the right kind of people, ones who will carry the torch. This emphasis extends to our training programs, which are as much philosophical as technical. It shapes our supplier relationships, our strategic relationships with our clients, and even positively affects our home lives. In fact, this is a way of life for us.

Focusing on our people is the foundation. The many other components that make up our company, the tools we utilize, and the theories by which we live all stem from this basic belief.

Just how we changed and the specific programs we put in place to help us make those transitions are explained in the coming chapters. We'll also take a look at the methods used to monitor our progress and the results we've attained along the way. But first, it might be helpful to know a little about us.

WHO ARE WE AND WHAT
IN THE WORLD DO WE DO?

We are a global travel management firm that operates five primary lines of business. Three travel-related lines of business are corporate travel, meeting and motivation management (programs that motivate and inspire people to reach goals their company has set, most often with travel as the reward), and leisure or "vacation" travel. The fourth travel-related business is our e-procurement arm. The fifth sector of our business is a service company offering customer care solutions. More about this in Chapter 11.

Our most explosive growth during the past twenty-five years has been in the corporate arena, representing 95 percent of our travel volume. By consolidating companies' business travel, we help them to realize gains in time and money. We do this through purchasing power, information, efficiencies, and comprehensive services that begin before the travelers even plan their trips and continue long after their return.

Outside our industry, we're not a household name, but our clients are. We are fortunate to count among them some of the most highly respected firms in the world, including a significant percentage of the

Fortune 500 *global* companies. We manage the corporate travel accounts of 1,500 corporations, and our client list is the envy of our industry. The firms we work with are clearly "best of class" in their respective industries.

There are more than 5,300 people in our company in nearly 1,000 offices covering 50 states and 53 countries around the world, on all 6 habitable continents, from Istanbul to Dubai; from Sao Paulo to Stockholm, and Copenhagen to Caracas. Our headquarters are in Philadelphia. At last count, our annual sales volume was more than $6.2 billion and growing at a rate of more than $1 billion in new business, annually. Rosenbluth International is a privately held company.

We didn't conduct any studies or create a plan for the changes we made in our company. We decided that as we grew from a regional to a global company we would need to formalize what we had captured, in order to retain and nurture it. So we began to look closely at the things we were doing and how we were doing them. From there, our theories took shape.

We've shared our philosophies and practices with a great many companies. In fact, one of the primary reasons for writing the first version of this book some years ago was to be able to offer written answers to the many questions brought to us by companies from all industries and parts of the world.

I hesitated, at first, when I thought about sharing our ideas in an open forum such as this—partly because I'm not overly comfortable doing so and partly out of concern about giving away competitive information. But I decided that what we have learned is too important not to share. Perhaps, by sharing what we have learned, we can help others have similar results. The best part of all is that it's the right thing to do, the right way to lead. Everyone wins.

A PREVIEW OF THINGS TO COME

The pages that follow do not tell just the "story of our company." This is intended to be a reference manual of factors that contributed to one company's success, of ideas that can be borrowed, adapted, elaborated upon, customized, and improved for application to your business.

I have tried to create a reference you can turn to periodically to try some of the ideas in your company. They can be implemented either together or separately. It's not necessary to employ them all in order for any one idea to be effective. They are intended to be cherry-picked as you find appropriate.

With these ideas, we turned our organization upside down and achieved results we never dreamed of. Ours is the story of an old company doing new things. Companies can change. We are living proof. It is our conviction that companies *must* change. We have that obligation to our clients and the people we employ, and it is the only way to ensure our place in the future.

The ideas I've included cut across industry and country. They center around *people*, so they can apply to any business. You will find them organized into two parts. Part One explains just how important it is to value and nurture your people, and explains ways to do that. Part Two extends people-first philosophies and practices to other aspects of leading your business, like technology, strategic planning, and partnerships.

An epilogue talks candidly about our journey forward since the events of September 11, 2001, in an industry affected like no other. And an afterword summarizes key ideas to put to work in your organization. I hope you will find these practices as helpful as we have. Happy reading.

PART ONE
The Power of People

It never made any sense to me that "telling people to care about their clients" could have any effect if those same people didn't feel cared about by their employer. Caring is an emotion. For centuries companies have lost sight of the fact that you can't delegate an emotion. Imagine if I sent out an e-mail to the six thousand people whom we employ in twenty-four countries, with the following message: "Starting next Tuesday, we must begin caring more about our clients."

I'll tell you, if I were to receive that message, the first thing I'd think about was whether or not the company cared about me. If it didn't, why should I care about what the company wants from me? Caring has to begin with the company, then emanate to its clients through caring people in the right environment.

People are truly the most powerful asset an organization can have. Without them, everything comes to a halt. Without their loyalty, motivation, and best effort, the most that can be expected is mediocrity.

It makes perfect sense, and these days it's popular to say the words. But it's not so easy to live them every day, everywhere. That's why most companies don't. But once the foundation is laid, and a "no-buckling-when-it-gets-tough" commitment is made, it can be done. It's well worth the effort.

To help you build that foundation, in Part One, you'll learn how to:

- Start out right
- Create a happy, productive workplace
- Find and attract the best talent
- Foster a learning environment
- Cultivate stellar service
- Nurture and grow a powerful culture
- Stimulate new ideas
- Prune your company to keep it healthy

CHAPTER ONE
How It All Begins

Most people can't sleep the night before their first day of a new job. They probably decided two weeks in advance what they'd wear. They can't wait to get started, meet new people, see everything, do great things.

After all the anticipation, their first day is usually a big yawn. They find themselves hidden away in a room somewhere, filling out forms. What a mistake! First impressions are lasting. Is that how most companies would like to be remembered? I doubt it. That's not the perception we'd like to create.

First days at our company are a little different. Every person who joins our team, regardless of position, department, level, location, or line of business, begins their career by spending the first day at work with their immediate leader. The day is spent having one's leader provide a personal orientation to the company. Leaders talk about values and work ethic, as well as introduce the new associate to everyone they will be working with. Typically, the leader will take the new associate to lunch or have a group gathering to celebrate their arrival. While every leader has a handbook on all critical information that needs to be imparted, each leader is free to do so in his or her own way. The key is to make the associate feel comfortable and welcome. With very few exceptions (like accelerated implementation of new business) every new associate, together with others who have recently joined the company, come either to our World Headquarters in Philadelphia or to our European Headquarters in London during the first quarter of their employment.

A lot of people never get to see their headquarters. They may never meet the top officers. Here, they do both. They also learn about what's really important in the company. And they have fun.

There are substantial benefits to this program. No doubt, it's a morale booster. It encourages buy-in from the start. It also prompts buy-out, which is important. Giving people an in-depth look at our culture lets them make a well-informed decision about whether or not this is the right place for them, and that helps us.

A new associate orientation program is a valuable tool to maintain culture as a company grows. Everyone gets the story straight. Everyone hears the same message. It starts people off on the right foot. It's really a tool from which all companies could benefit. I'll explain the way our program works.

The day begins with time spent learning about one another, followed by a historical look at the company they have joined. Next, we immerse the group in our people-focus, discussing the importance of perception and teamwork and the value of differences. We look into ergonomics and safety, communication and change.

We then focus on our clients, studying their expectations and concentrating on quality. Next is a business overview to ensure all new associates understand the goals, objectives, and workings of our business, which is built around our clients. We conduct an overview of the company's structure, so people know where to go for what they need. Finally, we spend some time on elegant service and elegant language (more about these in Chapter 6).

We immerse our new associates in the company's philosophies and values and they begin to see their role in the future of our company. People are always surprised to learn that they've been brought to headquarters just for philosophical training. Once we tell them how important these principles are to our company, they begin to see the emphasis we place on our values.

Next, the group tours our headquarters, stopping to meet as many individuals as possible. Then on to the culmination of the program, afternoon tea—with a twist. Our new associates are served by officers of the company. This is by far the most memorable portion of the program. People continually approach me years into their career, to tell me how much of an impression the tea made on them.

There's a service message behind the choice of a tea for the activity. A cup of tea can come from a vending machine, it can be tossed to you in a diner, or it can be elegantly served to you at a high tea. The tea is just a product; the service surrounding it makes all the difference in the world.

By serving our new associates, we're showing them that we're happy they're part of our team, they're important to us, and our people come first. We talk about what we believe in. We discuss what's on their minds. Nothing is off-limits.

Once when I was serving tea, a new associate asked me how much money I make. I told him when it's a good year I make a lot and when it's a bad year I take it on the chin. Another asked me what I would do if I weren't CEO of Rosenbluth. I told her I'd like to be the Philly Phanatic because I'm a closet clown and I love baseball. But most of the questions are about the future of the company.

One point we make very clear is that it's *their* company now, and each time they begin a comment or question with "Your company . . ." I correct them and have them start again, saying, "Our company . . ." I think it's important for them to feel a sense of ownership from day one.

While this is our core orientation, we have used a variety of approaches through the years to ingrain these points. For example, our orientations have included skits designed to elevate service, where small groups create the worst service experience they can think of. With scowls on their faces, they talk about all the terrible service episodes in their lives. The group decides which service experience is the worst and then embellishes it, making it as ugly as it can be. Next, they return to their groups and make their service story a positive one, improving on it in every way they can imagine. Then they perform the good-service experience in a skit.

When we've done this exercise, people expect that's all, but it's not. Even the very best of service can be improved upon. So back to their groups they go to create superior service—elegant service. But the point is that it shouldn't even stop there. Service can be taken from bad to good and from good to exceptional, but there are infinite ways it can go beyond exceptional—and that's the range we're interested in.

Starting Out Right

A SUMMARY

▮ Training should begin with an orientation program, which every new person completes before beginning his or her first day at work. First impressions are lasting and both good and bad habits begin early. Everyone should go through the same program, regardless of the job or location.

▮ Consider bringing new hires to your company's headquarters early in their employment (ours visit within their first quarter with the company).

▮ Orientation should include an overview of all areas of the company, so people know where to go when they need something.

▮ Be sure to include plenty of information on the philosophy and values of the company. This helps maintain the culture and encourages buy-in (or buy-out) up front.

▮ Try making a special tradition part of your company's orientation. Our high tea has long been one of our program's strengths.

CHAPTER TWO

Happiness in the Workplace

Does the proverb "A picture is worth a thousand words" really ring true? On a hunch that it might, we instituted a program, well over a decade ago, that has turned out to be one of the company's most memorable, and most emulated.

We sent a letter to one hundred associates asking them to draw a picture of what the company means to them. We enclosed construction paper and a box of crayons wrapped in ribbon.

Almost immediately, we began receiving people's drawings. The individuality of each was delightful. The company doesn't mean exactly the same thing to any two people. But there were some very common themes: happy faces; illustrations of service to clients and fellow associates; and lots and lots of salmon. (The salmon is our corporate mascot.)

Since our initial mailings we have repeated the program often. We've learned that while the vast majority of drawings we receive are positive, great value also comes from the *unhappy* pictures, and occasionally there are some. We're delighted to see that people feel free to submit negative drawings, and most importantly, these drawings uncover problems we can tackle.

The most chilling drawing I think I've ever received was on two pages. The first showed a family sitting around a fire, children playing, kittens and puppies. The picture was colorful, warm, and cozy. People were happy. I felt happy just looking at it. At the top it said, "BEFORE."

When I turned the page I was in for a rude awakening. The second sketch was in pencil. It was stark and cold. There was a person alone and shivering. The fire was out. The room was completely bare. I was horrified. At the top it said, "NOW."

I called and had a long talk with the artist and learned that an announcement had been made in her office that some of their work was being moved to another site. People there thought they were going to lose their jobs. In fact, plans had already been made for the people affected to be trained for a new function that was moving to their office, and it was to be a step up for everyone. Unfortunately, *that* information wasn't shared with them.

I don't think I could have understood her feelings any better from a conversation than from those pictures. And I wonder if that conversation would have happened without the pictures.

We are also concerned about those who receive the mailing but never respond to it, so we check with each person. Not everyone feels comfortable drawing, and that's not a problem. But there are a few who hesitate to tell us what they think, and that's a problem. So we talk with each of them to ensure any concerns are dispelled.

To really learn from this exercise, you need to discuss the drawing with the artist, unless they provide a detailed explanation. One recent drawing I received depicted a box with neatly drawn, colorful geometric shapes inside. Surrounding the box were squiggles and scribbles. During a discussion, the associate explained to me that the neat and colorful box was our office in New York City, and the chaos surrounding it was the outside world. It's unlikely anyone would have understood the meaning of the drawing without such a discussion, and discussions like these can lead to new ideas and solutions to challenges you might not even be aware you had.

We've learned so much from the program that we decided to extend it to our clients, and the response has been overwhelming. One of the most interesting findings is the clear similarity between the drawings submitted by our clients and those done by our associates. It is especially fascinating to match up drawings from specific clients with the drawings of the associates who serve their account. It has proven to be an effective gauge of happiness, service, perception, and communication.

How Can We Be Serious About This?
The Basis for the People-First Philosophy

Companies must put their people first. Yes, even before their customers. There. Now I've said it. I know it's controversial. It makes most people nervous just to hear it, but it works.

Once we were conducting a site visit with a potential client, who visited a variety of departments in several of our offices. At the conclusion of the tour one of the company's executives actually asked if we were some sort of cult. Everyone was so happy, that he was skeptical. I know he was half-joking, but it struck home with us just how different we are. He decided he liked that, and the company is now our client.

On the surface, it all might sound like a lot of fluff—but this is serious stuff. When we first tell people what we're all about they usually look at us kind of funny, but as the saying goes, "The proof of the pudding is in the eating." Of course the aim is to win, and this is how we do it.

There is probably nothing we believe in more strongly than the importance of happiness in the workplace. It is absolutely the key to providing superior service. Of course our clients are the reason for our existence as a company, but to serve our clients best we have to put our people first.

The principle behind it is straightforward. It's our people who provide service to our clients. The highest achievable level of service comes from the heart. So, the company that reaches its people's hearts will provide the very best service. It's the nicest thing we could possibly do for our *clients*. They have come to learn that by being second, they come out ahead.

It's kind of like the old story about the horse and the cart. Let's say our people represent the horses. If we put our clients in the cart and put them out front they aren't going to go very far. We can have champagne and caviar in that cart and our clients still aren't going anywhere as long as the horses are behind them.

We feel that way about our people. If we put our people first, they'll put our clients first. Sure, we have to do a lot of other things right too, but we contend that this is the aspect of service most often forgotten, and that's why it's the one I talk about most.

According to a theory of psychologist Abraham Maslow, human needs fall into a natural hierarchy from most to least pressing. These needs are related to physiology, safety, social acceptance, self-esteem, and self-actualization. People are driven to satisfy the most critical need and then will move on to the next most important.

If a person has food, clothing, shelter, security, companionship, and self-esteem, only then will he or she be motivated by self-improvement. While most companies provide for people's basic provisions, we contend that it's essential to create an environment in which higher-level needs are satisfied.

If people are concerned about job security, internal politics, or other typical workplace frustrations, they're not going to be concentrating on the customer. They'll be worrying about themselves. We try to create a climate in which our people leave those worries to the company so they can and will focus solely on our clients.

Companies are only fooling themselves when they believe that "The Customer Comes First." People do not inherently put the customer first, and they certainly don't do it because their employer expects it. Only when people know what it feels like to be first in someone else's eyes can they sincerely share that feeling with others.

We're not saying choose your people over your customers. We're saying focus on your people *because* of your customers. That way everybody wins.

Setting the Tone
The Importance of Accessible Leadership

In a 1991 issue of *Working Woman*, contributing editor and author Nancy Austin writes about Bill Arnold, then president of Centennial Medical Center in Nashville: "One of his first acts at Centennial was to shatter sacrosanct management tradition by yanking his office door from its hinges and suspending it from the lobby ceiling to underscore his commitment to an open-door policy."

Though I've always had an open-door policy, recently, I ripped down the walls to my office and replaced them with glass so everyone could see what I was up to. People emulate those who lead them, so starting at the top and emanating throughout the organization, leaders must always be cognizant of the examples they set. In our company, the leadership approach is to be approachable.

We need contact at every level. It's the only way to avoid the purification of information as it filters its way up the organization. It's human nature to want to share only the good news with those who lead us and to try to fix problems quietly.

But we often learn more from our failures than we do from our successes. We need to know about problems that are being solved as well as those that are not. We can't ever look at time with our people as an interruption. It's the most important thing we do, and we can never do enough of it.

My Day Is Yours
A Program to Reach People

About twelve years ago I initiated a program in which anyone in the company could spend a day with me. Whatever my day includes, their day includes. They read what I read. They are a part of every phone call, client visit, meeting, or whatever else makes up my day. The only exception is any confidential human resource issue that might betray another associate's privacy.

We call this our "Associate of the Day" program, and at first, to launch it, it was more formalized and structured. Today, associates spend a day or even an hour or two with any leader of their choice. Sometimes it's me and sometimes they choose a leader of an area in which they have a particular interest.

The program has been a tremendous success. Our associates learn more about the company, they get a good look at the overall picture of the organization, and they return to their jobs with renewed enthusiasm for the importance of their part in our goals. They also come away with a greater understanding of the level of responsibility their leaders carry.

On the other hand, the program has helped our leaders learn more about the needs, aspirations, and talents of our people. It has helped us spot future leaders and earmark growth areas for them. It helps people chart their career paths, as well. Someone may think they'd like a career in a particular department and after spending a day there, they might decide it's not for them. They learn what a department really does before working toward becoming a part of it and possibly being disappointed later.

The program also forces us to take a good look at how we're spending our days. Quite honestly, when someone is watching you, it's embarrassing to have a slow moment, to procrastinate on a project or decision, or not to give your best every minute of the day.

Feeling Like a Sandwich
A Program to Reach Middle-Level Leaders

They say that often the middle child in a family feels somewhat forgotten. The eldest child benefits from the sense of excitement that parents feel over their new role. The baby of a family is often spoiled not just by the parents, but also by brothers and sisters. But the middle child sometimes gets lost in the shuffle.

It seems to be the same with middle-level leaders. A great deal is expected of them. They're placed in the challenging position of communicating what comes from above to those on the front line and vice versa. They're caught in the middle.

It seems more and more companies are recognizing the benefits of supporting their front-line people. And we don't need to worry too much about those at the top—but what about the people in the middle?

In our company, the Associate of the Day program attracts mostly entry-level associates, and while the program is open to everyone, these are the people I most hoped would participate. On the other hand, I meet with our top leaders almost daily. So we needed a program to check in with our middle-level leaders.

I began by meeting with each of them on a regular basis, but soon realized how much they were missing by not having that same uninterrupted time to meet with one another, as busy as we all get.

So a few years ago, we began to hold an annual meeting of our entire middle management team. For our WorldWide Leaders Meeting, we gather together everyone, from our general managers (representing all lines of business, functions, and locations around the world) to our senior officers, in one place for a couple of days to meet face-to-face.

The senior officers present state of the company addresses to the leaders. Breakout sessions cover leadership development and team building; showcase our newest products and services (including live demos); share best practices; and include discussions with clients who attend to give us their feedback. The company's top officers hold a panel discussion for the leaders entitled, "Ask Us Anything," and they do.

We include plenty of social events to give the group a chance to spend time together and, on the final evening, we present our Outstanding Achievement awards for going above and beyond. The winners are presented with a crystal salmon (the salmon is our company mascot representing our contrarian approach to business and our desire to swim upstream against the tide).

In addition to refreshing our middle management team's overall company perspective, our WorldWide Leaders meetings bring together the great minds of our leadership to share ideas and provide our senior officers with a realistic view of the day-to-day microworkings of the organization.

Ambassador's Council
A Way to Gauge Happiness

The only way we can ever really know if we reach our goals is to try to measure our progress. The same goes with happiness in the workplace. We can't just assume our people are happy. We have to be sure they are, and that means finding ways to help them tell us.

About twelve years ago, we assembled a focus group we called our "happiness barometer." They met twice a year to give us a read on morale. Each meeting began with an anonymous questionnaire, and the rest of the day was left for open discussion. As we grew, particularly globally, we needed a more structured tool to ensure that we clearly heard the voices of everyone around the world, so we instituted our Ambassador's Council in 2001.

The council consists of twelve associates—two from each of our regions around the world—chosen at random for a one-year term. Like the happiness barometer group before them, the council meets twice a year at our headquarters, but prior to meeting, they survey the associates in their regions about issues, concerns, or questions they might have. We encourage them to use a variety of methods to gather input from their region—the more creative and assertive, the better. We really want to know what people think. Each member then presents their region's comments at the meeting.

I personally facilitate the two-day Ambassador's Council meetings along with our most senior officers. For our inaugural meeting, we divided our discussions into six key areas: leadership and communication; respect and appreciation; fairness; pride; "salmon spirit" (fun at work); and "final thoughts" (suggested changes, open questions).

To ensure that the meetings result in action, we designate a "lead ambassador" for each area, responsible for recording feedback exchanged and following up on any action items. Following the meetings, all associates around the world are informed of the issues raised and action items set, and they are invited to participate in the creation of solutions for the action areas that most interest them.

Associate Opinion Poll
A Global Diagnostic Tool

While traditional surveys can be useful, they can also be too slow for today's environment. By the time they are sent, completed, returned, tabulated, and reported on, many of the issues have changed or new ones have surfaced that are not addressed in the survey. To combat this, we instituted our "Associate Opinion Poll," a brief, open-ended diagnostic tool that can be administered quickly to uncover and address issues.

Topics include what people like best and least about working at our company; what single factor keeps them with us; reasons they would consider leaving; what they'd most like changed; and any additional comment they'd like to make. The one-page survey can be quickly translated into any language and e-mailed or faxed to any group, department, or location in the world. We always ensure anonymity. The results are consolidated and sent to the leader's leader, who then reviews the results with the reviewed leader, who in turn shares them directly with their associates. The team can then work together to resolve any issues.

We have found that the Associate Opinion Poll meets our requirements for an effective program: speed, fairness, global access, open communication, and a focus on what's important to our people.

Ask Us Anything
Using Communication Tools to Encourage Feedback

In the early '90s we created a voicemail program for our associates, through which they can call any time, from anywhere, about anything. Today, we also include an e-mail box, and we call the program "Ask Us Anything." The program makes it easy for our associates to share their views, ask questions, voice concerns, or present ideas. We review every message and get back to those requesting a response.

People can leave anonymous messages, but almost everyone seems to leave their name and number. We get a lot of questions, and that's good. People have made suggestions ranging from offering hang gliding at our corporate retreat (explained in Chapter 13, "Blazing New Trails") to establishing an exchange program with the educational system in which teachers could work at our company for a time while specialists from technology or other departments would teach in the schools. One associate from our Chicago office suggested that we work with the Red Cross to provide CPR training to all associates. Another in Daytona Beach recommended that we videotape meetings that take place at headquarters and send the tapes out to the field offices.

Several of the suggestions were cost-saving ideas, like the one from an associate in our Lancaster, Pennsylvania, office who proposed a program to cut down on unnecessary postage. He calculated that we could save up to $100,000 per year just by using plain white envelopes for internal purposes as opposed to our letterhead envelopes and by always using the smallest envelope possible. So far, his idea has saved the company nearly the estimated amount. Most recently, the state of our industry has prompted us to further uncover ways to reduce costs. This program has again been instrumental in allowing associates to recommend ways to save.

We hear from people suggesting certain accounts we should pursue, asking the status of potential accounts, and offering assistance with the sales process.

We've also uncovered areas of concern through the Ask Us Anything program. On a couple of occasions we've seen a pattern of several calls or e-mails from the same office about a variety of concerns from staffing to local office policies. That told us we had some underlying leadership and communication issues to resolve there that had not previously surfaced.

We've received many requests for more visits from senior leaders to our offices in the field. In response to that, my fellow senior officers and I held a series of Town Hall Meetings throughout North America, Europe, the Middle East, South Africa, and the Asia-Pacific region, with other parts of the world participating via conference call.

The Town Hall Meetings have been a great way to share company updates and strategies directly with our associates and to answer any questions on their minds in frank, open discussions. The meetings usually last about an hour, followed by an opportunity to just spend time with our people in their environment.

We found that two questions are asked almost everywhere we go. First, are we going public? The answer is that we are committed to a strategy of rapid growth and, when the market conditions are right, taking the company public is an option we may consider as a method to raise capital for our further growth.

The other commonly asked question is whether or not we will hold another company-wide meeting (see Chapter 6). Our associates cherish the chance to gather together from all parts of the world, and we try to do it every few years. Our answer is that if it is financially possible, we will try to have another company-wide meeting, perhaps next year.

As a result of the tragic events of 2001, our associates were yearning more than ever for constant communication from the corporate office. Therefore, we quickly created a weekly e-mail distribution entitled "Quick Connections" that contained an executive update, world news information, pertinent information in our industry, incentive program information, and human resources and benefit updates.

There's nothing radical about voicemail, e-mail, or face-to-face meetings. What's helpful is that something so simple could be so powerful when applied to making people's lives better. It's a way to make it as easy as possible for people to tell us what's important to them.

Business or Lifestyle?
Earning the Right to Be Part of Our People's Lives

Most of our waking hours are spent at work. Therefore, employers have a tremendous effect on the personal as well as business lives of their people—in fact, too much of an effect. As much as we all try, it's next to impossible to truly "leave work at work" and become a new person at home.

When something at work is on our minds, we aren't able to enjoy the little time we have at home. Then, the following day, we feel bad while at work for not having spent enough "quality" time with our family. We're concerned while at home over our lack of productivity during the day. The cycle repeats itself over and over again and people spiral downward.

This is no way to succeed either at home or at work, and it's no way to live. For that reason, our company ranks happiness in the workplace among our highest priorities. And I have made it my personal crusade.

Companies should strive to be as much lifestyles as businesses but they have to earn that right. They need to pay more attention to the humanistic side of business. It's said that it's not a good idea to work with friends. Hogwash. Friends don't let one another down. Who will people go that extra mile for—a friend or a detached business colleague?

To get people to "live" a company, it needs to more closely resemble life. Typical corporate structure is alien to the way people interact with one another naturally. We try to avoid the typical company design, which is often pretentious and isolating.

For example, we don't have layers upon layers of management and we don't have a large support staff. We strive to do most of our own communicating. To look at an organizational chart for our company you'd need an awfully wide piece of paper. We try to make our structure as flat as possible—that way, communication flows more freely both ways and we all open ourselves to closer contact with a greater number of people. This feeds creativity and makes our decisions more well rounded on every level.

A Holistic Approach
The Importance of Work–Life Rhythm

Increased stress at work and at home has given many people a burden that can't help but negatively impact both their work and home lives.

It's something most of us face on some level. Businesses need to ac-knowledge this very real stress and offer support to their people to help lessen it.

Our human resources group has been on the case for our associates for well over a decade. Through the years we have had a variety of ini-tiatives. As global awareness has heightened about the importance of the issue, a number of companies have created solutions to provide support, and we now work with a variety of those organizations to provide resources for our associates.

Through our "Associate Assistance Program" (AAP) associates can call a confidential hotline twenty-four hours a day, seven days a week. The services offered are available to not only the associate, but also their spouse, household members, and dependents, too. The services range from finding a certified day-care center within ten miles of their home, to advice on caring for an aging parent, adoption, summer camps, legal counseling and referral services, and mental health and substance abuse services. In addition, associates receive a monthly newsletter with topics like healthy eating, how to stop smoking, rec-ognizing and managing stress, and achieving balance.

Programs like AAP are the right thing to do, and while they're at it, they heighten morale, increase loyalty, lower absenteeism, reduce turnover, and raise productivity—the very results all companies seek.

Operation SAFE
Associates Helping Associates

Although we hope otherwise, there are times when an associate may face a crisis in their lives, and we want to be there when they do. So in early 2002, we launched Operation SAFE (Saving Associates From Emergencies), an associate-to-associate assistance program designed to provide financial aid to any part- or full-time associate, their chil-dren, parents, and spouse or partner, in times of personal crisis.

The fund is made up of strictly voluntary contributions by associ-ates, as well as periodic donations (of up to 50 percent of the fund) by the company. We're considering supplier contributions as well. The amount we recommended to our associates is one U.S. dollar (or equivalent) per day period, or $26 per year, but they can contribute whatever amount they wish. Associates are eligible to receive funds regardless of whether they have ever contributed or not.

The fund is managed by a non-profit charitable organization established by the company and led by a board of directors, which reviews requests and makes disbursement decisions. Associates volunteer to serve on the SAFE board for a one-year term. Members currently include our vice president of human resources and two leaders, and the balance are non-leaders from inside and outside the United States. They meet monthly and on an as-needed basis and conduct their reviews via conference call.

All requests and decisions are confidential, and payments are made directly to the institution or creditor requiring payment, on the associate's behalf. Some examples of appropriate requests include fire, flood, or other tragedy not covered by insurance, or medical expenses from treatments for associates or family members in critical condition.

While we were in the process of establishing Operation SAFE in late 2001, we were painfully aware that the furloughs that resulted from the events of that September (which you'll read more about in the Epilogue, "A Changed World") resulted in many financial hardships for the associates affected. An anonymous donor contributed a generous financial gift to establish a fund specifically for furloughed associates, to help them meet their financial obligations. We assembled an interim committee to review requests and distribute the funds to where they were needed most.

When I say this is a company of friends, I mean the best of friends—the kind who would reach out to those in need and not seek or accept recognition for it. We may never know who the donor was, but he or she will always be held dear to our hearts.

What Have You Done for Them Lately?
People Are the One True Competitive Measure

The happiness of life is made up of minute fractions—the little soon forgotten charities of a kiss or smile, a kind look, a heartfelt compliment, and the countless infinitesimals of pleasurable and genial feeling.

—Samuel Taylor Coleridge, *The Friend*

The big things in life certainly matter, but the little things can really add up. They can build happiness, commitment, and well being, or they can chip away at a person's self-esteem, security, and outlook.

So far, I've discussed the bigger issues—the foundation of putting our people first, programs to ensure accessibility of leadership, creative ways to measure happiness, ways to help people achieve balance in their lives. But I haven't talked about the little day-to-day things that help contribute to fulfillment among our people.

Even something as basic as celebrating each person's birthday, anniversary with the company, or other special occasion should be considered important business. My co-author tells me that in a company where she worked previously, these occasions were celebrated for years until a new company head banned such activity during the workday. Morale took a nose dive.

As hokey as it may have sounded at the time, thirteen years ago we started having "jeans days," which disproved the "dress for success" theory. We soon realized we were every bit as productive on those days, if not more. Today, even the most traditional Wall Street firms have "business casual" as their standard dress, as do we, but we've recognized for years that comfort and fun add up to productivity, more than formality and rules do.

There are also days when people dress like their account, wearing clothing that has the company's logo or keeping its products on their desk. Or sometimes, people wear costumes that reflect their favorite destination in a contest to win a trip there.

Our company offers "familiarization" trips (FAMs) for both educational and enjoyment purposes. This gives people the opportunity to learn more about the places where we send our clients, while traveling together and getting to know one another better. Our associates can also use their FAM time for educational programs or community service.

We give our people one to two weeks (depending on their tenure) paid time to participate, and we give them $100 to $700 (depending on the length of time with the company and the type of FAM taken) toward the trips, many of which are free to begin with. This is in addition to vacation time.

Most offices keep a scrapbook with photos of office events, letters of compliment to associates, and other mementos of shared experiences. These are all activities that foster happiness and encourage teamwork. Each office plans whatever programs they like. The important point is that they are not just permitted—they are invited—to do so.

I believe companies earn the bad attitudes of their people. Does anyone ever begin a new job with a bad attitude? No. They are "bright-eyed and bushy-tailed," filled with anticipation, excitement, and ambition. But companies with little regard for the happiness of their people find that their enthusiasm and open-mindedness are soon replaced by apathy and bitterness.

I was once discussing the concept of happiness in the workplace with the CEO of a company during a luncheon. We agreed that it's vital to a healthy workforce and to providing good service. But we disagreed on one important point—that it's the company's responsibility to ensure the happiness of its people. When I told him some of the things we do to encourage happiness, he said, "If they're not happy in our company, we fire them." I didn't take him literally, but at the same time, his message was clearly that companies shouldn't coddle their people.

Cries from the corporate world lament a lack of loyalty and motivation in the workplace. Turnover, absenteeism, apathy, lethargy, and a host of other evils drag down productivity and make companies less fierce global competitors. The origin of these maladies is a lack of happiness in the workplace. Without it, the best-planned processes, the finest tools, and the most marketable products fail. Without it, eventually all else breaks down.

I remember a conversation I had with an executive who had just been appointed CEO of a prominent airline. He asked me what I would suggest, as his client and partner, to turn the somewhat troubled carrier around.

I told him I certainly wasn't an expert in running an airline, but I do try to understand people and what motivates them, makes them happy, and helps them to provide outstanding service. My only suggestion to him was to put his desk on an airplane.

I said that if I were running his company, I'd make my office a different flight each day, and my time would be spent talking with my people and the clients on board. I never asked him if he did it or not, but I do know that his airline has come back strong and its service is among the best.

If more corporations paid as much attention to their people as they do to politics, public image, and increased profits, everything else would fall into place. Profits are a natural extension of happiness in the workplace. It doesn't work the other way around. We are consistently able to trace higher costs to cases of unhappiness in specific departments and offices. We take it very seriously.

Uprooting Unhappiness
The Story of a Costly Mistake

As important as happiness in the workplace is to us, we have certainly made mistakes. That's why it's so important never to waiver from our pursuit of it.

More than a dozen years ago we acquired a major account that warranted the opening of a new office. Our new client was anxious to have us begin service and asked that we start earlier than we planned. We didn't want to disappoint them so we rushed ahead.

We made a lot of mistakes by not following our normal process. We hired a leader for the office based on recommendation. We didn't employ our practice of placing potential leaders in uncomfortable situations and interviewing them under a variety of circumstances (explained in Chapter 3, "Finding the Right People"). We hired all of our new people for that office too quickly.

The first sign that things were wrong was our error rate there. We've learned that's almost always a symptom of unhappiness. The second sign was that our people in that location began to call my office to tell me they were unhappy. The third sign was when our client called to tell me that the company's travelers weren't pleased with the service in our new office.

What's interesting is that the client was the last to feel the effects of our people's unhappiness. There's a tremendous opportunity here. Unhappiness surfaces before client dissatisfaction. So by paying attention to our people, we can turn the tide before problems affect service. The best way to do it is to concentrate on building in happiness, up front.

To turn the situation around, a team of human resources associates set up shop in that office, talking with people, trying to get to the root of the problems. They went for a day and stayed more than a month. What they found was "old style" leadership: the treatment of people as a means to an end. We worked with our leaders there, but most of them just didn't fit, culturally. Only those with the human instinct were retained.

We met with our associates in small groups and asked which leaders were instilling fear and which cared more about their own advancement than their people. We asked them who neglected to make time for them and who was unfair. I went to that office several times to sit down and talk with our people. Those were some of the worst days in my career. I could see the negative effects our company was having on their lives. We had made the classic mistakes that so many others make.

We had to start over, to show our people the company was there for them, before we could ever expect them to feel they were truly there for our clients. And when we did, service improved drastically. Our clients are delighted with their service in that office, but it cost us a great deal to get there.

During the trouble period, there were twenty-seven turnovers—people whom we had trained at a cost of $61,290—and that was money out the door. To replace those people, we spent an additional $50,000 in recruiting costs (advertisements and search firms). These are just hard costs. More was lost in terms of time and perception.

Three human resource managers devoted what ended up being a quarter of the year to solving the problems created in this one office, so that adds up to 75 percent of a single person–year exhausted on the effort. In addition to the time, there were three legal complaints. We were successful in all of them, and while there was no cost in payments of any kind other than for our legal counsel, the complaints took time and energy, and morale took a beating.

In addition to lost productivity there were negative effects on our service to our clients in that city for a time, and shaken confidence on the part of our associates. These hurt most of all, and it literally took years to completely bounce back.

A company is only as good as its people. We can all buy the same machines and tools, but it's people who apply them creatively. We can hire consultants for direction, but when it all comes down to it, their advice is only as valuable as the people who will implement their suggestions. Our true competitive measure is our people.

Pillars of People
Building a Foundation for Happiness

Every company operates on a hierarchy of concerns. Ours is the following: people, service, profits. In that order. The company's focus is on its people. Our people then focus on serving our clients. Profits are the end result.

The pillars upon which many companies are built are primarily profit-oriented. We contend these pillars are not strong enough to hold the weight of companies, particularly in lean times. Human beings must be the pillars of a company. They provide an unshakable foundation. This might appear to be a soft strategy but, in our case, we rely on our growth and client retention rates to prove that this method translates into solid results.

Cultivating Happiness in the Workplace

A SUMMARY

∎ Happiness in the workplace is key to providing superior service. Continually create an environment where your people leave the worrying to the company so they can focus on your clients.

∎ People are companies' one true competitive measure. Take a look at areas with rising costs to see if there's a correlating morale problem.

∎ Measuring happiness in the workplace is essential. Five ways we have found to be effective are (1) asking people to draw what the company means to them; (2) using voice-mail and e-mail to encourage feedback; (3) holding Town Hall Meetings to hear directly from people; (4) assembling a regular focus group to test morale and bring issues from the field to the forefront; and (5) using a brief, easily administered opinion poll as needed.

∎ Make contact with your people at every level. Fight the purification of information as it rises to meet you. You will learn more about what's really happening in your company and morale will soar. Consider an Associate of the Day program. Leaders learn as much from it as their people do. A meeting with middle-level managers can give you a good read on morale within specific departments, and it brings everyone together to share ideas and expertise.

∎ Make your company a lifestyle—not just a place to work. Make it fun. Be ever cognizant of the effect your company has on your people's personal as well as professional lives. Remember always to involve your people in decisions; give them a sense of ownership in your company.

▌ Take a look at an Associate Assistance Program (AAP) to support your people in their pursuit of balance between their personal and professional lives. It's your obligation, and it's just plain good business.

▌ Recheck the ratio of financial to humanistic pillars in your company's foundation. We have found that the two co-exist in perfect harmony. The humanistic approach to business yields the financial results companies seek because people work better when they *want* to work.

CHAPTER THREE

Finding the Right People

Most of us choose our spouse with care and rear our children with nurturing and compassionate attention. Yet we tend to select the people who will join our company on the basis of an interview or two, and once they have joined, they often find they must fend for themselves.

This contrast illustrates the disparity between the environments of family and work. But given the amount of time we must spend at work, wouldn't we all be happier if we took as much care at the office as at home to create a supportive environment? Wouldn't we also be far more successful? I say yes, and yes again.

Service Begins in the Heart
The Importance of Looking for Nice People

Tenet number one is *Look for nice people.* The rest will fall into place. Too often, a person's job history carries more weight than his or her human values. What's in someone's heart can't be discovered in a résumé.

There's the type of person who pushes his way to the front of the line to snare a seat on the commuter train and the type of person who offers his seat to others. There are people whose favorite line is "That's not my job," and those who are quick to ask how they can help.

Some people can't wait until others finish their sentences so they can talk about themselves or their viewpoints. But there are those who really want to listen to what others have to say. Some look to gain; others seek to contribute.

In our selection process, kindness, caring, compassion, and unselfishness carry more weight than years on the job, an impressive salary history, and stacks of degrees.

It's something our competition always seems to try to figure out. At its most basic common denominator, the formula for our company's success is that we have more nice people than they do. Niceness is among our highest priorities because nice people do better work.

Our clients time and again tell us that they see our people as an oasis in the corporate desert. They actually look forward to talking with our people. This is no accident. We take pains to ensure it. There's no greater competitive advantage in a service business.

You can't teach people to be nice. You can't just say, "Thursday, begin caring!" Caring must be inherent in their natures—they have to feel it in their hearts. And if they do, their clients will feel it, too.

One of my proudest moments came during an interview with a prospective associate who was considering relocating to Philadelphia from the Midwest to work for Rosenbluth. Coming to the city for her third interview, she arrived at the airport and hailed a taxi. When the driver asked her where she wanted to go, she replied, "Rosenbluth headquarters." His response to her request will remain with me forever. He said, "Rosenbluth. Now that's where all the nice people work." After hearing that, our interviewee wanted very much to become a part of our company, and she subsequently did. In fact, she's the co-author of this book and has been a part of our company for fifteen years.

This particular reputation is more rewarding than any other we could earn and, in my mind, that justifies our ultrastringent criteria for joining the company. Each person selected must act as an ambassador for us and must be chosen accordingly.

It's important to remember that no matter how impressive people's résumés or previous accomplishments are, if they're not nice and don't fit they can't be right. Why run the risk of contaminating the team?

Only the Best
You Can't Afford Not to Be Picky

The differentiator that sets today's preeminent companies apart is the ability to attract and retain terrific people. When the earlier version of this book came out a decade ago, the employment market was an entirely different story. Jobs were scarce and companies were inundated with résumés from overqualified applicants eager to have an opportunity to just get a foot in the door.

I can't resist the chance now to say that at the time, we felt strongly that the tables were about to turn, and that there would be a human resource drought. In fact, in Chapter 14 of the original book, we had an entire section about how difficult it would become to find great people. At the time, a lot of people thought we were nuts, but now we all find ourselves in the midst of a global talent war.

Finding skilled, dedicated, thought leaders has never been more important or more difficult than it is today, yet even in this environment of scarce resources, it's as vital as ever that we retain our high standards.

We take a selective posture toward inviting people into our company. For each position, we interview eight to ten people before making our final selection. And the interviewing isn't easy—why should it be? We expect a great deal from our people and offer them a lot in return. We owe it to each other to select only people who will enrich what we have built.

Just as a money manager analyzes an individual stock by considering how it will fit into his portfolio, companies must evaluate prospective employees with this same unblinking eye. An individual stock, although possibly a good performer on its own, might have negative effects on the overall portfolio.

Likewise, individuals should be selected for what they bring to the team as much as for their personal potential. A key component to team fit is cultural fit. In order to make the right decision, companies must be able to get their arms around their culture and envision prospective employees within it. There's no place this is more important than in the area of leadership, because leaders are looked upon as role models for people throughout their companies.

Big Dogs, Tall Weeds
Selecting Senior Leaders

It's often been said, "If you want to run with the big dogs, you have to learn to deal with the tall weeds." Interviewing top leaders is a special process for us, because our leaders are a breed all their own. Candidates go through some pretty strange and stringent evaluations.

By the time leaders enter this company, we know what they eat for breakfast, when they lose their temper, and exactly where they will fit in. We've found that getting to know someone that well can only be achieved by observing them in incongruous scenarios that have nothing to do with the position, the company, or business at all.

Behind the Wheel or Under the Hoop
Unusual Interviewing Techniques

Take driving habits, for example. We think they say a lot about people. We don't want to hire the type of person who can't drive decisively or who doesn't look for alternatives to traffic jams, just accepting their fate of being at a standstill. On the other hand, we don't want someone who is reckless or distracted. We don't want anyone who puts "getting there" before the safety of their passengers. These are all traits that can be carried into the workplace.

Another acid test is sports. We like competitive people who are driven to do their best. But equally important are the ability and desire to work for the good of the team. Each player needs to possess that innate selflessness that comes from being secure enough not to need to be the star every moment of the game. We value the person who is eager to pass the ball to the open player as much as we value the superstar who can slam-dunk like Shaquille O'Neal.

We were once saved by a softball game. In the final stages of our search for a key senior leader, we invited a top candidate to join our leaders in a game of softball. His true colors really showed during that outing. He had to be the star, even at the expense of others. His team lost and he took it poorly, looking to place the blame on his team-mates.

We asked him to play softball because we weren't positive about him, but we never expected to learn so much. These were traits that went all but undetected during his interviews. Smooth operators *can* slip through the cracks, but when they are evaluated in nontraditional ways, they reveal much more about themselves.

It's important to get as many people as possible involved in the selection process, because we need to bring into the company only those who can work well with the team we have in place. For that reason, candidates for senior leadership positions spend time with our current senior leaders, and their input is crucial. To round out the process, prospective leaders are often interviewed by those they will lead as well. We're seeking people who will inspire their teams. Who better to make that judgment than the team itself?

Put to the Test
Employing Executive Assessments

Because finding our company's top leaders is handled like micro-surgery, many years ago we began an Executive Assessment Program to evaluate candidates for senior positions. These evaluations are conducted by our corporate psychologist and the team of leaders of which the candidate seeks to be a member.

Those new to the company as well as current associates being considered for promotion into senior leadership positions must participate. The assessments analyze values, personality traits, and strengths and weaknesses, as well as determining team fit. Each leader is unique, but it's crucial that as a group they complement one another's strengths and shore up one another's weaknesses. Most important, they have to enjoy working together as a team.

My co-author, Diane, recalls going through the executive assessment process. She completed the battery of written tests in about a half a day, which required her to dig deep into her values, priorities, and leadership style. In one test, she was asked to piece together some oddly shaped blocks to match a design provided on paper.

She noticed that throughout the timed test, our psychologist was taking notes. At the end, Diane asked what he had been so busy writing, since speed was supposed to be the objective. He told her that in reality, her *approach* to problem-solving was more important than the stopwatch results. Did she ask questions? Was there a method to her steps? Did she have a sense of humor? Was she interested in finding out, at the conclusion, what would have been the most effective method?

Because our assessments are conducted, in part, by our corporate psychologist, his understanding of our company's goals is key to the effectiveness of the program. For that reason, he is often included in our strategic planning sessions and other key meetings, though he is not employed by our company. We do, however, retain him to be available to help our people manage difficult situations either at work or in their private lives. He has been with us for many, many years. We think it's a sound investment in our people, so we have assumed the costs of even entirely personal consultations.

The Right Stuff
There Are Tools to Help You

Have you ever gone shopping, and after trying on what seems like a million things, bought something without trying it on? It's usually no surprise that when you finally try it on at home, it doesn't fit. Or how about the time you ordered something from a catalog or over the Internet that looked great in the picture, but when it arrived you were embarrassed to have ordered it? Then there's the day after Christmas. It's the biggest shopping day of the year—not because everything's on sale but because we're all returning gifts that don't fit or that we don't like, or maybe because we don't even know what they are.

The same bad fit happens with people and companies, but people aren't so easy to return. There are a lot of folks out there and they're not all going to fit in your company.

The recruiting and selection process is labor-intensive and expensive. Hiring mistakes take emotional as well as financial tolls. Every company wants to find the right people the first time around.

Experts can be helpful in establishing criteria for a good fit between employment candidates and your company, even its specific departments and positions. Two decades ago, our human resources staff worked with outside experts to create a selection process for new associates that helps identify the best people for our company. Part of that process includes specially designed profiles of the appropriate personality type and repertoire of skills needed for specific positions within the company.

For example, our front-line customer care associate (CCA) position calls for someone who will work with our clients on a day-to-day basis via telephone, e-mail, or electronic chat. A combination of technical, interpersonal, and organizational skills is required.

Our profile creation process had several steps. First, we put together a study group representative of our CCA population. Next, we created a job analysis to define the position as it was on a day-to-day basis and to determine performance ideals. We identified key skills and characteristics that were fundamental to the position.

Then we applied tests in these areas to the group, such as reading and clerical efficiency, math reasoning, verbal fluency, and perception. Personality traits were also evaluated, such as energy, flexibility, rapport, assertiveness, and team contribution.

We compared the test scores of each person in the group with his or her performance on the job, to look for correlations between certain skills, personality traits, and success in the position. From these, we were able to derive prediction formulas, which we can use to help us evaluate candidates during the selection process. These formulas are a way to determine the likelihood of success in a particular capacity.

A few years ago, we added formalized core competencies, detailing what it takes to be a part of our company. We then outlined additional competencies required for our leaders. We didn't stop there. Next we developed models for each area of the company, including specific competency profiles for each position. These profiles help us to find the right person for each position, but they are also highly useful in performance management, helping us ensure that we measure the things that really count.

The core competencies are made available to our associates worldwide through our Career Enhancement Guide (CEG), a PC-based tool also in binder form. In addition to the competencies, the CEG includes self-assessment tools for each area to help people figure out what it would take to work in a given area or position within the company, and it outlines career options. The resource also features résumé writing and interviewing tips and a directory of contacts to consult in each area for informational interviews.

A certain degree of science removes some of the inherent subjectivity from the interviewing and performance management processes. The profiles and core competencies help us spot people with the qualities that are likely to make them good candidates for a position and also more likely to enjoy their work—qualities that are mutually reinforcing. Utilizing the same information to enhance our associates' career options helps build loyalty, morale, and effectiveness.

While these tools are helpful as guidelines, they are not the sole criteria by which we select associates. We certainly don't want all of our people to be the same. But considering the fact that our company employs around six thousand people, these tools help ensure that we achieve our standards and provide consistent service.

Similar tools can be created for virtually any position in any industry, either through scientific studies like the one we employed, or simply through information gained from focus groups, performance appraisals, exit interviews, and other programs most likely already in place. Certainly, developing prediction tools can save time and recruiting costs.

Over the years, we have observed an interesting link. The correlation between excellence in tasks and people skills was incredibly high. One explanation is that when people have the tasks down pat, they're free to concentrate on people skills. We also know that nice people with a positive attitude instinctively master tasks so they can provide a level of service that supports their people skills.

The point is that the data support our belief that nice people do a better job. Those who get along best with their colleagues and clients also have the best skills. By seeking nice people, you'll benefit your clients in both the tangible and intangible aspects of service.

Mining for Resources
Attracting Applicants in a Tight Labor Market

You're probably thinking, "I'd love to find nice people, but how do I find candidates in the first place?" I don't think anyone has a revelation in this area. It's tough out there, but I can tell you that culture is the key. The right culture helps a company attract the right kind of applicant and retain the people it has.

I'm honored that our company has a reputation for being a great place to work. In fact, in 1992, just after we sent the original version of this book to press, we were selected for inclusion in the book *The 100 Best Companies to Work for in America* (Robert Levering and Milton Moskowitz) and in fact, we were named among the top ten. Since that time, *Fortune* has named us to its 100 best employers list and a number of similar distinctions have followed, including the Investors in People award in the United Kingdom, Western Europe, Asia Pacific, and South Africa, given to a company that best exemplifies a great place to work and a keen focus on its people.

As our visibility as a people-friendly employer has grown, so has the number of unsolicited résumés we receive each year—at last count about thirty thousand per year. The apparent benefit is in the broad spectrum of applicants from which we can select. A subtle but power-ful benefit also lies in the fact that those who apply more closely match our company, because they understand what we're about. Our reputation as an employer of choice leads the very type of person we seek to apply here.

The reputation is nice, but it's the reality that is effective. People can get an immediate sense of a company from even the briefest interac-tion, so every encounter is important. It all starts with the message that's on your website or your phone screening process. How do you make people feel from their very first contact? I believe you have to in-volve your best people in the process of attracting candidates. Every person must be an ambassador for your company, and they must look at recruiting as a priority.

Our top recruiting tool is our Associate Referral Program. We have found that associate referrals bring us candidates with a better cul-tural fit and more closely aligned skills that match because our people understand the company. So in 1999, we began a program to encour-age referrals (at the time, our third largest source of new hires).

Associates that make successful referrals receive a "thank you" gift of $500, and their names are also placed in a drawing that occurs each August during Associate Appreciation Month (you'll read more about this in Chapter 6). The grand prize–winner receives two round-trip air tickets and a weekend stay at a hotel.

We intentionally kept the referral bonus modest, so people see it as the gesture of appreciation that it is, rather than a race to submit names. This keeps the quality of applicant stronger. However, during critical hiring periods (for example, the start-up of a new account or other growth spurts) we have increased the offer to $1,000 per suc-cessful referral, plus a drawing with ten winners, each receiving $5,000.

Our second best recruitment tool is our internal job posting sys-tem. We are very proactive about making every job opportunity known throughout the company (through weekly job postings acces-sible to every associate) and diligent about promoting from within. On the surface, filling a job with an internal candidate still leaves you with an open position, but the key lies in our commitment to associate advancement. People know there will be real opportunities for them here. So they stay, they work to their full potential, and they recommend our company to friends. People who do apply hear the success stories of those who have joined the company before them. Promoting from within is a better recruiting tool than most realize.

Aside from these tried and true tools, we continually try creative approaches. For example, we hold job fairs, but they're not your typical résumé mills. We throw parties with great food, giveaways, and a fun atmosphere. We hold them three times per day, each time to make it easy for people of all schedules to find the time to attend.

One key to finding the best talent is broadening your horizons. Looking in nontraditional places, embracing diversity of background, culture, geography—every type of diversity—these are secrets not just to finding great people, but also to providing a certain richness of service.

Free from the Millstone of Ethnocentricity
The Benefits of Varied Backgrounds

People from a wide variety of backgrounds build depth into an organization. They offer a source of fresh ideas, new perspectives, and original applications for products, services, and resources. Because we commit extensive resources to our learning programs we are not limited to looking only within our industry for quality people. This opens up new worlds for us in finding the best talent.

Certainly, we hire experienced travel professionals, but more often we hire those who have excelled in their individual fields elsewhere. Rather than look for specialists in travel technology, for example, we seek technology experts from a variety of fields who will bring with them unique insight from other industries that may help change the future of ours.

Typically, our associates not only come from a wide variety of industries, but most often their experience is completely unrelated to travel. This broadens our horizons, bringing us perspectives that transcend our industry and giving us a more vast understanding outside our sphere.

It all makes sense when you analyze it. For example, a business systems architecture associate, who explains our technology products to our clients, came to our company from a career in special education. She has a gift of being able to explain complex concepts in understandable terms. She makes what could be a dry subject interesting. And she's an excellent listener.

One of our strategy analysts spent six years studying animal behavior and biology. He now uses highly analytical systems to optimize our clients' travel so they can achieve the best savings. His previous experience provided him with the ability to look at things in a very systematic, scientific, and strategic way.

A human resources business partner spent two years as a labor, delivery, and pediatrics nurse before pursuing a master's in human resources and joining our company. Her empathy, listening, and nurturing skills are called upon constantly, as are her strength, knowledge, and ability to withstand pressure, just as in her previous position.

The variety of backgrounds is endless. A member of our human resources team is an electrical engineer. She's charged with creating and updating human resource organizational systems. Her technical skills are being put to work in a creative application.

One of our account leaders holds an MBA in international finance. Working closely with a corporate client to manage a multimillion-dollar, global travel account requires her solid financial skills.

Our officer team is made up of best-of-breed individuals, all with diverse backgrounds. Our president and chief operating officer was a senior executive of the world's largest photo-imaging company; our chief financial officer held the same position at the country's fastest growing bank; our chief information officer, as well as our chief marketing officer, came from two of the world's most prestigious life insurance and casualty companies. I am extremely proud that I was able to extract each of them from their highly respected companies.

How do we find this vast array of people from such diverse backgrounds? Above all, we open ourselves to these possibilities by considering not *just* those whose résumés seem to fit the position. We take a great deal of care to interview a wide variety of people and to view their backgrounds with a creative eye. This is unquestionably a competitive advantage.

The "E" Word: Not What You Think
Finding Talent in the Electronic Marketplace

There's probably not a remote corner of the world that the e-environment hasn't touched, but I view it differently than most. I would argue that the secret to effective e-commerce is not the electronic aspects but rather the emotional aspects: "emotional commerce." The e-commerce road is littered with start-ups and bright ideas, but with no experience satisfying customers. On that same road are traditional companies eager to jump on the opportunity to drive their delivery costs down by marketing their wares and services in a people-less environment.

Pretty much the same people are buying from us all electronically that bought from us traditionally. They still want personalized attention, but they also want immediate answers and more convenient delivery. The biggest mistake companies make is to try to remove the people aspect from e-commerce.

Technology alone is not a sustainable advantage. It can easily be copied and as fast as things change, almost the moment you deploy it, it's obsolete. Our people are our only lasting advantage in the e-marketplace—in any marketplace.

People are so important to e-business that we did something that might sound counter-cultural. In 1999 we acquired Biztravel.com, and the first thing we did was to fire everyone. The staff they had on board hated one another. There were politics and in-fighting, and because of that, the architecture of the product suffered and customer service was an oxymoron. We brought in people with passion and compassion and created an environment of cooperation. We redesigned the product and put great people behind the process—people who were easily accessible through an 800 number on the home page, e-mail, or electronic chat. The human and emotional aspects made all the difference in the world, and Biztravel.com took off.

E-commerce is not as simple as everyone thought. It does level the merchandising playing field because anyone can get shelf space in cyberspace, but the costs to staff the business that backs sites up took many by surprise—companies large and small.

One common mistake is to understaff e-ventures, another is to staff them inappropriately, assigning them to inexperienced people. You can't just put a group of people together and make it work. You have to hire not for an IPO, but for the long-term, building a true team. And that's not as easy as it once was. There was a time not long ago, when e-careers were viewed as glamorous, and everyone wanted that type of experience on their résumé. The hype has settled now, and people are beginning to realize that while there are unique qualities to e-business, the same foundations still apply: hard work, teamwork, and the importance of the human aspects.

How do you go about finding the right people for this kind of business? For one thing, your recruiters have to have what your standard recruiters need (be ambassadors for your business, enthusiastic communicators of your culture, caring, nurturing, etc.) but they also must have a clear understanding of technology.

Speed is another imperative. The hiring process used to take a month or two, but today the best people are snapped up before you can blink, so companies need a well-defined recruiting process that all leaders understand and buy into. The steps have to take place quickly. In fact, the best process takes place over half a day, with a decision at the end. During that time, an IT expert assesses the candidate's technical competency; a human resource professional evaluates the cultural fit and people skills; leaders assess confidence, attitude, team fit, and other aspects; then everyone meets to discuss their views and arrive at a conclusion.

When recruiting talent for e-ventures, as with finding people for any aspect of your business, there are tips and tools. But at the heart of it all, remember you're dealing with people. Making your company the kind of place for which they'd give anything to work is the most powerful weapon you can have.

Play for Keeps
An Ounce of Retention is Worth a Pound of Recruitment

The rule of sales is that it costs more to get a new customer than to keep an existing one. We all know that's true not just for customers but employees, too. And with employee turnover, the costs run well beyond the financial. Turnover hurts morale, delays projects, damages recruitment efforts, and is a competitive risk.

With unemployment near its lowest point (in the United States) in nearly a half century, we can't afford to take our people for granted—not that we ever could. The shortage of talent is global and will not ease for some time. Add to that the "free agent" attitude prevalent among today's workers (particularly those just entering the workforce) and companies have a virtual crisis.

To fight the job-hopping trend, one of the best things you can do is to encourage your people to job hop within your company, making opportunities available to them to gain new experience, knowledge, and advancement. We have rules around here that mean we will not hold an associate back. We don't believe in waiting periods or red tape to keep people where it might be convenient for us. We encourage everyone to keep moving toward where they want to be—*within* our company.

A costly mistake we all tend to make is to spend excessive amounts of time with the least strong of our associates, because they need the most help. We need to spend time with them, but not at the expense of our strongest people. They need nurturing, too. They might not need our help, but they certainly need and deserve our appreciation, attention, and time. One of the best ways to nurture them is to seek them out and ask what's important to them, what makes them stay—and act on that information to keep them.

Another key to retention is to be as flexible and customized as possible in your employment offerings, catering to individual needs. We also have to remember that needs change, and checking back with people is a good idea.

A retention manager can be effective—someone whose sole responsibility is to keep your best people. Just focusing on the issue can dramatically affect it. Having a formalized retention plan can also help you keep all the balls in the air.

Our retention plan begins with some key elements that are essential, like executive commitment—leaders devoting time to strengthening retention and continually recognizing the highly competitive nature of the employment marketplace. It continues with specific actions, including a leadership development element geared specifically to retention issues, to help our leaders fully understand the needs of their people, establish mentorship, provide constructive feedback, and make performance reviews effective tools for career development.

Communication is also imperative for retention. People want to feel informed about the company they work for—where it's heading, how they fit into the future. They need to feel part of the team, involved in the planning, contributing ideas and being heard.

Fairness is another watchword for retention. People need and want to be treated and paid fairly, not held back by rigid policies and salary bands. In the end, to keep people we need to show compassion, common sense, and caring.

How Do We Rate?
Tools to Learn Your Retention Strengths
and Weaknesses

You have to know why people join your organization, just like you need to know the features and benefits that sell the products/services your company offers its customers. Our people tell us the things that attracted them to us are our culture, integrity, comfortable atmosphere, obvious opportunity for advancement, and a feeling of friendship/family. How do we know? We ask them, in a variety of ways, two of which I'll share with you here: our Engagement Study and our 30-60-90 day reviews.

In 2001, we instituted our "Engagement Study," sponsored and managed by my office. This global culture audit allowed us to benchmark our associate satisfaction against some of the best companies in the world. To get the highest participation possible, the survey was conducted over the Internet, and we ensured that every associate around the world had access to the web in order to participate. We also translated the study into all languages needed by our people.

In years past, we sent a satisfaction survey to all associates, but this study is more meaningful because it tells us not just how people feel about the company, but also how committed they are to staying. People who are happy at companies still leave them, and we want to know why they stay and what would make them leave.

This study looked at metrics we'd never studied before, like asking people to rank issues in the company and to compare the value of potential solutions. After all, why spend time, effort, and money on things you think will help, but might not be as meaningful to your associates as you hoped? They might view a different solution as the most beneficial.

Another important improvement over our previous surveys is the opportunity to benchmark our culture and associate loyalty against other world-class companies. This is made possible by the fact that the Engagement Study was developed by an outside organization, The Forum on Workforce Engagement, which is affiliated with the Corporate Leadership Council. The Forum is a membership of companies dedicated to understanding what drives career decisions. By utilizing their survey, we are able to compare ourselves to an audience of like-minded companies—those who seek to be best in class in associate satisfaction.

The survey assesses turnover risk, career preferences, job market opportunities, work/life issues, value alignment (how well what's important to our people matches what we offer), and the most effective ways to bridge that gap. It includes questions about things like the quality of co-workers and of direct managers; the amount of responsibility and accountability people are given; whether or not the work they do is cutting edge; and internal mobility and opportunities.

The Engagement Study is anonymous, confidential, and secure. Only the outside research staff has access to the data, and we make our people very aware of this so they feel free to be brutally honest.

An interesting facet of the survey is that it is personalized in two important ways. First, each company that administers it is allowed up to six customized questions, which are placed first in the survey. Ours had seven rankings from "very strongly agree" to "very strongly disagree." Our customized questions were about trust, caring, collaboration, balance between the bottom line and associate satisfaction, diversity of perspectives, and respect.

The second way in which the study is customized is that it branches in different directions based upon the associate's answers and rankings of importance. In other words, each section gets more and more targeted based upon how the person has answered. Toward the end, the person makes choices between hypothetical jobs and their own job with our company, telling us how likely they would be to leave and showing us the reasons why. This is powerful information to have and helps us to really understand how to keep our most cherished assets—our people.

The Engagement Study is a terrific retention tool. Another is our "30-60-90" day review process. Understanding why people join your company and why they leave it are critical pieces of information in the fight to win and keep the best talent. To do this, several years ago we began conducting follow-up interviews 30, 60, and 90 days after the first day of a person's employment with us, to track their perception of the company during those important first three months.

The same process is applied to those who leave the company, with the same 30-, 60-, and 90-day interview format. Through this, we seek to understand why they left. Multiple contacts over time have brought us very frank information, and in many cases have helped us win associates back.

We conduct the 30-, 60-, and 90-day interviews as often as possible, but we also have a "New Associate Follow-Up Questionnaire" to help us ensure we reach everyone at least once. The questionnaire is sent out sixty days after a person's start date. It asks them to evaluate our interview and hiring process; what, if any, resources they need; and how the work they're doing matches the description they were given at hiring. There's a place for open comments and, finally, we ask if the person would like to be contacted by a human resources associate to confidentially discuss any issues.

These efforts are all critical to finding great talent, but one of the biggest roadblocks to building the strongest team can be ourselves.

Political Animals, Egotists, and Other Parasites
Personality Types to Avoid

We work to avoid contamination of our environment because it's not fair to the people we employ to have to work alongside those who aren't nice or who don't work hard. Our environment makes this company special, and we need to protect it to keep it that way.

There are three basic personality types we can spot a mile away, and we try never to allow them into our company. They are political animals, egotists, and freeloaders. They are often attracted to an organization like ours because they see the openness in our culture as rich hunting grounds for their own pursuits. Open, yes; naïve, no.

Political animals. The quickest way out of our company is to try to get ahead at the expense of others. This is covered in detail in Chapter 8, "The Gardening Process." But I want to state here and now that I believe politics and a successful organization are mutually exclusive.

Egotists. There's a fitting proverb that sums up egotism: "Those who say don't know and those who know don't say." Egotists seldom have a clear view of things. They're blinded by looking at every situation to find the benefit for themselves only. Their talents are foiled by poor judgment and they destroy teamwork.

Confidence is fantastic but egotism is deadly. We'll take nice people with street smarts over arrogant "intellectuals" (who think they know it all) any day.

Freeloaders. Finally, there's the freeloader, otherwise known as the "travel hog" in our industry. Every industry has its own breed. They're along for a free piece of the product.

The travel industry has its share of shrimp-devouring nonprofessionals, carousing through trade shows in search of free travel. Obviously this is a stereotype, but it's a style we carefully avoid.

We're into minimal schmooze and maximum professionalism. Certainly, we provide excellent travel benefits to our people, and if they weren't interested in travel to a certain degree, they probably would not be drawn to a career in it. But free travel has to be so far down on their list of priorities that it's almost an afterthought. This can be ascertained through a thorough interview process.

It begins from the very first contact we have with a person, not just from the formal interview process itself. You can learn a great deal about someone through correspondence, phone calls, and casual interactions. Consistency is a good indicator of sincerity.

We're always on the lookout for nurturers and those who are mentally flexible. People who naturally and genuinely want to take care of others are ideal for service businesses, especially our company. Caregivers also make for strong team players.

Mental flexibility is critical in a dynamic environment. People need to be increasingly adaptable because of the rate of change and the fact that more things than ever before are being accomplished by fewer people. At our company, most of us think we know how we'll be spending our day, but it never fails to change. In fact, it's not unusual for our people to find themselves in a different city than they thought they might be on that day. People have to adapt quickly and enthusiastically.

Those who are ruffled by a change in routine won't be happy here, so we try to determine that during the selection process. We might ask people about a typical day in their life or on the job. We ask them what they find frustrating. Or we create hypothetical situations (most based upon a real-life day around here) calling for flexibility, and we see how they react.

One of the best indicators is adaptability in the interview itself. We try to cut down on interruptions when interviewing, but there's bound to be at least one. The patience, good humor, and flexibility people display in their reactions to those interruptions say a lot.

The people we select must be professionals in every sense of the word, and they must want to build a career with us or they won't like it here. It's tough work and requires commitment to excellence and complete dedication to the company, fellow associates, and clients.

The Element of Danger
The Dangers of an Open Culture

Our unique culture has been the focus of quite a bit of attention, and this actually can leave a company vulnerable to those who are attracted to it for the wrong intentions.

We wear our culture on our sleeve, and people know what we're looking for. Sometimes the wrong person knows how to say and do just the right things. We've made some hiring mistakes because of this.

Since people tend to hire in their likeness, unhealthy pockets may form around them. There have been occasions when we've had to rebuild entire departments to turn such situations around.

If leaders listen carefully, their people will guide them to the problem. When we do find the cause, we try to give that person a second chance, and often it will work. But when they don't change swiftly and completely, we have to ask ourselves if this one person has the right to have a negative effect on so many others. The answer is clearly "no."

The Annihilation of Arrogance
Tips for Conquering Pomposity

We believe strongly in the importance of combating arrogance. Trying to detect it during the selection process can help, but some is bound to slip in occasionally. Arrogance can even take root in those who normally are modest. The change comes about when turf is at stake or when they begin to feel they "own" a certain area.

Just to make sure we keep runaway egos in check, we regularly do teamwork exercises to illustrate the point that nobody has all of the answers. One of my favorites is "Green Vegetables," an exercise we learned years ago from a consultant.

In this exercise, people from all levels and all departments of the company write down all of the green vegetables they can recall in five minutes. Then each person reads his or her list out loud while someone from the group records all of the ideas.

Every time we hold this exercise the participants in the group are amazed at how many collective ideas were presented and how relatively few they could come up with on their own, compared to the group as a whole. The underlying message is one of synergy—not a new idea, but one that deserves continual emphasis. "The whole is greater than the sum of its parts." No individual's contributions will ever be as powerful on their own as they will be when strengthened by the contributions of the team.

Another ego-buster we rely upon is putting people in uncomfortable situations. People can often tell more about one another by spending an hour together with their guard down than they can by working together for a year.

One such experience for us was a fence-building project our top executives participated in during a strategic planning session. Our company holds these meetings three times a year for our team of top leaders to strategize about the future and to strengthen the bonds among us.

During this particular meeting years ago, our senior leaders and I set out to lay fence on a farm—not an everyday occurrence in corporate America. Suddenly, those who traditionally exude confidence—those to whom people come for answers—were wide-eyed and eager to tackle the new task that lay before them.

Everyone stood on equal ground, and to accomplish the job would require teamwork in the truest sense of the word. Interesting personality traits are revealed; heart and soul are bared when you manage to break down barriers and remove people from the environment they "own."

What happened surprised us all. Everyone was in charge. Everyone thought they knew how it should be done. We flew into action and the results were disastrous. The fence was finished in virtually no time, and it went in about as many directions as there were vice presidents. I think even the farm animals were laughing at us.

The farmer who owned the land was standing nearby. He possessed a wealth of knowledge about what we were trying to do. He had around twenty years of fence-laying experience under his belt. Tools that would have made the job much easier lay on the ground just a few yards away, untouched. They were unfamiliar to us, so they appeared to be of no value.

All chiefs and no Indians. All pride and not enough humility to seek guidance from those who could help. No process. No synergy. Poor quality. We learned some lessons that day that really made a difference.

Only after an hour of team humility did someone turn to the real expert, our farmer friend. Then, after two or three tries the fence stretched far beyond us around the perimeter of the pasture and stood as a monument to the bonds we all knew were strengthened on that hot, dry day on a farm in North Dakota.

Formula for Finding the Right People

A SUMMARY

█ Choose wisely—the emotional and financial costs of turnover are high. Projects are put on hold, service is interrupted, training costs are lost, competitive information walks out the door, and a host of other ills result from turnover. You have to be sure you find the right people from the beginning. Look for team and cultural fit.

█ When interviewing for leadership positions, place your candidates in situations beyond the normal scope of their work or in environments away from the workplace—try sports, driving, informal gatherings. Watch their interaction skills, see how they hold up in unexpected situations.

█ Include as many people as possible in the interview process for key leaders. Those they will lead, as well as fellow key leaders, should have a say.

█ You might consider utilizing the services of a corporate psychologist to help your company develop profiles for key positions or to help conduct executive assessments of potential senior leaders.

█ It's important to define the core competencies needed for success in your organization in general, specifically for leaders, and for each position. These competencies can be used for hiring, performance management, and career planning.

█ Having a reputation as an employer of choice can be very helpful in attracting talent, but it's the reality that counts. Make sure your culture attracts the type of person you seek.

█ Two terrific recruiting tools are an Associate Referral Program and promoting from within.

█ Open your company up to a variety of backgrounds—not just from your own or related industries; not just the traditional sources for people. Broaden your horizons, widen your areas of expertise, and increase your chances of finding good people.

▌ Finding and keeping strong people for e-commerce initiatives isn't easy. Consider the importance of the emotional aspects. Staff your e-ventures with enough of the right talent, and remember people are the most valuable component of e-business.

▌ An ounce of retention is worth a pound of recruitment. Make it easy for people to job hop within your company. Make time for your strongest people, too—not just those who need the most help. Consider a retention manager and a retention plan to keep your focus on this critical area.

▌ It's a good idea to have tools in place to rate your retention risk. Two that have been helpful for us are an Engagement Study and 30-60-90 day reviews.

▌ Avoid arrogant people, egotists, political animals, and those who have their eye primarily on the benefits of your industry, such as free or discounted travel in the travel industry, cars in the auto industry, or whatever perks your particular industry offers.

▌ Exercises to keep egos in check can be helpful. They break down barriers, strengthen bonds, and help diminish turf wars. Situations that are slightly uncomfortable put a spotlight on people's true colors.

▌ Above all, look for nice people who care. Everything else can be taught.

CHAPTER FOUR
Perpetual Learning:
A Secret Weapon

Leadership and learning are indispensable to each other.
—John Fitzgerald Kennedy, November 22, 1963

The growth of a company is really the aggregate of the growth of its individuals. Organizations that offer their people career-long learning opportunities are investing in the future, while improving their firms today.

We made a decision in 1980 to become such a company. We've come a long way since that time. Today, our learning goes far beyond the technical and extends outside our organization. It's been an interesting journey and one we've shared with a great many companies.

You might think, "Why would other organizations be interested in the learning programs of a travel company?" The answer is that much of our learning is philosophical, attitudinal, and cultural. A number of client and non-client firms have participated in our programs.

A very proud moment for our company came when we were cited as having one of the top ten training programs in the nation in the book *The 100 Best Companies to Work for in America*. The recognition is nice, but the affirmation that we are truly a learning organization is what means the most to us.

The Kindergarten Principle
The Importance of Making Learning Enjoyable

Most kids really enjoy kindergarten. After that, they seem to enjoy the academic aspect of school progressively less each year. That's because a lot of the fun is taken out of learning as we get older.

It's a fact that people retain more when they learn through interaction. We've also proven that people retain a great deal more when they have fun learning. We call that "The Kindergarten Principle." We try to put the fun back in learning.

Why is it that kids who hate math can manage to learn the batting averages of just about every player in the American League? How come kids can learn to work with computers at such an early age and can beat almost any adult at Nintendo? They learn what they have fun learning.

Learning is an attitude. For it to be effective, we must *want* to learn. Unfortunately, when we're required to learn something, we usually just memorize what we need to know. That's not learning.

True learning has become very important to this company. We consider it our responsibility to help each and every associate reach his or her full potential. If a hidden talent remains hidden and is not brought forth, nurtured, and developed, then we've failed as a company and as leaders.

We operate on the belief that there's nothing any of our associates couldn't learn if they wanted to. We try to select the type of person who thirsts for knowledge, and we keep rolling out new programs to quench those thirsts.

Our clients depend on our people to be highly knowledgeable about every aspect of our service. They don't want people to be limited to understanding just the technical functions of their work. They want to interact with multifaceted individuals who can take care of whatever needs arise. This is never going to happen by accident.

Broad-based learning prepares people to provide this level of service. Too many companies are so anxious to get their new hires working that they thrust them into their new positions without adequate training. I contend that this is a mistake.

At least the first two decades of our lives are dedicated to learning. Then we're propelled into the "working world" where these opportunities diminish. Sure, we learn on the job, but why stop the formal education process? The big yellow school bus pulls up to our house and takes us to learn for years, and then one day it just stops. Companies need to assume that role.

Training is as necessary as a road map in an unfamiliar place. Why let your people take a wrong turn, when providing them with information will lead them where they need to go? Providing them with the *best possible* information will get them where they need to be quickly, accurately, and with pride.

In any industry or any company, learning is essential, but when you're providing service, it's everything because you only get one chance. The people providing it can't just go that "extra mile." They need to know which is the best direction.

The programs we've found successful can easily be adapted to fit your company's environment, needs, and goals. Hopefully, these concepts will spark some fresh ideas.

Plato Would Be Proud
Philosophical Training Programs

When we first established our learning and development organization, we recognized the ongoing need for technical training only. It wasn't until after we had developed our technical programs that we realized there was a need for learning beyond the technical.

We saw an interesting phenomenon unfold. We found we were spending a great deal of time on the intangibles of service. Most of our people's questions were hypothetical, situational, and philosophical. Those questions flagged a need, and we began to add philosophical training.

People wanted to learn the philosophy behind service as much as the mechanics. When you think about it, culture and attitude have as much of an effect on service as skill. Learning really has to begin with philosophy.

Fluid Learning
Breaking the Learning Mold

The only irreplaceable capital an organization possesses is the knowledge and ability of its people. The productivity of that capital depends on how effectively people share their competence with those who can use it.

—Andrew Carnegie

In the original version of this book, we took great pains to spell out the number of hours invested in training, even down to the specific program. Interestingly, when we revisited those figures, looking to update them, we found them almost irrelevant. Not to say that we don't keep an eye on the investments we make in learning—we keep an eye on everything. But numbers of hours spent in specific classroom programs just misses the point today.

It would be almost impossible to pin down the exact hours devoted to learning, and that's great news. The secret to being a true learning organization is that learning is not restricted to the classroom. In fact, the walls have been blown off the classroom and learning is happening in every corner of the company, at any given moment, around the world. We certainly provide some core courses, but the just-in-time training that happens each and every day in the field is priceless. The key to it is an environment of openness, trust, and collaboration that makes sharing knowledge the norm.

Two secrets to maximizing learning are our "leader in learning" role and "Individual Development Plans." Leaders in learning are front-line associates who act as liaisons between our Learning and Development organization and the business unit in which they work. They assess training needs; research, develop, and facilitate courses; and work to make learning part of everyone's daily life.

All areas of the company have leaders in learning (there are more than 140). Some are full-time and others fill the role as part of their traditional responsibilities. Most are people who work frequently with clients, which means they're fully in touch with real-world issues.

To keep everyone moving forward, each person creates his or her own learning plan for the year. These Individual Development Plans (IDPs) include learning objectives for the associate's current position, as well as objectives to help them on the career path they desire (whether or not it relates to their current position). The plans include specific action steps, completion criteria, and time frames, ensuring we are all progressing on our learning paths.

Copies of everyone's IDPs are consolidated and studied to look for trends in learning needs across the company. The learning needs of our associates are then met by a variety of methods, such as classroom sessions, on-line programs, self-study modules, and outside offerings. Though much of the learning takes place beyond established courses, we'd like to outline some programs that are part of a core curriculum.

From Parsley to Relaxation Exercises
A Seminar Program for the Whole Individual

We're not running a spa at our company, although you might think we were if you walked into some of our seminars. One program we conducted on stress management found associates sitting in silence, breathing deeply, thinking about the most pleasant experience of their lives or the most peaceful setting they could imagine.

The room was silent. As I closed my eyes I could feel the tension of the day slipping into the past. I envisioned clear pools of cool water filled with resting lily pads, under a clear sky. I imagined the smell of freshly cut grass and spring flowers.

I was on an island with nothing around but gentle waves lapping up on powder-white sand. I felt everything in slow motion and nothing mattered, nothing waited, only the future stretching before me.

Then the unspeakable happened. I heard a voice on my island—it was the seminar instructor. Even though he was talking about relaxation, he was bringing me back to reality and that was a cruel awakening. You could see that everyone felt the same way. But we knew we had each learned the way to our own special hideaway where we can wrap ourselves in relaxation.

Do we really do this type of thing in the middle of the workday? Yes. We were learning exercises that can lower heart rates, reduce stress, and improve health. This session was part of our "Lunchtime Learning" program.

The idea is to offer material that benefits our people's personal as well as professional lives: topics like handling difficult situations, e-mail etiquette, presentation skills, food and fitness, organization skills, facing change, how to surf the Internet like a pro, and personal finance.

One of the more popular sessions we have held over the years has been "Perception vs. Reality." Participants discuss the importance of perception and of recognizing that other people's perceptions will differ from their own. We illustrate this through the following exercise.

The group attending divides into pairs. One person in each pair is blindfolded; the other is not. Containers of substances are placed before them. The blindfolded people can only touch the substance. Their partners can only look at it. Each person takes a guess as to what the substance is, and rarely are they in agreement. We use substances that could easily be mistaken. For instance, flour looks and feels like talcum powder; salt looks and feels like sugar. Some are easier to tell by touch and others by sight.

It's a tangible way to illustrate that others may see us, or something we do or say, from a completely different perspective. We emphasize that the viewpoints of others must be considered valuable, especially those of our clients, associates, and loved ones.

In addition to teaching us some really useful material, the Lunchtime Learning program brings together people who may not normally have the opportunity to work together. Someone from finance might be paired with someone in human resources; someone in maintenance might sit next to someone in accounting; or someone in our mail department might interact with one of our meeting planners.

Many of the seminar topics are submitted by our associates. It's a great way for them to express their developmental needs, concerns, and interests and to see the company helping to meet those needs.

The forty-five-minute programs are offered at lunch. We don't require anyone to sign up but rather to attend as they like, and attendance at the programs is strong. They are taught by content experts— anyone who has the expertise and inclination to put together and present a course with widespread applicability. These programs can be shared with other offices around the world and taught by our leaders in learning.

Other Starters in the All-Star Lineup
A Sampling of Programs

We have a wide variety of training programs—over seventy courses in all—everything from technical training to telephone techniques, emotional intelligence to elegant language, professionalism in the new millennium to diversity, coaching and development to project management.

I won't cover them all, but I'll outline a few and explain their objectives. These sessions are available to everyone, though some are geared toward somewhat specific audiences. The only requirement for attendance is that each person can work them into his or her schedule while not negatively impacting service to our clients or placing an unreasonable burden on fellow associates.

These programs are in demand. People really look forward to attending them, and the benefits to the individual and the company are far-reaching. If you stand back and look at what we're doing. I'm sure you'll see ways in which these programs could be applied in any business today.

We started our "Pre-Leadership" program several years ago because we noticed that as our company grew and became more complex, we saw a gap between the skill set at the entry level and what was required for our leaders. We needed early leadership training to close that gap and help our associates prepare for internal advancement opportunities.

So our Learning and Development team studied the skills, careers, and strengths of people throughout the organization who had successfully made the leap from front line to leader. Then they put together a program to build the right skills.

The program begins with a seminar, "Is Leadership Meant for Me?" It's held on a Saturday and explains the demands of leadership, illustrating what it's really like, day-to-day. In one exercise, participants are given an "in-box" filled with memos from senior leaders, client letters, a variety of phone messages, and other documents. Then small groups meet to prioritize the tasks, which represent far in excess of forty hours' work, yet the group must fit it all into a week's workload. It's a pretty good representation of a typical leader's schedule.

If they're still interested upon completion of the course, they can apply for our "Pre-Leadership Development Self-Study" program. Those who are selected for the program work together with their leader and the program manager to complete an IDP designed to help develop the appropriate leadership skills for each individual, to be accomplished through a series of learning modules.

Our "Team Leader Training" is an interactive, comprehensive leadership program created specifically for our team leader group. We began the program in 1997 as a pilot course and fully designed the curriculum based upon the feedback provided by the participants as well as studying the core competencies required for this key, front-line leader position. Today, we offer the course around the world.

Our team leaders (TLs) face the challenge of balancing their team tasks while leading the team. Topics like motivation, learning styles, team dynamics, communication skills, and "conquering the negative attitude virus" are introduced through a series of case studies, role-plays, and exercises, designed to support them in the unique demands of their position.

The course is supported by a network through which TLs share materials and consult with one another on issues that arise in their business units. Also available are quick study topics they can access to enhance their development.

The group tells us that one of the best parts of the program is the opportunity to spend time with their peers. For most, this is their first chance to meet TLs from other offices. They usually work in situations where they are the only one, or one of a few. We've heard countless stories from team leaders that they have solved challenges in their business units by calling on TLs from their training class and putting their heads together. This helps the TLs, while providing value to our clients.

Our "Fundamentals of Corporate Operational Standards" (FOCOS) course is a study in boosting companywide productivity and effectiveness. It's a model from which virtually any company in any industry could benefit. I think of it as "Rosenbluth 101" for new operations leaders. We make it mandatory for the general managers and account managers that lead our business units.

The three-day course covers our *Corporate Operations Standards Manual*, which is packed with recipes on how to run a successful business unit. What makes the course so important and so effective is that it takes all the hard work done by our leaders over the years and documents their trials, tribulations, and paths taken. For that reason, we are able to avoid reinventing the wheel and repeating mistakes. This represents a huge savings in time, energy, expense, and thought-drain.

During the FOCOS course, our new leaders learn about the support structure at headquarters and meet many of the associates there who will support them—also a time and energy saver when they return to the field and need help with something. The final portion of the course is a relaxed session with senior leaders, during which they learn about the state of the company, ask questions, and discuss ongoing and upcoming initiatives.

"Business and Financial Training" is designed for our leaders to expand their knowledge of topics like analyzing financial statements, measuring financial key performance indicators, tracking trends, reviewing budget variances, and analyzing cash flow. These are skills they use to better manage their business and help our clients achieve their travel program goals.

Participants are invited to "put fresh batteries in their calculators and grab their P&L statements," because this course is very interactive, combining class lecture with group activities using their own, live financial data and real-world issues. They are challenged to explain what's behind their numbers and to share best practices with one another.

A favorite part of the session is when participants "run their own company for a day." Using a third party business simulation, they are challenged to make decisions from an overall, "big picture" perspective and to see the effects on the entire organization. The course evaluations we receive tell us that attendees anticipate a finance course to be somewhat dry, perhaps boring. But they leave saying it was fun and, therefore, memorable. And that tells us we're making an impact in a key area that helps ensure the health of our company.

In our "Leadership Development" program, we lead attendees down a path of development that builds on the basics and then challenges them on more nontraditional theories through each topic. Those topics include "Leadership at Rosenbluth," systems thinking, strategic planning, motivating associates, decision-making, marketing techniques, impact and influence, the power of information, and work/personal balance. The course is mandatory for all new leaders and has been adapted for all of our global locations. I'll share a few highlights of the course with you.

We ask everyone to bring in an article to share, which has had an impact on them. One person brought in a paper from an educational magazine, talking about different learning styles in children, and this spurred an interesting discussion about the various learning styles of our associates. This tradition encourages class participation and broadens the knowledge brought to the classroom.

Another favorite part is a brief video featuring associates from around the world discussing how they define a great leader. This is powerful. We need to never lose sight of what our people value and the fact that leading them is a privilege.

A fascinating portion of the class to sit in on is the discussion of power, which is part of the "Impact and Influence" section. It's interesting to hear how many associates view "power" in a negative light. We spend time talking about different types of power and share examples of power used positively and negatively.

During the "Power of Information" portion, each person brings a document that they have used internally or shared with a client. After we define the terms "data," "information," and "knowledge," they look at their document and determine what is being shared. In many cases it's merely data and information—not knowledge. They then take the same document and build knowledge into it, for example, creating a scenario using the data, which could positively impact a client's program. Everyone shares their changes, and a powerful best practices forum results.

The marketing section is a personal favorite because we get to taste-test Oreos—lots of them. We bring in four different types of Oreos and have four different groups write new marketing strategies for their product—each for a specific target market. One group came up with an easy snack box, containing cookies and milk. They designed a terrific marketing plan, complete with some great slogans. Next, we ask each group to design marketing strategies for *our* products.

The Oreo part is fun, but in all seriousness, the most important part, to me, is "Balancing Act," a two-part session on striking balance between our work and personal lives. Part one is done at the end of day one, and it talks about the importance of balance, offering how-to advice. Part two is presented at the conclusion of day two, and we do some things that really make people think.

We ask everyone to draw a circle and divide it into slices representing the roles they play, like spouse, parent, manager, son or daughter, volunteer. The size of each slice reflects the amount of time they currently devote to each role.

Then everyone leaves the room, and while they're wedging in calls to the office, checking voicemail, and putting out fires, the room is transformed. The lights are turned down, place mats are put on the floor, scented candles and soft music fill the room. We invite everyone back in and ask them to lie down on a mat. A gentle voice guides them through a relaxation exercise.

At first, there are usually some giggles and uncomfortable fidgeting, but within minutes, guaranteed, nobody is moving. Inevitably someone snores. After twenty minutes, we gradually bring everyone back to reality, and we ask them, in this newly relaxed state, to redraw their circle with the optimum size for each role they play—how they *really* want to spend their time. While this is happening, we bring in some apple pie and slice it up. Then, we discuss how their pictures have changed and what they need to do to change their lives to meet this all-important goal.

From Novice to Pro
Comprehensive Technical Training

Most companies have technical training, so I've focused mostly on the philosophical aspects of our learning programs. But there are facets of our technical training that can also have broad applications to businesses outside our industry.

I'll use our training programs for customer care associates (CCAs) for illustration, because these associates comprise most of our company. As you read earlier, CCAs are our front-line associates who primarily make corporate travel reservations for our clients. Every industry has its own parallel position—front-line people who work with clients on a day-to-day basis.

We require all CCAs, no matter their level of expertise, to participate in our technical training program. Depending upon their level of experience, that ranges from five days to six weeks (and in some cases, eight) of instruction.

When people start at square one they move from our "New Associate Orientation" straight into our six- to eight-week training program to teach them the process from scratch. They don't show up at their workplace until they have successfully completed the course.

This program enables us to lessen our dependence upon our industry, broadening our potential labor sources. We try to hire as many people as we can locally, to become part of the communities in which our clients are based. Our training gives us a competitive advantage because we can do that without worrying about finding people with prior travel experience.

We are able to hire the type of person who will excel in our culture and provide our clients with the service to which they have become accustomed. The technical can be learned. Our training program ensures that we will always have qualified CCAs.

We do hire a number of people with experience as well, but they too must complete technical training. Even those with extensive experience in corporate reservations still are not ready to serve our clients. We have our way of doing things, our own style of service that includes elegant language, the use of our proprietary technology, and knowledge of our clients' corporate travel policies and programs. We teach these and other aspects of our service in our "conversion" class.

From there, most of our CCAs attend account-specific training, where they learn all about the client company they'll be serving— what they do, where they most frequently go, their policies and preferences. Often, our clients are involved in this portion of the instruction, and that adds terrific value.

All CCAs participate in recurrent training to keep up with technological enhancements, industry trends, and client needs. No industry or company is exempt from the need to provide ongoing training to keep people current.

TLC
Coaching to Success

Coaching is important for every person, every day, but nowhere is it more vital than for new people. They can't be thrown from the training room to their workstation to fend for themselves. They should be coached by experienced people, to encourage them and guide them through situations that might not have been presented in training.

They say true life is stranger than fiction. There will always be a need or idiosyncrasy you couldn't anticipate in preparing your people to serve your clients. There's no end to the variety in people's needs, wants, and tastes. Experienced people need to be accessible to share their knowledge with those less experienced.

The philosophical and technical training of these new associates is followed by on-the-job instruction in a protected environment, provided by experienced coaches. We call this our Transitional Learning Center (TLC). In some offices this is a classroom setting and in others it is a special section on the reservation floor. The key is that each new CCA who has successfully completed the course takes his or her first calls with a coach standing by to assist them through the process.

The new associate stays in this environment until they are ready to take calls on their own. Even then, they are placed beside experienced CCAs who will continue to assist them as they become fully proficient.

Though the specifics of this program are tailored to our industry, the concept of a transitional learning program could be utilized in any department of any organization to ease new hires into the mainstream.

5,000 Computers Later
Training by Challenge

Not all training programs are formalized. People learn by example and through experience, so you need to ensure that those examples and experiences are the ones you want to reinforce. If you continually provide a variety of projects, people will rise to the occasion and develop new talents. In fact, without being challenged, people may never discover a talent they possess—and that's a crime.

Change is a great motivator to learn new things. But it's vital to provide security so people won't fear change. New products and new ways of doing things don't replace people. Lack of training in these new things does. As leaders, it's our responsibility to provide that training.

Today, technology is a part of our everyday lives. We do most of our banking through ATMs, but two decades ago, people didn't trust computers on the street to manage their financial transactions. We conduct a large portion of our business via e-mail, the Internet, and voicemail. Annoyingly enough, computers even call us on the phone during dinner trying to sell us something.

I remember when more than two decades ago, technology invaded our workplace and everyone was afraid that somehow computers would replace them. They resisted using them, but at the same time, saw their inevitability. We broke down fear by assuring our people that whatever our company did and however we did it, they would play an important part. But in order to do so they had to embrace change. To help them do that, we provided thorough training on our new computer systems. And today, five thousand PCs later, we're a better company, with more opportunities for our people than ever before.

It's our continual responsibility to make our associates aware that their roles *will* change. As technology advances, those roles will continue to evolve. For example, as our clients utilize self-booking tools more frequently, our people will find themselves spending more time on the consultative issues, the more complicated transactions, and the human aspects of service. This is great news. Automation tends to move our people toward more interesting, fulfilling, and meaningful work.

As with all other aspects of change, we provide the appropriate training to help our associates successfully shift their roles. It's part of the implementation process for on-line booking tools for our clients. It's facilitated by our account managers and general managers, and in many cases, the client.

Our distribution methods may change, but our people will always come first. Loyalty to our company is high—in part because our people know that rather than hiring new people to use new products, we train our own associates to use our new products. That's not only job security, it's an endless opportunity to learn new things.

Currently under development is Rosenbluth University on-line, through which all of our associates in every corner of the world can develop their skills in order to fulfill their professional goals. We plan to offer curriculum in a wide variety of subjects on-line, to be followed by classroom sessions that are more workshops, offering our associates the chance to interact with one another and explore the practical applications of what they have learned on-line. This will truly be learning free of boundaries.

From Travel Agent to Teacher
A Learning Organization Calls for Original People

To be able to teach a wide variety of programs, we need to choose our Learning and Development team carefully, knowing they have the same effect on people's lives that teachers do. There are certain backgrounds that lend themselves to training. Teaching experience and training within another company are ideal credentials, but we don't limit ourselves there. We've also found that a theater background can prepare someone beautifully for a corporate training role.

We've discovered some strong trainers by promoting from within. We rely more upon personality traits than specific backgrounds when selecting people for training positions. The best traits are poise, polish, outstanding communication skills, a sense of humor, and enthusiasm. It's also essential that each and every trainer be a role model.

In addition to creating and presenting a wide variety of programs, our Learning and Development department serves as a resource for the company, diagnosing learning needs, facilitating meetings, and creating customized learning tools whenever the need arises.

Today, we have less than half the full-time training staff we had when the original version of this book came out, yet we're learning so much more. At the time, 27 full-time trainers instructed 2,600 associates. Today, a staff of 10 supports more than 5,000 people.

We're not making less of an investment in learning. The secret is that it has shifted out to the field where it belongs, pursued by individuals seeking knowledge and by leaders in learning alongside to support them. Learning is individualized, customized, self-paced, time-efficient, and much more effective.

Our clients are delighted with the new training design. It means that their specific needs can be addressed immediately. They don't have to wait for a learning need to be spotted, a program developed, and the associates who serve them to travel to a centralized training site to attend a course. Learning takes place on the spot.

It's important to look at learning as a long-term investment. Companies that look for immediate returns on the time and money spent on training will be disappointed. The investment in learning should be viewed no differently from any capital project. Its success should be gauged by the benefits over the entire life of the project, not just by looking at years one and two. Similarly, trainers shouldn't have to waste time trying to justify the investment. Their time should be spent developing and conducting learning programs and serving as a resource to guide individual learning. And time and resources must be committed toward *their* continual development as educators.

Well Worth the Investment
A Look at Training's Bottom Line

Training isn't free, in any sense of the word. Highly effective training doesn't have to be exorbitant, but it takes commitment of time and money. And time *is* money when you're taking people away from their work to learn.

We do keep a close eye on our long-term return on investment for training. Our Learning and Development team tracks it as a matter of pride. They like demonstrating the tremendous value it offers. In one recent study, the team analyzed the typical training costs for a business unit of two hundred for a one-year period. Extrapolating that across our associate base of five thousand, our estimated annual training costs come out to $11.4 million—and these are only the costs to develop and customize the programs and materials. This does not include any related travel and entertainment costs, and it does not include associate time spent in training—the most significant expense.

Training is well worth the investment. It benefits both the front and bottom lines. How else can you bring out the talents in your people and prepare them and your company for tomorrow and the years to come? Training provides a more proficient workforce, improves quality, and cements loyalty.

Training Tips to Consider

A SUMMARY

▮ Consider training an essential part of your company. It means the difference between success and failure in the service industry, and more and more manufacturing companies are finding the competitive battleground is becoming one of service.

▮ Remember the kindergarten principle: *Make learning fun.* People retain more when information is presented in a creative, interactive, and interesting manner.

▮ Training must be attitudinal as well as technical, and it must be perpetual. Culture and attitude are as important to service as skill is.

▮ Think of learning without boundaries. If you have the right tools in place, learning will happen continuously, on the spot, all over your organization. Two secrets we have found to maximizing our learning are the Individual Development Plan (IDP) and our leader in learning role. IDPs keep everyone moving forward, and leaders in learning help ensure that learning is part of daily life in every corner of the company.

▌ Try offering training programs on general subjects, to all of your people, on a regular basis (we offer ours at lunch). It creates cohesiveness and consistency and fosters team-work. Offer material that benefits the personal and profes-sional lives of your people. You'll be pleased with the results.

▌ Consider a pre-leadership program to help close any gaps between front-line skills and what's required for internal advancement. We begin ours with a course on a Saturday designed to bring forward those who are serious about ad-vancing. From there, we offer a self-study program to strengthen the right skills.

▌ If you have people in roles combining front-line work and team leadership, a learning program that brings them to-gether to sharpen skills and share ideas can be a wise in-vestment. You might find, as we have, that those who attend will build and utilize lasting networks.

▌ A course (accompanied by a comprehensive manual) that outlines operational standards and procedures can be a powerful productivity tool, especially if it documents the trials, successes, and paths taken over the years. It can help you avoid reinventing the wheel or repeating mistakes.

▌ Business and financial training can have a significant im-pact on your leaders' ability to run their portions of your business, especially if the sophisticated and, at times, dry material is presented in a fun and memorable way.

▌ A comprehensive Leadership Development program is essential to prepare leaders for the vast array of challenges they face today. The topics we cover include systems think-ing, strategic planning, motivation, decision-making, mar-keting, impact and influence, the power of information, and work/personal balance. We make the two-day course mandatory for our leaders around the world.

▌ Continually sharpen your technical training and be sure it's comprehensive enough to enable you to hire people with no experience in your particular field. This will broaden the scope of people from which you hire—a distinct human resource advantage.

▌ Offer a "conversion" training class to even the most experienced new hires to confirm their level of expertise. It ensures that they'll do business the way *your company* does, not the way their previous employers did business.

▌ Always provide training for your people for new products or methods you plan to employ in your company. This will eliminate the need to find new people to use these products and will go a long way to ensure that your people won't resist change as a result of fear. It also builds loyalty and drives down turnover.

▌ Try training by challenge. Your people will surprise themselves and you with what they are capable of doing when challenged. Provide a variety of new projects and employ new tools. People will develop new skills to rise to the challenges.

▌ Daily coaching of your people by their leaders will strengthen the skills of both. It's particularly important for those new on the job. You may want to consider creating a Transitional Learning Center to ease new hires into the mainstream.

▌ In selecting your training staff, consider people with theater and other varied backgrounds as well as those with experience in teaching and corporate training. Grooming your own trainers by promoting from within can also be very effective. Be sure to offer ongoing training to your trainers, too.

▌ Commit the training resources necessary for your company—both financial and in terms of time. It's a long-term investment that you'll never regret.

CHAPTER FIVE

Service Is an Attitude, an Art, and a Process

The 1991 movie *The Doctor* illustrated the importance of compassionate service in a very gripping way. In the movie, a callous but mechanically highly skilled doctor becomes very ill and faces hardships others must face in the wake of his work: difficult things like pain, fear, disrespect for a person's time or feelings, and even possible death.

He is a changed man because of his experience. After struggling with himself, he realizes there's more to medicine than science. He chooses a surgeon whom he once belittled to perform his crucial operation, on the basis that he is a caring person. He begins to spend time with his family and to nurture the relationships he has neglected. He learns a great deal from getting a taste of his own medicine—an eye-opener for most of us.

We're all in the service business. Even companies in the manufacturing sector are service companies. Gone are the days when a company could merely produce and distribute products. Consumers want service surrounding those products and they'll give their business to those who provide it.

It's not easy to provide good service. There's no one way to do it. We all have to do our best to develop our own formulas for service. In this chapter, I'll share our formula with you. Then I'll break it down and analyze its components.

Attitude + Art + Process
A Formula for Service

Our formula is *Service = Attitude + Art + Process.*

Attitude encompasses many things. Finding the right people—people who care and who want to be the best—is the core of attitude. But attitudes can be influenced by external factors. If a person who cares is placed in a non-caring environment, for example, or if her efforts to go above and beyond are foiled or discouraged, her attitude can be smothered. So good attitude is really a matter of the right person working in the right environment.

Next, *art.* Anything done with conviction, with style and flair, is art. Service is—or should be—creative. There are endless things one can do to enhance a service experience. That's one of the most exciting aspects of service. There are literally endless opportunities for improvement. There is no 100 percent, only close and closer. Service is a continuous creative pursuit—an art.

Finally, *process.* Finding the best way to do things is also perpetual, and it's incredibly important. Process makes things possible. It brings order to the components of service so that the people executing them are free to concentrate on the finer points and added touches that make service come alive. Process makes measuring progress possible, which is the key to continuous improvement. Process also facilitates consistency across a large, and particularly a growing, organization.

Service is an attitude, an art, and a process, but none of these is possible without happiness in the workplace. Service is demanding, if performed well, so it inherently breaks down if those delivering it are not happy.

ATTITUDE

Let My People Go
Giving People Room to Be Outstanding

People need to be given space to provide truly outstanding service. They must be given the freedom to create and the support and encouragement they need to do great things. We like to call this a "mental safety net."

Too many managers make the error of holding their people down, fearing the mistakes they might make if they are given freedom. But by doing so, they are also forgoing opportunities for potentially outstanding results. This type of manager has no place in the leadership of this millennium. There's no room for such a person in our organization.

We all make mistakes. Anyone willing and determined to strive for something special will probably make more mistakes than someone who provides only status quo service. But mistakes are a small price to pay for the successes that often follow failed attempts. A true test of exceptional service can be found in the actions a company or individual takes to turn mistakes into positive experiences. But when we make mistakes, even when we turn them around, we've got to feel them in our stomachs—yes, our stomachs.

I contend that providing less than stellar service should make us physically nauseated. I know that after a client tells me we've erred, I usually wind up planning our recovery strategy while drinking antacid. Some people blush uncontrollably when they're embarrassed; some people's palms sweat when they're nervous. I get sick when we mess up—I literally become physically ill.

Once I ran into a client in the airport and he shared with me his dissatisfaction over a recent trip on which it seemed everything went wrong from the start. I spent the entire flight between the air phone and the lavatory. And I'm not the only one who's affected this way.

Many of my colleagues are plagued with the same consequence to one degree or another.

But as with performers or athletes who fall, the best thing they can do is pick themselves up and keep going. In providing service, we have to discipline ourselves to keep moving forward in spite of any fumbles we've made. We can only learn from them if we see them as steps to improvement.

Remaining "Busied In"
The Service Attitude at Work

The Chinese philosopher Confucius was once on a journey with his disciples through dry terrain. One of his followers discovered a hidden puddle, filled his rice bowl, and offered it to the Master. Confucius was about to raise it to his lips when he caught sight of the faces of his disciples. He emptied the bowl on the ground, saying, "It would be too much for one, too little for all of us. Let us continue our walk."

Many years ago, we learned a valuable lesson about teamwork that we use as a reminder of the power of group effort. It's the story of a principle we called "busied in/busied out."

We serve our clients in business units so our people and clients can get to know one another. When a client calls to make a travel reservation, the call goes to the next available member of the team. Our system enables our CCAs to take themselves out of the loop if they need a break or feel overloaded, and when they do it's called "busying out." When they're ready to take a call they "busy in" and return to the loop.

A number of years ago, we started serving a new account for which the volume was greatly underestimated. Our people were swamped with calls. They felt overloaded and morale was dipping.

One of our vice presidents spent some time with the team to help ensure smooth service until we could shift additional resources to that account. While she was there she developed a theory and asked the team to give it a try for just one week. They did, and they discovered they didn't need more people after all—and productivity and morale soared.

Here's how it worked. There were ten people dedicated to serving the account, and it seemed as though the phone never stopped ringing. Each would take several calls in rapid succession and then busy out for a breather. Let's estimate that at any one time, half of them were busied out, leaving five people to bear the burden of calls. When they busied back in, they would be in a group of about five, taking calls for ten.

What was happening was that their tendency to busy out was creating an overload of work for those remaining, and when they were the ones taking calls, they were overloaded by the same burden created by their associates busying out. It was a vicious cycle.

Our vice president asked the team members to stay busied in all day (with the exception of their breaks, lunch, etc.) so that the calls would be distributed among ten, as was intended, as opposed to five, which had become reality. Rather than create a cycle in which they faced an overload of work, then needed a break, *everyone* made themselves available for the right amount of work, all day.

The concept is just common sense, but when people become overwhelmed, it's easy to slip into a reactive mode rather than a proactive one. The busied-in principle instilled confidence in the team that they could manage that level of work.

The busied-in principle can take on life-and-death proportions in the military. It did for the famous *Memphis Belle,* the first B-17 bomber to finish all of its required twenty-five missions during World War II. The Eighth Air Force crew flew out of England and over Germany. Ten percent of all World War II casualties were troops who did the same.

There were ten members on the crew—the pilot, co-pilot, bombardier, navigator, engineer, radioman, tail gunner, belly gunner, and left and right waist gunners. Every position was critical. They each had a job to do and if even one person had busied out, the crew would have faced death or capture by the enemy. Every man's life rested not just on his own shoulders but on those of each fellow crew member. They all survived by staying "busied in."

In industry, the principle doesn't carry the same dire consequences, but it can mean the life or death of a company if people relax into letting others pull some of their weight. In the manufacturing sector, when people are busied out, it can halt production. In the airline industry, a flight is grounded until it has the proper ratio of crew to passengers. So if a flight attendant doesn't show up, the customers have to wait until a replacement arrives.

Have you ever waited in line at the supermarket or bank, and the checkout person puts up a "COUNTER CLOSED" sign? You know what happens next. You move to another line and wait for a very long time along with everyone else. And by the time people reach the front of the line they're steaming, and often not very pleasant to the person who *does* serve them.

There are also sports that closely parallel the service attitude we're describing. Two in particular are rowing and tug-of-war. In these two sports, everyone has to literally pull his or her own weight. Trust is a must. You can be rowing or pulling with all your might, but unlike other sports that more clearly demonstrate individual effort, how do you *know* each of your teammates is giving their all?

You can't know, so you have to trust, encourage one another to be your best, and keep your goals in synch. You have to choose your teammates wisely and you have to work together to make the strengths of one offset the weaknesses of another.

The key is for us all to stay busied in, especially management. It's top leadership's role to extend the busied-in technique across departmental lines, so that companies as a whole perform like a rowing team.

ART

Frances Russell
The Story of a Service Hero

I had perhaps the best service experience of my life on a trip to San Francisco in 1989. The combination of an experience beautiful in its simplicity and completely unexpected made it what it was—and I don't think I'll ever forget it.

My wife and I stopped by a restaurant for breakfast before starting our day, expecting little except a hurried and possibly grumpy waitress, serving some pretty good eggs and very good coffee. Up walks Frances Russell, of Sears Fine Food, the creator of an exceptional service experience. She was polite, friendly, and efficient. You could tell she took a great deal of pride in her work, and I began to see that the service would be good. But the unexpected came when she prepared to pour my coffee.

Normally, if 90 percent of your coffee in a standard restaurant lands in your cup, you're doing pretty well. But before serving my coffee, Frances asked if I was right-handed or left-handed. Living in a right-handed world, I was surprised to be asked, but I was even more surprised to be asked by a waitress in a restaurant. When I answered that I was left-handed, she proceeded to reposition everything on the table to be more convenient to a southpaw, including setting the coffee cup to my left and moving everything else aside.

Before that time, I was quite accustomed to moving the cup and other items myself. In fact, I was so accustomed to it that before this experience, I never even realized I was doing it! But now, Frances Russell has spoiled me for life. Every time I go into a restaurant and my waiter or waitress assumes that I am right-handed or really doesn't care either way, I will move the items myself and think of Frances Russell.

The point is that once you have had an extraordinary service experience, nothing else will do. People shouldn't have to settle for less than outstanding service. People shouldn't *give* less than outstanding service, but the dilemma is that they most often do. That makes us appreciate it all the more when we receive truly fine service.

When you're dedicated to providing excellent service, you become jaded to the point where it begins to infringe upon your life. You become less and less tolerant of poor, even average, service. You begin to analyze the service you receive with a trained eye.

My colleagues and I may not be able to relax in a restaurant because we're too busy analyzing the service, but we think that's great. Why shouldn't we have the highest expectations of service? Why shouldn't our clients demand the best? We hope they will, and we hope we can rise to the occasion. Our goal is to spoil our clients beyond the point where anyone else's service will do.

Frances Russell is a service hero. I'm proud to say we also have a few of our own. We consistently get our clients seats on sold-out flights, rooms in sold-out hotels, and last-minute passports and visas. We try to get them complimentary upgrades to first class on flights and suites in hotels.

These perks might seem appropriate from a travel company. You may be surprised to learn that we also locate lost luggage for our clients; act as a message service, calling spouses or assistants; greet our clients' special guests at the airport; and when our clients return from overseas, then have a coast-to-coast flight, we'll deliver their mail to them to read on the flight home. Beyond that, we often make arrangements for our clients for theater tickets, sporting events, restaurant reservations, baby-sitting services, and golf tee times. We even get requests for wake-up calls.

Then there are those unusual situations when we really get an opportunity to come through for our clients. In two such instances we were literally going to the dogs.

The general manager for a National Hockey League team, one of our clients, bought a dog as a gift for the general manager of another team. The client asked us to take care of the dog's flight arrangements. What did we do? We rented a kennel and flew the dog with a personal escort to ensure his safe arrival. Our associate delivered the dog, in person, and returned home on the next flight.

Another client had to make an emergency trip at the last minute. When he called to make his reservations, he mentioned he was worried about quickly securing someone to take care of his dogs while he was gone. Our associate spent the week dog-sitting.

A client called us at 3:00 A.M. in a panic because he was on the road and his wife was in labor. We chartered him a flight and he made it home in time for the birth of his first child.

One of our clients who suffers from severe asthma called us when an airline lost the luggage containing her medicine. Our associates were so concerned that while one traced the luggage and arranged for its immediate delivery to the hotel, another stayed on the phone with the client the entire time to make sure her breathing was stable until the medicine arrived.

Probably my favorite story took place during the Gulf War. It begins as a story of friendship and, along the way, becomes a story of heroic service. A number of years ago, we expanded to the Middle East, and I didn't really know what to expect, particularly how Rosenbluth International would be received as a potential business partner by companies in the Arab nations. But I knew from our first meeting with the people of Kanoo Travel (a division of the Yusuf Bin Ahmed Kanoo group) in Bahrain that we would forge a special friendship with them.

Their company is very much like our own in many ways. Both have been family-owned businesses for more than a century, and their commitment to excellence and caring attitude toward their people mirror ours. But we had no idea the dimension this relationship would take on over the years.

When the Gulf War began, a number of our clients found themselves faced with trying circumstances, but probably none more than Chevron. Amidst the chaos at the onset of the conflict, some Chevron employees were not able to get out of Kuwait. The U.S. State Department couldn't provide information, and our stateside friends at Chevron were determined to explore every possible resource to ensure the safety of their associates. They called upon us to help in any way we could.

We immediately called upon our friends at Kanoo. They mobilized a team to reach any and all contacts they had in Kuwait to try to get information on the Chevron executives. Within a matter of days, they were located. What happened next was something only a friend, in the truest sense of the word, might do.

A team of Kanoo associates assembled to travel into the midst of the war in Kuwait to assist the stranded Chevron executives, whom they had never met. Their mission was to find them, help them depart

Kuwait, bring them into Saudi Arabia, then safely on their way home to the United States and their families. Our friends at Kanoo were willing to risk their own safety, possibly even their lives, to protect the safety of people who were important to us.

In the end, the Chevron executives in Kuwait reached safety without the Kanoo team having to travel into the war zone, but the point is, they were ready and willing to do it. Caring can triumph over even war.

Every company will have its favorite service stories. But the secret is to make this level of service the norm and not the exception. The attitude and art components of our formula are vital, but without process, it is very difficult to master service and make it routinely excellent.

PROCESS

Cook with the Best Ingredients
The Importance of Building in Quality Up Front

Just having a process won't cut it. You have to have a quality process, and it's hard work to develop one. In order for your company to operate at peak performance, there must be a quality process for everything you do.

I regret the overuse of the word *quality*, but no other word means quite the same thing. There are words that come close, but they don't accurately describe what we all strive to achieve. I guess that's why the word has been used by virtually every company to describe their products and services. I'll use it anyway because it's the best word we've got.

Quality has to be built in up front. It doesn't work to try to make up for it at the end. Quality built in, up front, to every single product, process, and service costs less, though one might think the opposite to be true. We have examples to prove it.

There's no substitute for doing it right the first time. In a company providing quality service, the need for a customer service department should be minimal if not nonexistent. Over the years, we have significantly reduced ours, shifting those resources to more productive purposes. For quality products and services, problems and complaints are the exception, not the norm.

There's an advertising campaign that paints a clear picture of what I'm saying. You know the one: The appliance repairman bemoans his loneliness because he is never needed. The message: The company's appliances work, and if you own one you will use it for years and years without needing a repairman. Quality should be so good in America.

A person dining in a restaurant that prepares its meals with the finest ingredients will normally enjoy the meal with no additional seasoning or condiments. On the other hand, when bland or inferior ingredients are used, those who are dining will reach for salt and pepper and ask their waiter or waitress for mustard, catsup, horseradish, and all varieties of condiments to enhance the flavor, or lack thereof, in the food.

The same can be said for service. When quality is built in at the outset, clients have little need to ask for corrections after the fact, thus diminishing the need for a customer service department. In the end, it takes a certain number of ingredients to make up service. Why not use the right ones in the first place?

Quality Control
An Oxymoron

I think "quality control" is an oxymoron. True quality needs space to breathe. If quality is built in, then where's the need for control? Why on earth would you want to control quality? It should be allowed to run rampant.

Give your people the proper tools and freedom to use them, and in the right atmosphere, they will create and perpetuate quality.

The Right to Be Pygmalion
Tailoring a Quality Program for Your Company

In Greek mythology, Pygmalion was the king of Cyprus who carved an ivory statue of the maiden of his dreams. He fell in love with his creation and pleaded to Aphrodite, the goddess of love and beauty, to bring her to life. She granted his wish and the statue became Galatea, Pygmalion's love.

We're all Pygmalions to a certain degree. When dating, everybody's probably found themselves wishing they could take one person's personality and combine it with another person's appearance and add to that the timing of another relationship. Through this process, we'd try to create our ideal.

When selecting a home, there's that special room in one, another is in the neighborhood where we'd like to live, and then there's the question of price. We want the ideal home for the ideal price.

Of course, all of the above is not always possible in our world, but I have some good news. We've found that you *can* selectively mold your own quality/service philosophy—one that takes the best attributes of each and fits them together to create the ideal model for your organization. That's exactly how we built our approach to quality at Rosenbluth, and we have discovered that it works beautifully.

Our eclectic approach to quality has enabled us to understand and utilize statistical process control but not be controlled by it. One very important thing we've learned is not to let process stand in the way of progress. A key element in our approach to quality is common sense.

Extensive Research in the Quality Lab
Doing Your Homework to Make a Quality Choice

After a very humbling experience we began to see quality in a whole new light. Our company has always applied quality principles. We've long maintained the highest accuracy rating in our industry. Our clients have always been pleased with our service. So we assumed we were a "quality" company. We were in for a surprise.

Many years ago, when one of our new clients was awarded the prestigious Malcolm Baldrige National Quality Award, the company encouraged its suppliers to pursue total quality management and apply for the award as well. We got an application and intended to apply immediately. When we took a look at the application we were put in our place.

For those of you who might not have had the pleasure of reading this application, it calls for statistical measurement of just about everything a company does. It looks for every person in the organization to be utilizing these measurements as tools for continuous improvement. A history of consistent improvement must be proven statistically.

This was quality of a different species. We knew we operated on the principles of quality, but we didn't have the tools to prove it, the same tools that help a company to improve. We had some decisions to make about what type of program we wanted. We thought that our level of quality deserved measurement. Continuous improvement was one of our most important goals. So we went for it.

The first thing we did was to study the quality processes of our clients and the research of the complete line up of quality gurus. We developed a pretty good idea of what we wanted out of a quality program and a clear understanding that we couldn't do it ourselves. So after an exhaustive search, we hired a total quality management consultant.

We selected the consultant not just based on his knowledge of statistics, although that's essential. It was important to find someone who would make the material interesting and fun so we would all be enthusiastic about learning it and applying it on a day-to-day basis. Because for most of us, sophisticated applied statistics seemed intimidating.

With our partner in place and sights aimed high, we were ready to convert to total quality management. Quality was about to become serious stuff at our company.

Building a Quality Program
Where to Begin

We decided that a serious approach to quality would demand dedicated resources. We created a small department to analyze the company's quality needs, to develop training and implementation programs, and to continually evaluate our progress. This team ensured that all of our quality programs worked together toward the results we wanted to achieve as a company. We created new and more demanding goals and they helped us measure our way to success.

We built this team from inside our organization. Rather than hire quality experts and teach them about our company, we hired people who live the company and trained them to be experts in quality.

Our quality team completed rigorous training on quality principles and tools. Then they went into a week-and-a-half-long course that prepared and certified them to teach their fellow associates throughout the company.

In the first year of quality training, about half of our associates completed the program, and by the second year, the entire organization was trained. Once all of our associates were trained in the fundamentals of quality, we incorporated quality into our core learning programs.

For example, as new associates join the company, they gain exposure to quality principles during our orientation program. We introduce it during the client focus portion, discussing our clients' expectations of quality service and how we must exceed them. It is reintroduced when we talk about the technology tools we have to help us build quality into the front end. We talk about frequently used quality tools our associates rely on in the field.

Over the years since its inception, our quality program has evolved to truly become a way of life. That was our initial goal, and our associates have achieved it. When we embarked on our quality journey in the early 1990s, our quality team was told that if they did their jobs right, they'd be out of jobs, as quality became integrated into daily work life.

They did their jobs expertly, and once the initial training was accomplished and our associates were accustomed to using the tools, our quality team disbanded, and those associates took their in-demand skills and put them to work in all areas of the company. One quality team member went to operations and developed company-wide measures for our goals and objectives. Now she's a leader in one of our key new lines of business.

Our European operations have recently embarked upon a quality initiative much like the one we implemented in the United States. An internal team of "quality champions" provides expertise in the use of quality tools, techniques, and processes. And they consult, train, advise, and share best practices throughout their region. Monthly meetings monitor key performance indicators and help close gaps using a six-step problem-solving process to analyze problems, find root causes, develop solutions, formulate action plans, and track progress. In Europe, as in all regions of the world, wherever we are in our quality journey, our approach is to view quality not as the goal, but rather as a tool to achieve our goals.

True quality is not an add-on, but a seamless part of daily life. We describe quality as "defining client expectations, developing processes to meet those expectations, measuring our performance against those expectations, and empowering associates to improve processes." If these principles are interwoven into the tapestry of our business, then we are "doing" quality.

On any given day, it's not unusual to walk into one of our offices anywhere in the world and find someone analyzing Pareto Charts and cause-effect diagrams, brainstorming, discussing critical path methodology, or utilizing any number of quality principles or tools.

Current processes are being studied by teams across the company, all putting quality tools to work. Human resources is working on reducing the cycle time on résumés. Accounting is reviewing their cash receipts procedure. Our industry relations group is studying the negotiating process with our suppliers. We use quality in our learning programs by compiling data about participants' knowledge before and after courses, to see what's been learned and if the new skills are being put to work in the field.

Our use of quality runs the gamut from scientific to fun, all with intensity of purpose and measurable results. To be effective, quality must permeate an organization and begin and end with people. It's equally important for us to measure internal service as well as external, and never stop improving.

Rewarding Quality
An Incentive Program

In 1997, we instituted a front-line incentive program for our business units, designed to support our company's goal of being the highest quality provider at the lowest cost. Each business unit can institute the program at their discretion and can customize the program to meet their unique client and/or business needs.

Our "Customer Care Associate Performance Incentive Plan" is administered quarterly and is designed to meet three goals: business unit performance, improvement in an elective category, and individual productivity.

The first goal, the business unit's performance as a whole against predetermined goals, is based upon both client satisfaction and the financial health of the business unit. This criteria can only be met if client satisfaction survey results meet or exceed a rating of 4.5 out of 5.

For the second goal, each business unit selects a specific area to improve, which they'd like to focus on for that quarter, such as telephone service or transaction quality. The goal must reflect an area in need of improvement or a critical success factor for the business unit.

The third goal, individual productivity, calls for the leader to set a daily goal for each associate, for example, transactions per day. We also encourage each business unit to include their team leaders in this goal, rewarding them for helping each individual achieve his or her goal.

No incentives are awarded unless the first two goals are met. Our clients must be satisfied and each business unit must continually improve. If these two goals are met, every associate on the team receives a set payout for that quarter, regardless of their individual productivity. The associates who reach their individual goals receive additional individual incentive awards.

In our Intellicenters (large customer care centers), we have a front-line incentive program driven by quality first and quantity second. Associates must meet a quality threshold each month to qualify, and they can then earn additional incentive payments for exceeding quality and productivity expectations, for teamwork, and going above and beyond for our clients. Front-line associates who do not interact with clients can earn incentives based on their support of those who do.

Programs like these are a boost for our people. They improve service for our clients, helping our company achieve its goals. That's quality.

How Do You Know How You're Doing?
The Importance and Methods of Measuring Quality

The key to being a true quality organization is to keep setting goals higher and higher, always moving forward. "Raise the bar," as high jumpers say.

We use internal and external barometers to measure our service. Internally, our company measures things like average speed of answering the phone or e-mail, age of oldest pending e-mail, average response time for chats, average length of chats, percentage of accuracy in obtaining the lowest fares, phone hold time, on-time delivery of tickets, and so on. We also measure aspects that have a long-term effect on service, like turnover, associate satisfaction, completion of required training, and support to fellow associates, business units, and lines of business.

Each department has its own services to gauge. We use measurement as a tool for further improvement. And we take these measurements seriously. Our leaders' bonuses are dependent upon successful results in these areas.

An important component of our quality program is our associates' access to the tools that make it possible for them to measure their performance. It's not just management that's involved in continuous improvement. Each associate takes personal responsibility for the company's performance.

What about our clients? We keep a close watch on their perception of our service through a variety of tools. Like many businesses, we have two distinct client audiences: our business-to-business contacts (in most cases, the client companies' travel managers) and the end users (the individual travelers from those companies).

For our business partners (travel managers) we hold client focus groups, business planning sessions, quarterly account reviews, and an extensive process we call diagnostics (which you'll read about in Chapter 12 on open partnerships). We gauge our performance against predetermined measures that we have established with each individual client, taking into account their business needs, goals and priorities, their corporate culture, and everything else that makes each company unique. These customized measures are outlined in service agreements, determined by our diagnostic process. We then compare our performance to these baseline expectations.

To measure traveler satisfaction, we have an automated customer survey process. For many, many years we have surveyed our clients to assess their satisfaction with our service, but recently we automated the process with a web-based tool. After considering outside tools, we decided to develop our own so that we could tailor it to our exact needs.

Each client company determines the number of travelers they wish to have surveyed, and an e-mail invitation to participate in the survey is sent to the random travelers (although we ensure that no traveler is surveyed more frequently than three times per year). The invitation includes a hyperlink to the web-based survey, which can be quickly completed on-line and submitted to an automated data collection point. The system is available twenty-four hours a day, seven days a week, so travelers can respond at their convenience.

The survey asks travelers to evaluate our performance in areas like ease of reaching us, courtesy and professionalism, knowledge of products and client policies, acknowledging individual preferences, communication, accuracy, and overall service, calling for open comments at the end.

The results are consolidated weekly for each account and sent electronically to the management team responsible for serving that account. The surveys with the lowest scores are automatically flagged for immediate review and action, although the account management team reads the comments on every survey. A key benefit of the electronic format is that it provides the opportunity for quick action on not only areas for improvement, but also recognition of outstanding service on the part of our associates.

Security is a priority for us and for our clients, and because we designed our own system as opposed to subscribing to a third-party service, we can ensure that the e-mail addresses of our clients are not shared with anyone or used for any other purpose. The survey is not sent as an attachment (the invitation directs the customer to the separate survey) so firewalls don't prohibit travelers from accessing it. We own the process and the data, and we can ensure safety and security.

The system was also designed to gather traveler feedback on the performance of specific suppliers (such as airlines, hotels, and car rental companies). This information can be used to improve service as well as for negotiation purposes. This added dimension takes the service improvement process to the next level.

To complete the picture, we also seek the evaluations of third-party audits. We carefully measure our service and accuracy levels, but when outside parties evaluate our performance it assures impartiality and objectivity. We have a minimum of two audits being performed at any given time, and I'm proud to say that our average audit results have consistently exceeded 99 percent accuracy. We encourage our clients to use these companies to reconfirm that they have made the right choice in selecting us to serve them.

Service Is Not an Advertisement
Guaranteeing Service

To many, service is an advertisement—cleverly crafted words that claim excellence in service. But service has to be a lifestyle. Companies that are serious about service have to be able to put their money where their mouth is. We like to do it in a big way.

Research tells us we have the highest accuracy rate in our industry—consistently more than 99 percent. We're pretty sure that rate could hold its own in any industry, anywhere. We want our clients to know it. We like to show our associates how proud we are of their hard work and level of success, and to give them venues to proclaim it to the world. One that created quite a buzz was our "Biztravel Guarantee."

Biztravel.com was a Rosenbluth Interactive company—a successful venture until travel came to a virtual standstill after the events that changed the world in September 2001. One casualty of the terror that was unleashed was this promising business. We were left no choice but to close it because there was no longer a market for it, but for the years that it was in existence, it was a shining star.

It was Biztravel.com's service guarantee that turned our industry upside down. Imagine a service guarantee so unusual that it was featured on the *Today* show, Fox network, MSNBC, and in *The Wall Street Journal, The New York Times,* and *USA Today.* What made this service promise so groundbreaking was that it not only stood behind *our* service, but also guaranteed the performance of our key suppliers.

In 2000, we announced that we would offer $100 for flights arriving thirty minutes late; $200 for those one hour late; and a complete refund for flights arriving two hours late or cancelled. Yes, including delays due to weather and other factors beyond our control. We also offered refunds for lost luggage, seat assignments not honored, and other inconveniences travelers frequently face.

The program was based upon what travelers told us aggravated them the most. More than one thousand fed-up travelers responded to an on-line survey calling for them to vent their frustrations, and the result was a flood of comments (many hilarious, but all serious) painting a not-too-pretty view of our industry. Here are a couple we received.

One traveler wrote: "I wish the airlines would designate a 'family section' so all the kids could kick each other's seats and not my full-fare coach middle seat number 42B." Another said: "What do hotels have against power receptacles? How am I supposed to deal with a one outlet when I'm traveling with a laptop, zip drive, external CD-ROM, printer and PalmPilot charger?" Still another wrote: "I hate it when an airliner taxis away from the gate and the flight attendant announces, 'Another on-time departure for *XYZ Airlines*' and then they say that we're 86th in line for takeoff."

We wanted to alleviate frustrations for our customers, but we also wanted to make a loud statement about the quality and reliability of our own service, so we offered payments for phone calls not returned within ten minutes, e-mails not answered within two hours, not being connected with an associate for an on-line chat within five minutes, customer service issues not resolved within forty-eight hours, clients waiting on hold for more than ninety seconds (twenty seconds, by contract, for our corporate clients), and other measures of service.

In many corporate environments, you might hear mumbling like, "This really puts the pressure on," or "Does this mean that if I make a mistake I'll have to pay for it?" Our intent was certainly not to add pressure to our people's lives. And their accuracy rate was so spectacular it would have been unfair to ask them to pay for the very few errors they did make. Our goal for the program was to encourage our clients to look closely at the work our people were doing because we were so proud of it.

Our people weren't afraid of the program—they loved it, and so did our Biztravel.com customers. Traffic to our site increased by over 400 percent and bookings by over 50 percent after we implemented the program, and that's great, but what really mattered was that we could proudly stand behind our service. We hope to have the opportunity to reintroduce it one day.

Service guarantees force companies to look closely at their accuracy rates and influence their suppliers and clients to do the same. It's a great way to keep yourself on track. It's better to spend money refunding clients when they aren't satisfied than to forfeit money in lost accounts for the same reason.

Aspiring to Perfection
99 Percent Sounds Good, but We Have to Keep Trying

No company will ever be perfect, but the bottom line is that even the smallest mistakes aren't acceptable. This is a beast we all have to struggle with. And the service sector presents probably the most difficult terrain because of the perishability of the product a service company offers. You can't just return a travel experience to a manufacturing plant to be repaired. Once it has been defective, that service is over forever—consumed instantly, to the lasting dissatisfaction of the consumer.

Not only are they perishable, services are personal—they actively involve people. They affect lives. If a service company had an error rate of 1 percent, that would be considered very good, translating to 99-percent accuracy or only one error per every one hundred transactions. Most companies would be proud of that.

Let's relate that to another scenario. If a surgeon has a 99-percent accuracy rating and operates on five hundred patients per year in life-and-death situations, that means five people will die because of his 1-percent error factor.

Do you suppose their families will kindly appreciate the fact that he has an accuracy rating of 99 percent? Of course not, and the same goes for any other service. Who wants to be the person on the receiving end of the error? Any alternative to total client satisfaction is unacceptable.

Dealing with the Realm of the Possible
Reconciling with an Unattainable Dream

I once learned something in a grade school math class that parallels service. It's an illustration of infinity: If you stand any given distance from a wall and proceed half the distance, and then half the remaining distance, and then half again, you will never finally cross the room.

In service, there will always be room for improvement. Even if you manage to get all the basics right, there are literally infinite enhancements you could place on a service experience to make it that much better. That's one of our favorite aspects of being a service company. What would we do once we reached the wall anyway?

There Is Always Room for Improvement in Service

A SUMMARY

∎ Examine your service as an attitude, an art, and a process. Attitude starts with the right people in the right environment. Art is important because some of the most memorable aspects of service are creative ones. Process brings order to service so people can concentrate on the added touches that bring it to life.

∎ Make sure you maintain an environment in which people feel encouraged to reach for the exceptional. They won't if they fear the repercussions of failure.

∎ Check for potential applications of the "busied-in" theory in your company. It's the same principle that a rowing team works on—distributing the burden among the many, not the few.

∎ Recognize your service heroes. Look for those who add special touches—don't let them go unnoticed. Frances

Russell put a touch of caring in her service that went a long way.

∎ To build your own quality program, start by studying the many quality gurus as well as your clients, companies admired for their quality, and even your competitors. A cafeteria approach can be effective in determining the right program for your particular needs.

∎ A total quality management initiative takes commitment of time and resources—both human and financial. But it's well worth the investment. It costs less to do it right the first time. Consider working with a professional who can make statistics fun. Once established, quality becomes a way of life, not a separate initiative.

∎ Consider an incentive program that rewards quality along with productivity. Design it to meet your company's specific goals. Our program has three components: business unit performance, improvement, and individual productivity. Such a program rewards people for their hard work, enhances service for clients, and helps the company achieve its goals.

∎ Set measurable quality and service goals for your company and keep raising them. Measure your progress both internally and externally, with separate tools for business-to-business customers and end users (if you have both). Automating measurement tools can help you respond to service issues and to reward exceptional performance in a more timely manner.

∎ Consider guaranteeing your service. It's reassuring to your clients and motivating to your people. It will cost less to refund an unhappy client than to lose his or her business.

∎ Never be satisfied with the service you provide. Never feel you have finally "reached the wall," because if you do, there's nowhere to go but backward.

CHAPTER SIX

The Creation of a Culture

The great law of culture is: Let each become all that he was created capable of being.

—Thomas Carlyle (1795–1881)

Most organizations are steeped in culture, whether positive, negative, or nondescript—even a seeming lack of culture is a culture, in and of itself. The best way to describe ours is one in which our people feel protected and embraced by the company. But it wasn't always that way.

When I joined the company, I would have described the culture as one that demonstrated the highest concern for its clients, integrity, and tradition. The culture was certainly admirable, but a stark difference from what it is now. And it was largely the transformation of that culture that brought us to where we are today.

We engineered a concerted change that puts our *people* at the forefront. And there's been a surprising level of interest from the outside in the forming of that culture. A number of our clients, as well as non-client companies, have requested "cultural change" training from us. They've spent time in our offices talking with our people and studying our environment. They've talked with us about the steps we took in building the culture we have today.

We sought the input of our people, because they "live" the culture. We spent a lot of time in those early days daydreaming, as a group. We didn't know the technical terminology for the way we wanted to be, but we came up with a plan all the same. Looking back, it was probably better that way. We didn't mold our culture on principles we were *supposed* to believe, but on those we *naturally* bought into.

For example, I don't think any of us had ever heard of the "inverted pyramid" style of management, but we knew we needed to support our people on the front line. We understood that their input was key because they were the ones closest to the client on a day-to-day basis. They were the ones "in the know."

We were much smaller then, but we knew we were building something special. We wanted to find a way to preserve it as we grew. Growth seemed certain. Our clients began telling us they wanted us to provide them with service nationwide. As word spread from client to client, we began to receive requests to consolidate national travel accounts, and today we manage their global accounts.

Our clients told us they looked forward to talking with our people because they were happy and took pride in their work. They said our associates showed a sense of ownership in the company. They had a "buck stops with me" attitude, and our clients liked the results.

This presented us with an enormous challenge because our culture wasn't formalized. As we grew rapidly from, at the time, a regional to a national company and scores of new people joined our organization, how would we preserve what our clients had come to trust?

Live the Spirit
The Capturing of a Culture

No longer could we rely upon our culture to take root naturally, in new locations and in new associates. It was time to formalize our culture. We even gave it a name ("Live the Spirit"), corporate colors (blue and white), and a mascot (the salmon).

The first step was to capture what we had built and put it into words we could share universally. We created a mission statement and an official set of philosophies and values. We coined our own service language: "elegant language." This language is part of our overall service approach, which we call "elegant service."

The principle behind elegant service is to create a service experience far beyond that which is expected. We all know it when we experience it. Elegance by its very definition means refined, polished, graceful. Likewise, we strive to offer elegance in service that means those same things to our clients when they work with our people.

Elegant language is a way of speaking that truly reflects the way we feel about ourselves, our clients, and what we're doing. It's easy to slip into a lazy way of speaking that, when you stop to think about it, doesn't say what we mean nearly as well as do more expressive words.

Answering the phone "Hello?" doesn't say anything. People taking pride in themselves and their work would want to identify themselves and offer to help the caller. A better greeting would be, "Welcome to Rosenbluth International. This is Hal Rosenbluth. How may I help you?" It takes a little longer. It takes a little more effort. But it means a great deal more to both the caller and the person answering.

The closing you would expect from most calls is "Good-bye." How inexpressive. How final. How uninspiring. This closing leaves both caller and answerer empty. Doesn't the following say it much better? "Thank you for calling Rosenbluth International. It has been my pleasure to assist you."

We never refer to our people as *employees.* If you look in a thesaurus, you'll find listed such harsh and demeaning words as *hireling, servant,* and *subordinate.* These words far from reflect the way we regard our people. We refer to our people as *associates,* which the thesaurus describes as *colleague, partner,* and *friend.*

Once one is shown the benefits of expressing one's self in a more elegant, more meaningful manner, there's no turning back. But it's not just language; it's attitude. Our people have to feel it on their own. That's what gives meaning to the words.

Pentimento
True Colors Will Shine Through

There's a phenomenon in art called *pentimento*. It occurs when an artist paints on a canvas and then "erases" the image by painting over it. Years later, the original image begins to shine through. So pentimento is the reappearance of the original image through the new painting.

For example, if an artist painted a bowl of fruit and decided he didn't like it, he might paint over it in black or white and then paint a scene of a garden. As time elapsed, the bowl of fruit would begin to appear in the garden.

People's true colors shine through, and so do companies'. It's not enough for our people merely to answer the phone with the right words. Any faceless corporation can train its people who spend time on the phone to use special language. A lot of companies have stopped calling people *employees*. What makes it work?

What is called a sincere work is one that is endowed with enough strength to give reality to an illusion.

—Max Jacob (1876–1944)

It's easy to provide helpful words but no help. What makes elegant language meaningful is that the people using it are ready to back it up with action. The words and the attitude with which they are spoken make our clients feel special, pampered. The service that goes along with those words is what makes them matter. To instill the confidence in our clients that we are qualified to serve them, our people need to possess good communication skills, be positive, use proper grammar and vocabulary, and have a thorough knowledge of our products and services.

But it's more than that. Our people must understand our clients—be able to put themselves in their shoes, know their policies, needs, and wants. It's important for each client to feel like he or she is our only client. And we need to perform accordingly.

What makes the term *associate* significant is that our people are treated with respect and care, hour after hour, day in, day out. A person's attitude about his company is a direct reflection of the experiences he has within that organization.

It's the depth behind the demeanor that counts. That depth comes from the individuals who make up the organization and the organization's commitment to them. There's no faking it. The real state of a company will shine through in its daily interactions with its clients.

Reputations are not destinations, they are journeys. Each and every encounter between a company's people and its clients holds the power to enhance or diminish the company's standing.

What's the Bottom Line?
Our Answer to a Frequently Asked Question

We've been asked repeatedly what type of financial incentives we must be offering in order to get our people to care the way they do. The answer is that for the most part, that's not at all how we do it.

I asked our human resources team what our people say motivates them and why they feel committed to this company. The answer is that they look forward to coming to work in the morning. They don't tremble at how they're going to be treated or lie awake at night worrying. A lot of people in other companies live in fear of their jobs.

Our people say they feel happy and comfortable, and that kind of peace of mind holds a great deal of value for most people. It's not financial rewards that leave an indelible impression on people's behavior. It's quality of life.

The impact is significant—not just warm and fuzzy. Most companies can calculate the economic impact of turnover by equating it to six months salary of the person leaving. This accounts for costs to recruit, hire, and train a replacement. These are costs most companies can't afford to waste.

Spreading the Word
Communicating a Culture

None of the formalized elements of our culture are forced upon our people. We didn't invent them. We just looked around and saw what people were doing best and made sure everyone had the benefit of knowing what those things were.

When we set out to "capture" our culture nearly twenty years ago, a team of five associates visited all of our offices and observed people at work. They defined the elements of our service that made us the way we were. Next, we met with the top training executive of Ritz-Carlton hotels, because we greatly admired their style of service and sought to learn from it.

We then put together communication programs to clarify our approach to service and share it with everyone who makes it happen. For example, elegant language was already being used by most of our people. But to make sure that the people who joined the company understood the concept and took pride in it, we made display cards for each person to keep on his or her desk with examples of elegant phrases. Everyone really seemed to enjoy it. A number of associates took the cards home to their families, who liked what they heard when they called our offices and wanted to learn more.

There were laminated wallet cards with our mission statement and philosophies and values; daily computer briefings (before e-mail); and follow-up training programs to ensure a unified message. To kick it all off, we introduced our newly coined culture at a company-wide meeting. Anything this important calls for a face-to-face gathering of everyone.

Today our culture is firmly ingrained and is reinforced through a variety of ongoing programs and vehicles. It's a never-ending process. But our most valuable tool is the protectiveness our associates feel about our culture. They guard it ferociously.

One Face
Keeping Culture Sincere

The root of the word *sincere* is a fascinating one. It comes from the Latin *sine* (meaning "without") and *cera* (which means "wax"). In the days of the Roman Empire, to possess marble was a sign of wealth and prestige and the smoother the marble, the more value it held.

Vendors in the marketplace would fill cracks in their marble with wax to make it appear flawless. But when the new owner returned home, the wax would melt in the heat of summer and the marble's true form would be revealed. Thus, the word *sincere* is derived from the term "without wax." After all, the cracks are what make marble so beautiful.

A key to making a culture work is sincerity. We place the same emphasis on "Living the Spirit" with one another that we do with our clients. Of course Caller ID enables each of us to know whether an incoming call is internal or external, yet we answer the same way each and every time the phone rings.

I think everyone finds it disconcerting to hear someone speak courteously to a client and then "switch off" the charm when speaking with a colleague. Demeanor has to be consistent to be sincere. People should treat one another like clients. What we should all strive for is the absolute antithesis of the Jekyll–Hyde complex.

The code of ethics has to be as strong as the work ethic. Happiness in the workplace has to be recreated day after day. In our company, we have an unwritten code of ethics that says we'll never let one another down. We believe that if we accomplish that, we'll never let our clients down. If our sales team was to tell a client that we had a technology product that we didn't really have, they would let down their associates in technology, who would then have to attempt to make the product a reality in an unrealistic time frame.

How dependable a company's people are with one another is a good measurement of how dependable they are for their clients. Ultimately, in the example above, the client would be let down. Who's to say it's even possible to develop the product in the promised time frame? Furthermore, a product developed in haste wouldn't be as effective as one that was carefully planned.

We believe that when associates let one another down, they negatively affect one another's lives. And when they've done that they've overstepped their bounds. Around here, an associate who places another in a compromising position has signed his or her own ticket out of the company.

Corporate Salmon
The Selection of a Company Mascot

> I shall be telling this with a sigh
> Somewhere ages and ages hence:
> Two roads diverged in a wood, and I—
> I took the one less traveled by,
> And that has made all the difference.
> —Robert Frost, "The Road Not Taken"

Our company thrives on being atypical. We like to be different, to blaze new trails, stir up commotion. Our heroes are those who have dared to do things differently. If the stream is flowing one way, we're almost sure we should be swimming another. There have been times that by doing this, we think we may have actually changed the tide.

Because we're a group of contrarians who always insist on swimming against the tide, we selected the salmon as our corporate mascot. Our people love having a mascot. It's a great morale booster and team builder. And they particularly like the salmon.

I've received salmon of so many varieties since the adoption of our mascot. Associates, clients, and suppliers from around the world have sent some very unusual varieties. I have a statue of a salmon on wheels in my office along with a beanbag salmon, a chocolate salmon, and of course the salmon stuffed animal we designed and produced for our clients. We recently made beanie salmons available to our associates, and on the day they were unveiled, we served salmon for lunch in the cafeteria at our world headquarters.

We know that those who journey down a different road may have a tougher trip. But along it they will experience things that those who travel the traditional paths might never see. And most important in business, they will get there first.

The outside pressures of the world and the climate of our industry conflict with the way we operate. But we're sticking to our guns because we know we have created a culture that withstands fads and trends. Above all, it offers happiness, which is the key to success.

A Unique Environment
Setting the Stage for Creativity

You can tell a lot about a company's culture just by a walk through its facilities. Its "personality" is easy to gauge. I'll take you on a mental tour through our world headquarters to give you an idea of what I mean. Our entrance features large flags representing each of the many countries around the world where we have locations. The richness and positive influence of each of the cultures represented and the hard work and great input from our associates in each of those countries are among what we value most.

Our cafeteria is lively and fun, with a jukebox and big, comfy booths. It's a favorite meeting spot. We made it that way so people could share ideas, build friendships, and have a place to just kick back, relax, and feel refreshed. When clients visit, we always have meals there rather than in a restaurant. We want them to feel a part of our family and to get to know our associates.

Our corporate library is not what you'd expect either. We call it "The Gathering," and it has overstuffed couches that people feel very free to put their feet on. Our associates go there to read newspapers in a variety of languages, to spend time on-line, or to have casual meetings. There's also a work–life station there with materials and resources to help our associates achieve balance.

There's the high-tech aspect of our personality, too. Our Network Operations Center houses a video-wall that displays our quality statistics, our phone system activity, the latest weather and current events, flight delays, and other key information our experts track that may affect our clients. It resembles a NASA control center. You'll also read about another high-tech area in Chapter 12, on partnerships. It's our future center, The Continuum, the entrance to which looks like the helm of a spaceship.

Our world headquarters has a name: Riverplace. We call our meeting rooms "thought centers" because the name more accurately reflects what goes on in them. We have an open meeting policy. Every meeting is open to all associates (with the exception of performance reviews and other meetings that might betray associate confidence). To make it easy for people to attend, all meetings are posted so people will know where and when they will take place, what they'll be about, and who's leading them.

These things are not gimmicks. They're part of who we are. They wouldn't work for everyone. Each company must look deep within to find what makes it unique, and design everything else around that. The result is a culture that permeates the organization, from which its people gain strength.

It Has to Be Fun
Celebrating Success

I've always had the theory that we can usually measure how successful we are by how much fun we're having. Think about it—does anyone ever have fun while failing? Not normally. On the other hand, winning is fun and hard-fought victories are even more fun.

Just look at Disney. One of the most highly respected and successful companies in the world, they made "fun" a business, and it is legendary for being a great place to work. For instance, the company opens its parks one evening every year for a holiday party for its employees (or, as they call them, "cast members") and their families. Management, all the way to the top, operates the parks that night.

You'll read in the coming pages about some of the lengths we go to, to ensure our associates have fun. Here are a few examples to start off. We held a "Fifties Day" where every associate in each of our call centers who achieved their cost reduction goals had a fifty-dollar bill dropped in their lap. We include a karaoke session at virtually every meeting we hold at our executive ranch (which you'll read more about in Chapter 13, "Blazing New Trails.")

We always try to incorporate fun into our learning events because we know that when people learn through experiences they'll never forget, they don't forget the lessons taught, either. To that end, we've held city-wide scavenger hunts, talent contests, and some all-out learning extravaganzas. Two particularly memorable ones were an Olympiad and a Decathlon.

The Olympiad was a two-day meeting of leaders, in which the goal was to win business. Senior leaders played the role of clients, while teams made up of general managers, sales associates, and other leaders were called upon to sell our services to the mock executives. Each support department was represented to provide resources (as they do in reality) and the teams competed for those resources.

Each team assembled a war room and worked together to build and deliver a customized presentation for each client. There was only one winner for each account. Medals were awarded to the winning team, and a best practices review deepened the learning. During this intense, competitive process, everyone learned a great deal about the sales process and the value and impact of each department within the organization.

The learning Decathlon was a follow-up event to the Olympiad, and it was so effective that we made it an annual event. This meeting is for the leadership of the company (general managers, directors, vice presidents) who compete in ten events. One was a storytelling competition, in which we provided information about disparate, hypothetical events and asked each team to connect them into an interwoven story. For example, an air strike in Israel, a war in Kosovo, a growth burst of hotel rooms in Japan. The events were seemingly unrelated, but they all had some effect on each other. The team who explained the chain of events best, won. The point is that if you don't connect the dots to form opinions, and use information to predict and prepare for the future, then you're not adding value.

Another event was an unusual twist on musical chairs. Anyone caught without a seat had to answer a question about our value proposition. If they couldn't answer it, they had to sing a song for everyone. Participants could score "charisma" points by distracting the judges' attention away from those still in the game who were able to answer the questions correctly. The lesson was that someone can come in at the eleventh hour and steal the trophy. It certainly happens in business.

Other events included rock-climbing, "Full-Contact Poker," "Virtual Golf," "Site Visits of Terror," "Peace, Love, and Presentations," and more. The meeting began with a giant pep rally and concluded with a half-day meeting with the top officers. It was definitely a memorable event, and one in which a great deal of truly usable learning took place.

To me, fun and success are so intertwined that I can't tell anymore which comes first. Are those who enjoy their work and have fun at it the successful ones? Or is it that those who happen to be successful seem to have all the fun? I'm not going to chance trying to figure this one out. My philosophy is just to do both. Guaranteed fun. Guaranteed success.

When you have fun, it shows. Haven't you ever talked with anyone who had a talent for "smiling over the phone"? It's a pleasure doing business with people like that, and the finest organizations are full of them. It's something that can't be simulated.

In fact, we make having fun part of our official strategy. Seriously. Ensuring that our people enjoy their work and have fun here is always a top priority for us. We want people to enjoy the journey and when they do, it shows on their faces and in their work.

Salmon Happy
Recognition Programs

We learned from our friends at Federal Express about an internal recognition program they have that they call "Bravo Zulu." So we asked more about it and created one of our own centered around our company mascot, the salmon.

The program recognizes associates who go above and beyond to help one another and our clients. We wanted the program to be alive on a day-to-day basis, so we created salmon materials our associates can use to recognize each other. For example, when we receive a letter complimenting an associate, the associate's leader sends him or her a copy with a salmon sticker on it. And associates send each other salmon note cards with messages of thanks or encouragement.

The highest honor in our company is the salmon pin. We also have service pins to recognize length of service, but the salmon pin is reserved for associates who far exceed even a salmon's expectations.

August Is for Associates
An Annual Event to Say Thank You

It's important to take time all year to recognize the contributions of our people, yet we all get busy and time seems to slip away. But we never forget in August. That's "Associate Appreciation Month" at our company, a time set aside each year for special events and activities to thank our people.

Every August, something special happens each day of the month. Some activities are centrally planned and implemented company-wide, and others on a local level, by associate volunteers. Every office has its own celebration. We encourage our suppliers to each sponsor an aspect, providing free airline tickets, hotel stays, car rentals, or hosting parties, breakfasts, lunches, or special treats for our associates.

One event everyone looks forward to is our VP barbecue, where our senior officers prepare and serve their associates a barbecue lunch under a tent in the parking lot of our world headquarters. Another favorite is the internal open house. Each department comes up with a theme. For example, one department was set up to resemble the TV series *Survivor*. A new line of business held a first birthday party to mark its first year of operation. Our associates can tour each area, get to know their colleagues, and learn about the different areas of responsibility.

During Associate Appreciation Month, we also designate Rosenbluth International Volunteer Days, when associates have the opportunity to give back to their communities.

Some of the events center around getting to know and appreciate one another better. For example, we'll have a contest to match people with their favorite story about themselves. It's a great way to get to know more about people you *think* you know.

One of our associates appeared with John F. Kennedy in a publicity photo, as an infant. One was an NFL cheerleader. Someone had a brown belt in karate, and another, who's been with the company for twenty-five years, was a child actress who starred in dozens of TV commercials.

Our accuracy rating on matching the people with their stories is usually fairly low. There's so much we don't get to know about one another during the course of a workday, but these stories are part of our lives. They make us interesting people. They helped make us who we are.

We always end Associate Appreciation Month with our leaders sending a personal note to each of their associates, thanking them for their efforts and contributions. It all takes a little time, but our people really look forward to it each year. It's a concept anyone could adapt for use in their business. The point is just to say thank you, and that's something we all need to do.

Face-to-Face
Company-Wide Meetings Boost Morale

When we celebrated our culture at that first company-wide meeting, we found it to be such a good investment that we have held one several times since, at first every other year, then as we grew, every five years. The meeting is educational, motivational, productive, and most important, enjoyable. Because after all, it has to be fun.

It's one of the best morale boosters we know of. Somehow bringing everyone together from all lines of business, departments, and regions of the world creates a magic that's hard to duplicate.

The meeting takes place over a weekend, and we bring our people in from everywhere. For the last one, in 1997, we brought together more than four thousand people, speaking twelve different languages, from twenty-five countries.

There are educational seminars and social events. We host a trade show in which every department and line of business exhibits, to help associates chart their career paths, learn the latest developments, and see how everything fits together.

One unusual event from the most recent meeting was a life-size game of Chutes and Ladders (you'll read more about our connection to this game in Chapter 8, "The Gardening Process"). For the meeting, we built a two thousand square foot board game covering the floor of an entire room in the Philadelphia Convention Center. We had full-size ladders, chutes, and dice that were a couple feet wide. Our associates acted as game pieces, and 250 clients divided into teams to play the game. Along the board were ways to reduce their travel expenditures. The event was informative and one of the most memorable of the meeting.

We invite our clients and suppliers to speak to our people. We also hold client-specific gatherings, where everyone from around the world who serves a particular client meets together with that client, face-to-face. We talk a lot about the future and what it holds, to make sure we're all headed in the same direction. It's a great forum for communication. It's a program we can't recommend highly enough.

Global Professional Development Plan
A Learning Opportunity of Global Proportions

We recently developed a program to encourage the sharing of knowledge around the world. Our "Global Professional Development Program" provides the opportunity for associates to indicate their interest in a specific region or country (out of fifty) and/or a specific department for a short-term assignment (most often three months to a year). Likewise, offices indicate their short-term needs. The information is compared to match associate interests with business needs.

The only requirements are that the associate be in their current position for at least one year, that they be fully proficient in that position, and that they be in good standing with the company. We ask candidates to outline their professional goals and business objectives for their participation in the program and that they provide a comprehensive action plan and résumé.

The associate works together with their leader to determine program goals and objectives. A "foster leader" within their new department will temporarily act as the associate's leader throughout their stay in the temporary location. Many associates make their home available to visiting associates, should they wish to stay with a local colleague.

The program has many benefits. Through it, people gain understanding of new cultures, departments, and responsibilities. It provides a great forum for sharing best practices globally. It helps us fulfill immediate short-term needs in various locations. Most important, it helps our associates reach their career goals, while providing them with personal growth.

Service Day
A Simultaneous Celebration of Service

In 1989 we had a unique experience. Tom Peters named Rosenbluth International "Service Company of the Year." We were speechless (for about a week).

Then we decided to celebrate. We planned a company-wide celebration that would occur simultaneously across the United States. I hopped in a small charter and visited as many offices as I physically could in one day.

There were four of us traveling from city to city in a very small plane. The day turned out to be one of the stormiest I can recall. Up in the air, thunder was rolling and lightning striking all around us. None of us was positive we would survive. There were at least forty white knuckles in that plane—probably more, but I was afraid to look in the cockpit to find out.

Then all of a sudden, out of nowhere, the storm lifted and we flew into a stretch of sun-streaked, billowing clouds. One in the group said, "Are we safe or is this heaven?" That was the joke for the day, but actually that day was a bit like heaven. It was not only one of the best days of my career, it was one of the best for our company. What better occasion to celebrate than the occasion to serve our clients?

Ensuring Happiness in the Workplace

A SUMMARY

▌ Every organization has a culture: Is yours the one you want? If not, change it. Seek input from your people. After all, they will be living the culture.

▌ Formalize your culture. Capture it. Name it. Make sure it withstands growth and change. Have organized programs to reinforce it—for example, a company-wide meeting. If your size or geography prohibit a company-wide meeting, then consider programs that bring together as many people as possible who do not normally have the chance to meet face-to-face.

∎ Try instituting your own form of elegant language—one that fits your company's personality. You'll feel the difference and so will your clients. Announce the program with plenty of fanfare and encourage your people to buy into it and have fun with it.

∎ Encourage your people to treat one another like clients. Service and professionalism must begin in the office and emanate outward to your clients. Look closely for any traces of the Jekyll–Hyde syndrome.

∎ Think about adopting a company mascot. If you had to choose one today, what would it be? What would you like it to become?

∎ Work to make fun a part of daily life in your organization. Fun breeds productivity. For example, the more memorable a learning event is, the more the lesson is retained. The power of fun is greatly underestimated.

∎ Consider an "exchange program" that matches short-term department or location needs with individual career goals. Programs like our Global Professional Development Program can help encourage idea sharing, strengthen morale, cut down on the expense of temporary help, and foster greater understanding of varied cultures, company functions, and people.

∎ Celebrating success is essential. Formalized recognition programs can be effective, as can setting aside a special time each year to thank your people.

CHAPTER SEVEN

The Birth and Nurturing of Ideas

For every really bright idea any of us ever comes up with, we've had plenty of poor ones. I once had a bad idea that actually cost me a job. When I was in college, I studied criminology and had an internship with the state department of corrections. I worked with inmates to help them pass the high school equivalency test prior to their release. In my spare time, I organized athletic programs for the inmates, and I really enjoyed it. I could see these activities were important to them, and that was rewarding.

One day I had a great idea, or so I thought: I would put together an "away" softball game against a team of inmates from another prison. Needless to say, the idea didn't fly with the administration. They decided I was too trusting to continue to be responsible for the inmates in these programs. There's a fine line between creativity and naïveté, and I'm not sure to this day whether it would have worked or not.

That was three decades and thousands of ideas ago. Some ideas are worth pursuing and some are not. The important thing is to keep ideas flowing and to see failures as steps toward success. Even the greatest of innovators guesses wrong sometimes. Around here, everyone's favorite example is the story of a meeting between my grandfather, Joseph Rosenbluth, and an airline sales rep in the 1930s. At the end of the meeting, Joseph said to him, "Son, get into another line of work. The commercial airline business will never amount to anything."

The meaning of the word *idea* found in the dictionary is "that which exists in the mind, potentially or actually." The key words are *potential* and *actual*. Because we all know there's a world of difference between thinking about something and doing it.

Everybody has ideas, some better than others. But they live in people's minds. They need to be brought out, refined, tested, and implemented. Ideas are the lifeblood of a company. They weave the fabric of its future, but they're fragile.

Ideas come to the curious—those who ask, "What would improve our lives?" But ideas have to be nurtured and cultivated. The stifling of ideas starts when we're young and are told, "Just do it and don't ask why," or "That's just the way it is." Creativity and innovation aren't emphasized enough in our schools, homes, or professional lives, but people who seek these gifts can and will find them in the right environment.

Lure the Muses
Creating an Environment that Inspires Ideas

There's a group of four of us who began years ago to get together periodically on Amtrak to develop new ideas. We started riding the "creativity train" by accident. One day the four of us were on our way from Philadelphia to New York for a meeting. On the train we started kicking some ideas around. We came up with at least a dozen that we planned to implement. When we arrived in New York we hesitated to leave the train, because we accomplished more on the journey than we knew we could in the meeting.

We decided to hold train meetings to come up with new ideas. It sounds crazy, but something just happens when the group gets together in that setting, and we're taking advantage of it. It's not that odd when you think about it. The great masters of creativity each have their own style, so why can't we?

Ernest Hemingway wrote many of his classic works in the south of France and Cuba, in its former splendor. But some of his greatest works came out of Casa de Botín, a restaurant in Madrid that's still open today. He would sit in the cellar and create masterpieces while drinking wine. In fact it was there that he wrote much of *The Sun Also Rises* and he gives the restaurant a mention in the final scene.

When Claude Monet set out to create an impressionist painting of the Rouen cathedral, he wanted to capture it at all different times of day, so he set up a series of twenty-five canvases, side by side in a shop across the street from the beautiful structure. There he would view it through the window and paint it over the course of an entire day. At sunrise he would work on the first canvas, moving to the second canvas a short time later, then the next canvas, and so on, until he carefully recreated the cathedral in each distinct light.

It took him nearly three years, but the result was twenty-five masterpieces, each of the cathedral from the same view, but all completely different. Most artists would paint one picture at a time, but not Monet. What an ingenious way to do it—the way that made sense to *him*.

For centuries, artists have surrounded themselves with sources of personal inspiration and they've insisted on working the way they desire. The legendary muses work their best magic where they are not constrained.

Maintaining a creative, energetic, and caring environment in which to work enhances the spirit of innovation in people. Incorporating individuality into the workplace is essential. Just giving people the freedom to create is an important beginning.

It is said that Henry Ford once hired an efficiency expert to evaluate his company. The report was positive except for an observation of one employee. "It's that man down the corridor," he said. "Every time I go by his office he's just sitting there with his feet on his desk. He's wasting your money."

In reply, Ford said, "That man once had an idea that saved us millions of dollars. At the time, I believe his feet were planted right where they are now."

Brilliant ideas will spring forth only in a nonbureaucratic atmosphere. Nothing creative ever comes from a slow-moving organization that crushes the entrepreneurial spirit in its people. Ideas must never be suppressed. They need to be championed. While their flow should be continuous, an organized call for ideas can spark people's thoughts and keep creative talents sharp.

In 2000 we began a program we call "Renew for the New Year," in which we ask every associate to set aside time to brainstorm ways to improve our company. We hold Renew just before the first of the year, and we designate a day for thought, encouraging people to free their calendars and their minds and spend an entire day contemplating making us a better organization in the coming year.

Most of the ideas are ways to eliminate processes, reduce costs, increase efficiency, and automate daily functions to free time for more creative pursuits. As part of Renew, we hold a contest to reward the strongest ideas. The winners each receive two free airline tickets.

One idea from an associate in Massachusetts was to buy jugs of ink to refill printer cartridges (for $2) as opposed to buying new cartridges (at $26). Reusing the cartridges not only saves money but is also better for the environment.

Another idea came from a business unit in Arizona. During 2000, the client that business unit serves had a 50 percent increase in their meetings volume, so we increased our staff there accordingly. However, a shortage of on-site office space called for some creativity. Because our meeting planning associates travel on-site to meetings, they were already laptop equipped. So they decided to come up with a plan that incorporated telecommuting. On the other hand, the nature of their work called for team meetings and face-to-face time.

The team paired up in a buddy system, where two associates share a desk equipped with two phone lines. Each team member also has a phone line at home. On Mondays everyone comes in to the office, and most meetings are scheduled for that day (though everyone agreed to come in for meetings as needed). Everyone then spends two days in the office and two at home. The plan maximizes department growth while minimizing the need for physical expansion. The results have been terrific, and both client and associates are delighted.

To help associates in one of our offices in Southern California work toward their career goals, a leader there came up with a program called "Walk in My Shoes," which provides for associates to act as if they were in their leader's position.

Each leader lists the tasks that he or she can delegate, things like planning and conducting a staff meeting; analyzing error trends and providing solutions for recurring errors; staffing plans; and charting productivity statistics. Associates then carry out tasks from the leader's list.

The program goes a step beyond traditional shadowing, giving participants a portion of the leader's responsibilities. It provides the associate with valuable experience and a broader perspective, while freeing leaders to concentrate on strategic issues and spend more time with their staff.

Some great ideas have come from Renew, but more have come as a result of our open and nurturing style and our continual emphasis on creativity. Really, every day should be a "Renew" day.

Four Disparate Origins
Tracing Innovation to Its Roots

When we hear a great idea, we say to ourselves, "Why didn't I think of that?" Some innovations come from great scientists and others come from everyday people who asked a question and turned the answer into an invention.

Ideas can come from every imaginable source. We just need to train ourselves to recognize the opportunities around us. Studying the roots of good ideas can help us spot the potential for an innovation.

I chose four ideas from our company with very different origins, and I'll trace each to its inception. I'll talk in depth about the first in Chapter 13, and discuss the second idea in Chapter 10, so here we'll look only at how these two ideas came about. The final two ideas call for a little more detail.

These are just a few of the springboards for ideas that surround us all: (1) social responsibility; (2) finding a way to do something better;

(3) filling a need in the marketplace; and (4) creating a solution to an existing problem.

A Company with a Conscience
Origin #1: Innovating Through Social Responsibility

As you will learn in Chapter 13, our practice of opening customer care centers in rural communities has been one of the most fruitful ideas in our company's history. The origin of that idea was a desire to make a difference—to do something socially responsible. In an effort to come to the aid of a small farm community in North Dakota devastated by drought, we located an office there. And in the process, we gained outstanding human resources situated in an ideal place to do business, where quality is high and operating costs are low.

Not all programs designed to help people will further a company in such tangible terms. But there's nothing wrong with looking for opportunities to make them mutually beneficial to your company. There's no better way to encourage the commitment to these projects on the part of associates, clients, and shareholders than to have them add value to your company. In fact, it only helps ensure the life of the programs.

The origin of our idea was just the desire to help, but the way we implemented it was what led us to our discoveries about rural resources. If we'd made a financial contribution rather than opened a temporary office, we never would have learned that rural communities can be fantastic places to do business.

To make our decision, we looked for a way to benefit both a community and our company. The idea started with a perspective that spanned beyond our own company or industry, but we brought that idea home to come up with the plan. The result was a *permanent* benefit to the people of that community and many others, to Rosenbluth International, and to other companies who have since followed our lead.

How Can We Do this Better?
Origin #2: Creating Through Self-Improvement

If we ask ourselves each day, "How can we do this better?" we are bound to find ways to improve. Whether large or small, these improvements can lead to discoveries. As I discuss in Chapter 10, our Custom-Res point-of-sale software was the answer to the search for a way to improve upon our processes and our service to our customers.

To quickly explain, Custom-Res guides our CCAs through the steps of booking our clients' travel, incorporating both the individual's personal preferences and his or her company's travel policy.

More than fifteen years ago, a couple of associates from different departments were saying, "This process constitutes the majority of our day-to-day service to our clients. We have to be able to do it faster, more accurately." Their pursuit of an answer ultimately led to the development of a product that changed our company.

Systems can be designed to facilitate any process in any organization. We just need to ask ourselves what we'd like to improve upon, and the answer becomes our innovation.

Smoke Signals for a Need
Origin #3: Filling a Need in the Marketplace

My office is a revolving door. Everyone is encouraged to walk in and run suggestions by me. One of those suggestions became a product that filled a void in the marketplace and provided a service from which countless companies have benefited.

In recent years, the airlines have deepened their discounts to large corporate clients, while hiking ticket prices to offset the costs of those discounts. The result has impacted small- to mid-sized companies that have limited, if any, structured deals with suppliers. This client segment has become disproportionately profitable for the airlines, who are looking for cost-effective ways to interface with this market.

Likewise, the companies were lacking a forum through which to negotiate with the airlines. The answer to these needs: mytravelbid.com, an electronic marketplace.

The idea originated when an associate who worked with our DACODA product (a yield management system for our clients which you'll read about in Chapter 10) came up with the idea to load airline offers electronically into DACODA to quantify their true value for our corporate clients. This ultimately would become an application of the mytravelbid.com idea. However, it was a different application of the original idea that became the initial focus.

The DACODA associate approached her leader with her idea, and he suggested she map it out and present it at the next vice presidents' meeting, which she did. She received the go-ahead to pursue it. After extensive research and planning, she and her leader discovered the need in the marketplace for an on-line procurement exchange for small- to mid-sized companies. So that's the application of the idea we jumped on.

At mytravelbid.com companies can post their annual travel segments at no cost and have suppliers bid on their travel business. The site is now the industry's hub for connecting corporate travel buyers and suppliers. For the companies, it saves time and money, giving them buying power. (The average discount received is 17.5 percent.) For the suppliers, it reduces the cost of pursuing this market and offers the opportunity to capture a larger share of a company's business by rewarding its loyalty.

This powerful tool was arrived at by spotting a need in the marketplace and going after it, even if it meant putting the original plan on hold to pursue the opportunity. This kind of flexibility and proactiveness led to the realization of an innovative idea. There was a need in the marketplace for this service. It makes you wonder how many other needs there are just waiting to be filled.

Creative Problem Solving
Origin #4: Developing a Solution to an Existing Problem

Every company experiences an occasional, sudden need for additional resources, and temporary help from the outside is not appropriate for many types of work. Our immediate needs are normally caused by two factors: our approach to growth and the seasonal demands of our business.

Years ago, we made a strategic decision that our growth would be client driven. Rather than pick a spot and hang an "OPEN FOR BUSINESS" sign, we'd grow when and where our clients required us to have a presence. This approach has served us well, but it has presented its share of challenges along the way.

There are certain locations where it's important for us to have an office, but with only a handful of people. These associates need to be able to take vacation and sick days, but even one person absent from an office that size can impact service. Sometimes clients have an immediate need for us to be in a new market on short notice—for instance, when a client opens a new office in a city where we don't have one and they want local service. Or a company consolidates its travel and wants us to be in all of their key markets. Whatever the case, the demand for our services in a new location is often sudden.

Any business has its peak and off-peak periods, and that presents its share of staffing challenges. In our business, summer is generally a slower period for corporate travel, while fall through early spring is extremely busy.

Where do we find people who can fill in for the small yet important locations? Where do we find people who can "jump in" to assist where we've opened a new office, in which we've hired local people who are new to our company? How do we staff for the busy winter and slower summer, while offering full job security to our associates? The answer we came up with was what we call the "Rosenbluth reserve corps."

This idea originally came about during a strategy session many years ago where we were discussing these very challenges. We began joking about taking some of our most experienced people in a mobile home across the country and stopping wherever they were needed. We carried the idea out to the edge of the envelope, picturing our people in SWAT team uniforms armed with pagers and laptops. Soon, we modified the story to a team of professionals, ready to help on a moment's notice.

Years ago, the reservists traveled to offices that needed help, but today we shift business electronically to where resources are, rather than send people to where the work is. To build our reserve corps, we call for any interested associates with reservations experience (who do not currently work as CCAs) to sign up. We currently have thirty reservists. These exempt associates must be available to drop whatever they're doing during designated periods to take calls during peak times. Of course, they must keep up with their primary responsibilities. By just agreeing to take calls for a minimum of twenty hours, they receive a $1,000 bonus and two round-trip domestic airline tickets.

Utilizing current staff creatively to meet peaks in demand makes service seamless, holds down costs, and rewards those willing to pitch in. Everyone wins.

From joking about a travel SWAT team that day, we created a solution to an existing problem. If we hadn't pursued the idea, and then updated it for use in our business today, we would have never realized these benefits.

How Many Paths Do You Let Yourself Cross?
A Broad Approach to Idea Generating

It seems that well-rounded people not only get more out of life, they contribute more to it as well. The broader your horizons, the broader your scope of understanding and, ultimately, the areas in which you can make a difference. If you stay on only one road, you limit the possibility of crossing so many paths that could lead you elsewhere. This is true in both our personal and business lives.

That's one reason we seek a wide variety of people to join our company. And well roundedness is encouraged throughout their careers with us. To come up with ideas, we try to look not just at what's happening inside our industry, but what's happening all around us.

A wider focus helps a company spot trends early and discover emerging needs in the marketplace. This might present opportunities to diversify. Or it can lead to a larger share of a company's current market through gaining a clearer understanding of the pressures potential clients face and developing ways to ease those pressures.

Protect Them, but Not Blindly
The Importance of Germinating Ideas

Ideas must be championed, but not blindly. There's a delicate balance between encouraging ideas and recognizing the ones that won't be productive. One of the best methods to evaluate and refine an idea is "germination." Every idea is like a seed that needs to be cultivated, but the plant has to be strong to survive. Ideas need to be put to the test to see if they will work.

The best place to start is to objectively study each and every idea with the person(s) who suggested it, to ensure that it can and will work, and to determine whether or not it should be modified or even expanded. In an open, honest, and encouraging environment, this will be possible without people feeling threatened or defensive. A spirit of teamwork has to surround the building of ideas because they become stronger with input from other people.

To test my own ideas, I like to "sprinkle" them around to associates in a variety of departments, regions, and levels within the company. I particularly like to run them by people I know will regard them with the least reverence. Their constructive criticism improves the ideas because we all have a natural tendency to be too personally involved with our own ideas to see them objectively. The more often ideas are put to the test, the more powerful they become.

That's why I think "weekend thinking" is dangerous. Most truly dedicated people can't completely get their minds off work, even in their free time. Opportunities, problems, and solutions pop into their heads, and their natural reaction is to work through those thoughts and return to the office with solutions. The dedication is great, but creating solutions within our own limited boundaries narrows our ability to envision how the answers we've arrived at will play out. The solutions can have a ripple effect on the entire company.

People come back to work on Monday morning all fired up about the ideas they came up with over the weekend. They set them in motion right away. But without input from other departments, their ideas can be redundant, counterproductive, even destructive. Ideas need to be shared to be enhanced. Otherwise we limit them to just our own creativity. We should seek to surround ourselves with imaginative people and help bring one another's ideas to fruition.

Besides, people need the outside stimulation that time away from work can bring. Louis Brandeis, associate justice of the U.S. Supreme Court from 1916 to 1939, once said, "I find that I can do a year's work in eleven months, but I can't do it in twelve."

Steps to Encouraging Ideas in a Company

A SUMMARY

▌ Encouraging fresh ideas to spring forth from your people starts with the right environment—an energetic, creative, and caring environment from which you remove the fear of trying something new.

▌ Consider a Renew for the New Year program to encourage people to be thinking of new and better ways to do things. Innovation is an art that needs to be practiced. Every day should be a Renew day, but it helps to set aside an official time for ideas.

▌ Continually squelch bureaucracy in your company, because slow-moving organizations crush entrepreneurial spirit and stifle ideas.

▌ Recognize that ideas come from a variety of sources, such as the four outlined in this chapter: accepting social responsibility; finding a way to do something better; discovering a need in the marketplace; and finding a solution to an existing problem.

▌ Examine the origin of innovations, inside and outside your industry. Study the steps in developing successful ideas and re-create those steps.

▌ Never, ever allow an idea to be suppressed in your organization. People will come forth with idea after idea if they know their suggestions will be respected and acknowledged.

▌ If an idea is implemented, give plenty of credit and recognition to the originator of the idea and allow him or her to be involved in its implementation.

▌ Keep a wide focus because you never know where your next innovation will come from. The best thing that can happen to an idea is for it to be shared with as many people as possible. Well thought out ideas are the most powerful.

CHAPTER EIGHT

The Gardening Process

We've all become couch editors. In our hands is the power of the remote control, and we use it like a weapon. Whenever we don't like what we see on TV, we just switch the channel. When a commercial comes on we cruise the stations, and if we don't find something we like, we mute the sound. When we rent a movie and it's moving slowly, we fast-forward to the parts we like. I've even found myself at live sporting events clicking my thumb in search of my remote, to fast-forward time-outs.

There are a lot of situations in life where a remote control could come in handy. Most of us have people we'd like to mute. I'd like to fast-forward service and product development and to edit out mistakes the way you can with videotape. There's no remote control for that yet, though, so the best we can do is to develop processes to edit our organization to be the best for our clients, because they don't have a remote control for it either.

The selection process is a great start, but even the most thorough selection process isn't foolproof. Companies need to make an ongoing effort to keep the right people and encourage those who aren't pulling their weight to move on. This might sound incompatible with our philosophy of putting our people first.

On the contrary. We owe it to our people to create an environment where they are surrounded by others who care as much as they do, and who work as hard—who have a positive attitude. And we owe it to our clients, too. Which client should we pick to be served by someone who doesn't measure up? We can't do that to any client and we won't.

We liken it to carefully tending a garden. In order for the crop to grow, the weeds need to be pruned away. It takes a sharp eye and a steady hand to weed the one without damaging the other. But it's a never-ending process that's essential.

Chutes and Ladders
Creating Clear Routes to Advancement and Demotion

As a child I was quite fond of the game Chutes and Ladders. I guess when some things hit home, they stay home. Even today, that game plays an invisible role in our company. At Rosenbluth International we live our own version of Chutes and Ladders. Here's how it works.

In the game, the objective is to work your way up the playing board until you reach the top. All players start at the bottom, and with the spin of a wheel determine how many spaces they may advance each turn. There are ladders on the game board that enable the player to advance rapidly. When players land on a space that intersects a ladder, they get to jump over spaces. Ladders are shortcuts to the top. On the other hand, players have just as much chance of landing on a chute, which sends them back to square one.

While we don't keep game boards in our offices, we certainly have chutes and ladders. But the fundamental difference is that the moves people make are completely of their own choice, not left to the spin of a wheel. What's more, everyone in our company knows just where the chutes and ladders are.

Figuratively speaking, every company has its form of chutes and ladders. The secret is to keep careful watch over how they're working. Are the right people being lifted to the top, or are all the wrong ones climbing their way up?

Recognition systems send loud messages to people and affect their behavior. People who advance become role models for others. We've found that frequent evaluation of what type of person is moving in which direction can be helpful in making sure the system encourages the right values.

In the corporate arena, people often perceive that the climb to the top requires stepping on others. Perhaps it does in some organizations. But in ours we make it an instant chute. We have a rule that no one progresses at someone else's expense.

Conversely, being discovered helping someone else in the company is an instant ladder. There is no faster way to rise to the top. Our people delight in seeing someone ascend a ladder, because it's a given that they deserve it. Usually it's the people they've helped along the way who make the noise that gets them recognized.

'Tis the Season
Watch People's Contributions
So They Don't Have To

We have eschewed traditional management styles and created what we refer to as our "Santa Claus" style of management. Yes, you've got it—we know who's been naughty and who's been nice and we reward people accordingly. We do our best to eliminate politics by creating an environment in which it doesn't work. Customarily, people make power plays to catch the eye of those who can promote them. In our company, people know that all the grandstanding in the world won't get them as far as excelling at what they do and helping those around them shine.

It's a fun way to manage. Our leaders enjoy promoting those who truly deserve it yet do not expect it, as opposed to those who expect it and may or may not deserve it. But more important, it's an *effective* way to manage. People begin to spend more time *doing* their work and less time promoting it.

Unfortunately, politics exist in every organization, to a certain degree, and it's a tremendous time waster. Internal political efforts don't add value. In fact, they take time away from value-adding activities. If people are spending 25 percent of their time covering their tails, 25 percent documenting what they have done, and 25 percent figuring out how to get ahead, then all that's left is 25 percent. That's not enough. With profit margins as narrow as ours, we need 100 percent.

People fear that without positioning, their efforts won't be noticed. It's up to the company to assure them they will. Most people are just behaving the way they've been conditioned to behave. We find they welcome the opportunity to drop the politics when they learn it's not necessary.

It normally takes a while before new associates learn to relax, cut back on the memos and backtracking, and begin to trust. But when they do, their productivity soars. If companies could reduce politics by even half, think of the gains in productivity they could achieve.

This management theory, in practice, is only as good as the leaders who carry it out. It's nothing more than propaganda if, in reality, the grandstander is the one who's promoted. To make it work, leaders have to walk the talk. One way to ensure it is to make it part of the performance appraisal system. Objective performance measurements will determine who's really working. Leaders have to actively seek those who are quietly contributing, by carefully evaluating actual work completed by each individual.

Our company has a policy that says a written performance appraisal with objective measures (which have been established up front) must be submitted before a merit increase can take effect. This helps ensure that those who are rewarded are deserving. Our performance appraisal system is job-description driven, and therefore highly personalized. Each job explanation includes specific core competencies, accountabilities, predetermined measures for success, and time frames for completing those actions. Every position incorporates our culture, company goals, and teamwork.

Teamwork has to play an important part in the performance appraisal process. To ensure it, it must be measured and rewarded. We've found that the best way to find out who's helping others is by asking. It won't work to ask people how they've helped others. To find out the real story, people should be asked how they've *been* helped and by whom.

"Zero-Base"
Question Your Business

Grown-ups never understand anything for themselves, and it is tiresome for children to be always and forever explaining things to them.
—Antoine de Saint-Exupéry, *The Little Prince*

Children have a delightful way of looking at things. They always bring questions to mind—things we haven't thought about in years. Every other word is "Why?" They take nothing for granted and make everything new. Somehow they cut through to the truth. They find the most direct route to where they want to go.

An airline executive who's a friend of mine keeps a drawing in his office showing a soccer team trying to find out which goal is theirs as they prepare to drive down the field. He had it made because he never wanted to forget a lesson he learned from his son.

His son's first-grade soccer team had a losing season and their coach asked them what would help them win. They told him they sometimes got confused about which goal was theirs. Something so simple, so easy to remedy, but so crucial to success. Their coach promised his team that the next season, he would stand on the sidelines and point the way to the goal throughout every game. Guess what—they were undefeated that season.

These are the kinds of lessons that might seem simplistic to an adult, but how many businesses get off track from their real goals? And how often are team members running in all different directions? We believe there's plenty we can learn from a childlike look around us.

At least twice a year, we zero-base our business to make sure our business model doesn't get stale. When you build something from the ground up you don't fall into habits. You simply think, "What do we need in order to be successful?" You set objectives, identify potential barriers to success, build a plan to remove those barriers, figure out what you need to sustain the business, identify what to build and what to buy, and go from there.

Our first try at zero-basing resulted in the most sweeping and effective change in our company's history. In 1992, we completely dismantled our business, breaking it apart into business units, making what had become a very large organization into a collection of small, fast, entrepreneurial companies providing customized service to their clients.

Our goal was to come up with a design that put our clients at the very center, and emanated out from there. Prior to that, our structure looked like most companies, with functional areas resembling stovepipes. Information flow was sluggish, and our structure felt like a ball and chain.

In the new structure, we combined a number of key functional areas. There are no jobs that perform single tasks, and this role diversity enables everyone to shift their focus to accommodate whatever needs to be done. These business units can turn on a dime, and our clients and associates love it.

A change this sweeping called for new positions virtually across the board, as well as new learning programs, compensation systems, and financial systems. Every area of the company had to redesign itself to meet the needs of the business units.

Today, a decade later, we operate smoothly under the business unit model, but we never rest because we know that unless you continually, mentally dismantle your organization and build it again from scratch, you'll never know if you're as good as you could be.

There was a splendid article in the July/August 1990 issue of *Harvard Business Review* about the need to re-engineer companies. It contained one passage that stuck in my mind: "At the heart of reengineering is the notion of discontinuous thinking—of recognizing and breaking away from the outdated rules and fundamental assumptions that underlie operations. Unless we change these rules, we are merely rearranging the deck chairs on the *Titanic*."

Leader Reviews
Question How You're Doing

When was the last time you asked the people you lead to honestly evaluate you? To make suggestions on how you might improve? We have a tool to help us do just that: our "Leader Review by Direct Reports." It works from the bottom up, but it has to start at the top.

Leader Reviews began many years ago at Rosenbluth International when at the end of a review with one of my vice presidents, I asked her to honestly evaluate me. I must admit, that day I was humbled. She told me a lot of things. One was that I didn't listen when I had a lot on my mind. And usually that's when it's most important for me to listen. That's when there's something going on in the company that's concerning me.

She went on to say that when I'm not listening, people read the wrong cues from me and it affects the decisions they make. The consequences of such a flaw could be disastrous. I found myself endlessly reviewing hypothetical situations in my mind, and it really bothered me.

So I asked our director of learning and development to work with me to improve my listening skills. We set up a program to meet once a month to evaluate my progress and to practice techniques that help me keep focused on the conversation at hand. One of the most helpful suggestions from these meetings was to bring one meeting to a close before beginning another. He told me he had noticed that because I allowed no time between meetings, my mind was often a meeting behind. Now I take a few minutes to jot down thoughts or put plans into motion before tackling the next subject. The feedback I've gotten from those around me is a great motivator. I think I still have a way to go, but it's a good feeling to know I'm improving.

After the initial experience, I was eager to have each of my vice presidents evaluate me, and today the process is spontaneous and ongoing. But at least once a year, I still hold a formal Leader Review with each person who reports directly to me.

Sometimes I take all the written reviews I've received and read them aloud during a meeting with all who have reviewed me. I ask them to hold me accountable for improving in each of the suggested areas. I really feel the heat, and that's good.

Leader Reviews are both difficult to do and to accept. At first, people were cautious. They'd only give me one or two suggestions, followed quickly by compliments. But with each Leader Review the constructive criticism increased. I don't think it's because I was losing ground. It's because people began to feel more comfortable with the process and secure that they could be frank. Today, people wander into my office freely to let me know how they feel I'm doing, and that's what I hoped would happen.

Sure, the truth hurts, but it helps to hear it. You know you're open to self-improvement when you look at constructive criticism as a gift from a friend. In my case, it must be Christmas every day in my office.

Once our associates saw how effective Leader Reviews were, the process began to filter throughout the organization. Today, vice presidents are reviewed by directors, who are reviewed by general managers, and so on. It's a mutual process.

Today's Leader Reviews are more structured than those early reviews. Associates complete a standardized form (either in hard copy or electronically) and send it to an outside company who collects and consolidates the information, to ensure anonymity. The data is then sent to our human resources department, which produces reports for each leader. Copies are sent to the leader as well as to *their* leader, who review the results together and develop an action plan to continue the leader's development.

The evaluation tool rates our leaders in eight skill categories: commitment to our values, concern for associates, understanding of internal and external business environment, client focus, results orientation, impact and influence, flexibility, and teamwork. The specific questions are about things like accessibility, listening skills, recognition, open-mindedness, delivery on commitments, fairness, and respect. At the end is an opportunity for written comments.

Leader Reviews are a good barometer of morale, leadership skill, and, ultimately, client satisfaction. Everyone should be given the opportunity to review their leader. To kick off the initial process, we sent a special team to all of our offices to help encourage full participation and offer people an additional chance to say what was on their minds. It also happened to be a great way to cross-pollinate ideas throughout the company.

Lipomanagement
A Process to Keep Lean

Even the best-laid plans have to be adaptable enough to withstand outside pressures. The downsizing of the late eighties into the nineties was a crash course in learning how to operate a leaner organization. Management experts have preached for years that lean is the way to go, but it's easier said than done. No company wants to lay people off. Then it becomes a numbers game in which some really good people can come up short.

A more fair method is to keep a trim organization based upon merit. We've actually found that in an environment like ours, which squelches politics, a natural attrition occurs, and the best people stay. This is a different culture, and people who don't buy in generally wind up leaving. It's just a matter of time. Those who don't know how to operate without politics become frustrated. Those who aren't pulling their weight begin to feel out of place, surrounded by those who are.

Every company's goal is to keep the muscle and lose the fat. To achieve it, they can't be afraid to cut out nonproductive programs or people. They can't hesitate for a moment to make room for the muscle—programs that work, people who make things happen, people who care. "Fat" just makes a company move more slowly, and in today's competitive environment, who can afford that? It's a demotivator to those who make up the "muscle."

Natural attrition is helpful, but it's often not enough. Marginal performance will weight a company down. To be fair, it has to be made crystal clear, up front, that marginality is not condoned and that the company can't make room for it.

We compare it to preparing for a trip. Those who travel frequently have learned the secret: Pack lightly. Only neophytes drag half the things they own with them. They bring everything they might ever possibly need . . . just in case. Experienced travelers know they can find whatever they need when they arrive, if they have to. They don't burden themselves with what they *might* need. They bring what they *know* they need.

The same applies to companies. Fit organizations don't carry excess baggage. They keep a pure environment with their best people. They don't make room for those who are marginal, because it's not fair.

Leaders must be strong enough to give their people frequent and honest feedback. Those who are marginal need to know it and be encouraged to improve, because marginality is contagious. It discourages those who give their best and is a sure way for a company to be left behind.

Run from the Dinosaurs
Keep Moving as a Company

Two dinosaurs took a break from their lunch of tasty treetops to observe a caveman trying unsuccessfully to cart his belongings along in a crate resting upon square stone wheels. With every bumpy turn, the dinosaurs would hear a loud crash and his cart would tip over. They laughed uncontrollably and said, "We dinosaurs will rule the world forever." Unfortunately for our two friends, their analysis wasn't quite accurate, and they haven't been heard from for millions of years.

For companies to avoid becoming dinosaurs, they need to keep things moving; stir up change. When people are given the opportunity to move around, complacency is replaced by energy. Change is exhilarating and it keeps people on their toes.

How appetizing would it be to eat the same thing for every meal, every day of the year, year after year? Not very. How inspired would the person be to prepare that same meal over and over? Not at all. Variety is the spice of life. We all crave it. We need to remember that in business.

To keep things fresh, we regularly make structural changes and reorganize regions, lines of business, and departments. While our long-term goals remain the same, we take these opportunities to reevaluate our strategies. As a result, we've seen some very positive effects in terms of creativity and energy. But we go a step beyond just changing the structure of the company. We also move individuals around the organization, throughout their careers. As a result, we've seen a new breed of leader emerge, one who is flexible, multifaceted, and well rounded.

Dismantling Compartments
Encouraging Cohesiveness

Most companies have departments of some sort. We have them, too. The danger lies in the fact that departments easily become "*compartments*," each with its carefully drawn boundaries and closely guarded domain.

There are certain efficiencies that can be captured by the sharing of resources and procedures within various areas of specialization. But there is a natural tendency for those areas to metamorphose into territories when people become too busy to look beyond their own niche. Fresh ideas can't flow in this type of environment. When people and ideas are guarded, their growth is stunted. Conversely, ideas breed ideas and often, input from people "outside" our specific area brings a new perspective to things.

Departments may be a necessary evil, but the natural barriers they erect should be continually torn down. One way to do it is to base leaders' compensation largely on the company's performance as a whole. The bonus system for our leaders is weighted equally between individual and company performance. This puts emphasis on teamwork that extends beyond department or line of business.

Another method to decompartmentalize departments is to encourage the cross-utilization of resources—both human and capital.

The Cross-Pollination Principle
Keep People Moving

Cross-pollination has brought us some of the most spectacular varieties of plants and flowers known to the world. It's an old science that perpetually creates new wonders. Its value is the strength that results from exposure to diversity. The same principle is true with people.

The more a person knows about a wide variety of subjects (or in the case of a company, a variety of departments), the more of an asset he or she is. And access to a variety of leaders strengthens people as well.

There is a theory in academia that a person reaches the scholastic pinnacle when subjects begin to relate to one another. When knowledge of biology makes a literary work clearer. When understanding of geometry enables one to appreciate a work of art. When erudition in geology begins to put events in history into perspective.

Cross-pollination facilitates well roundedness and heightens teamwork to astounding levels. The more people know about the "big picture" and the company's goals and objectives, the more they will be empowered to contribute. One tool that can be helpful is focus groups, or "blue teams." They aren't new, but they're a highly effective means of cross-pollination because they offer a full spectrum of viewpoints upon which to base decisions. Furthermore, they give the people involved a chance to "buy in" to the program or policy being developed.

Like it or not, people usually come to the table with their own agendas, which can bear on decisions that affect many. For example, let's say there's a company that operates an employee cafeteria in which those responsible for preparing the food are also responsible for selecting the menu. Chances are, they will prepare food that (1) fits their personal taste and/or (2) they find easy to prepare. There's a good chance the lunchtime crowd will choose to bypass the cafeteria and eat elsewhere.

The best decisions are made with input from as many people as possible. It's vital to include the widest possible cross section of people in the development of processes, procedures, and products.

When we held focus groups around the company years ago to assess our benefits program, we learned that our policy on "sick days" was not current with our people's needs in one very important aspect. Our former policy allowed for six paid days per year for personal illness. What we learned was that people needed days off for important family events more than they needed sick days. People need to take their children or parents to doctor's appointments or to attend parent–teacher conferences.

Our policy was changed so that people can stay healthy and use these days as they need them. Our "family responsibility" policy supports our people for what's important in *their* lives. The plan is based on flexibility. Time may be used either in partial or full days and is taken at the discretion of the associate for illness, family obligations, or medical appointments. Without asking people what was important to them, we probably wouldn't have made this simple change that positively affected their lives.

Accordion-Style Management
Preparing Your Organization for External Pressure

All industries fall upon good and hard times. In our company's case, potential danger can be found in reduced corporate travel programs. Cutbacks in budgets and personnel in corporations around the world affect us immensely. We manage the travel accounts of 1,500 corporations, and when times are hard for them, we share the burden.

When budgets are slashed in cost-cutting measures, travel is one of the first discretionary expenditures to be cut. And when our clients make the choice to reduce their travel programs, we can suffer huge losses because we have assumed the resources to provide service for their original volumes. In fact, in 2001 our clients cut back by over $1 billion in travel volume, and we suffered those losses without losing a single account.

We try our utmost not to subject our people to layoffs, downsizing, or cutbacks in personnel. Undeniably, there are times when it has been imperative to do so, but our associates know it's only as a last resort, when all other efforts have been put into action. We truly believe that creating as secure an environment as possible is the right thing to do. It's also good business. When people feel secure, they're more productive and more likely to resist when competitors attempt to lure them away in better times.

Do All Accordions Come with Monkeys?
The Trials of Flexibility and Steps to Success

Yes, all accordions do come with monkeys. In this case, the monkey on our back is the threat of the imminent squeeze after expansions. But our accordion-style management means maintaining a flexible organization that can expand quickly and effectively with the acquisition of a major account, and tighten its reins just as rapidly and efficiently when times are lean. Businesses continually face growth and decline, but we think a secret is to minimize layoffs, cutbacks, and drastic downsizing. And we have developed a four-step plan to help us conquer downturns in volume.

The first step in our accordion process is to fuel our sales effort in order to maintain the proper balance of productivity. We then redirect underutilized staff to serve those new accounts. You might be thinking, "Why don't they fuel their sales effort all of the time?" We do, but we plan our growth very carefully to ensure consistency without straining our resources.

We used to target the accelerated sales efforts to the particular region or city in which the squeeze took place. But years ago, an interesting opportunity presented itself. The volume of an enormous account dropped dramatically in a cutback. Simultaneously, we acquired a major account in another city, where our presence was minimal.

We presented to our new client the idea to service their account out of another city, where we had an operation in place that ran like clockwork. The start-up costs had already been absorbed. The staff was already a team.

Our client was sold on the idea. And since that time, we haven't limited our "accordion" sales effort by location. We can provide service from any location. We simply move business to where our resources are.

The second step in the accordion process is a combination of promoting from within and eliminating unnecessary work. Ultimately, the goal is to identify positions that are not essential and move those resources to where they are needed, providing chance for advancement in the process.

As a fail-safe to detect wasted resources, senior leaders routinely review hiring requests. When a current position is vacated or a new one created, it is analyzed for its value to the company. If the position is justified, it must be filled from within if at all possible. This creates another opening, which is then evaluated for its contribution to the company, creating a cycle of objective evaluations of positions throughout the organization. Through this process, we have discovered a significant number of jobs that are not vital to the organization: positions that are draining resources from what's really important.

The third step is to cross-train our people, which enables them to shift from one position to another successfully. This is a hybrid between the cross-pollination principle and dismantling of compartments discussed earlier in this chapter. Our business unit structure thrives on the cross-utilization of associates.

In many companies, a standard reaction during lean times might be for people to try to *look* busy in order to justify their existence. People need the opportunity and the security to seek new challenges. We painstakingly maintain an environment where our people don't have to be afraid to say, "I'm not busy. Find something worthwhile for me to do."

This brings us to *the fourth step:* to instill confidence in our people that each will have a challenging, fulfilling, and enriching position in good times and in bad. It may not be the position they have today, but it will be a position that is vital to the company, because we don't have positions that are not.

An interesting test of our accordion management theory came in 1991. The Gulf War and the recession rendered it one of the worst years in our company's history. Travel came to a virtual standstill.

We couldn't have weathered the storm without the dedication of our people. First, our associates initiated a program they called "Operation Brain Storm," which generated over two hundred cost-saving ideas. The second action was a pay freeze (*not* a cut). Third, our top leaders took a voluntary pay cut which spurred the fourth move, in which associates from across the country took voluntary time off without pay. Through these four displays of support, we made it through in good shape.

A decade later in 2001, during one of our most difficult years, again our people rose to the occasion, helping lift us above outside pressures and on to a successful future. Our accordion style has stood the test of time and continues to prove that a genuine focus on our people and a commitment to do the right thing will earn their loyalty, and with that, we can face anything.

Developing a Gardening Process

A SUMMARY

▌ Terminations are a fact of life. We should never get used to them, but we should prepare for them. Preparation is the key to minimizing the trauma and helping separated associates move ahead.

▌ Make sure you have clear routes to advancement and demotion in your company that send the right messages to your people.

∎ Watch people's contributions so they don't have to spend their time measuring their worth and bringing it to your attention. Give Santa Claus management a try.

∎ Visibly reward those who help others—make it a requirement for promotions and see how your teamwork improves.

∎ Take a hard look at your company. Mentally tear it apart and reconstruct it, on a regular basis. You might find out just how good your organization can be.

∎ Make Leader Reviews a practice in your organization. Offer the opportunity for everyone to evaluate the leadership that guides them.

∎ Encourage leaders to make room for the muscle (programs that work, people who care) by eliminating fat (marginal performers).

∎ Keep people moving. Stir up change. It keeps people on their toes, develops cross-departmental understanding, and breeds innovation and fresh ideas. Dare to rethink your structure every now and then.

∎ Discourage departments from becoming compartments by tying leaders' compensation to company performance as much as individual contribution.

∎ Encourage cross-pollination of people. Generalists better understand the "big picture"—the company's overall objectives.

∎ Create an "accordion" management plan that works for your company to enable you to shift resources and stretch or shrink for the peaks and valleys in business.

PART TWO
Inventing the Future

People touch every aspect of an organization, yet there are undeniably outside factors that affect business in very real ways. At first glance, they may appear to be areas difficult to impact—moving forces against which organizations have little control. You might think the people principles apply inside the business, and these other factors affect the rest, existing in parallel.

Not true. Our approach to people has helped us to conquer every outside force and harness every marketplace pressure to our benefit. We've talked about how critical people are, and we've studied ways to find and keep them, value and nurture them. Now it's time to look at some of the ways in which people-first principles can be applied to other aspects of your business—aspects you might not have considered.

In Part Two, you'll learn how to extend the people-first foundation to help you:

- Design the future with a leading place for your organization
- Maximize the benefits of technology
- Develop strategy to help you defy marketplace pressures
- Build unshakable partnerships with your clients and suppliers
- Find untapped talent and a fresh approach to doing business

CHAPTER NINE

Inventing the Future

In every neighborhood there's a kid who's always in charge. In mine, it was Billy. Whatever he said was final. He invented the rules of the game so it's no wonder he always won. He was small but fast, so when we played football it was always touch football, not tackle. And he was always either the quarterback or the receiver. He made sure he'd be the one to score.

He happened to be ambidextrous, so when we played dodgeball, he would suggest that everyone play with the hand they didn't favor. He always placed himself at an advantage. People seldom questioned why. Everyone wanted desperately to be like him and he knew it. He made sure it was that way.

I've never forgotten the power people hold when they invent the rules of the game. For that reason we strive, as a company, to continually invent the future of our industry. That way we secure a prominent place in it for ourselves and our clients.

To illustrate some of the ways in which a company can boldly redefine itself. I'll identify five pivotal decisions that were instrumental in taking us from a local company, to a national company, to the global firm we are today. Our ventures into uncharted waters have always told us that it's worth the uncertain journey.

First—Taking Deregulation by the Horns
Turning Change into Opportunity

The changes brought upon our industry by deregulation of the airlines were seen by many, if not most, travel agencies as a closed door.

Agencies saw the uncertainty of their future role as a death sentence for their companies, and for many it was. But we looked at deregulation as the opportunity of a lifetime.

We knew that from that point on, we'd no longer be limited to the role of reservation taker and ticket deliverer. We were about to enter the business of information management. Open skies meant "all's fair," which in turn meant rapid changes in schedules and airfares. We knew people were going to need a lot of help. We said, "Bring on the commotion!" Then we positioned ourselves as the solution.

A small group of us used to work late and then go to a place called "The Top of the Two's." Believe it or not, we'd sit and talk about how exciting the new world of travel would be. Over a few beers, we'd map out our dreams for the future. From our viewpoint, the change in regulation made room for a higher level of service. We took deregulation by the horns and delivered it to our clients in the form of solid advantage.

This was the point at which we realized that corporate travel would be affected the most by deregulation. Now companies had opportunities for savings that didn't exist before. Prior to deregulation, the airfare choices between cities were basically limited to first class and coach. Suddenly there were new routes, new carriers, and, almost daily, new fares. There were so many choices for business travelers in this new climate, and we made it our job to find the best ones for our clients.

We ran out and got computers for everyone in our corporate travel department and set out to make sense of the chaos. We did our research and we showed companies that travel was now a controllable expense (which we were prepared to manage for them). They took us up on our offer, and our corporate travel business boomed.

Prior to deregulation, corporate travel represented less than a quarter of our business. Today it's over 95 percent. Because we hungered for change rather than being afraid of it, we seized an opportunity to completely redefine our business.

Changes in regulations, a competitor's new product launch—any restyling that takes place around you—holds promise for you to capitalize on it. Sometimes even changes we dread can be the best thing for us. They force us to face the future.

Second—Strength in Numbers
Reshaping for Growth

Demand for our services in corporate travel management grew and we expected that growth would explode. We banked on that projection, and in 1981 we opened the travel agency industry's first reservation center and hired more than one hundred people to take corporate reservations.

This was a big investment for us. It called for significant human and capital resources. A lot of people in our industry thought we were strapping ourselves with a "white elephant." We were convinced otherwise.

We invested in advanced technology that would enable us to capture data on the travel patterns of our corporate clients. We used that information collectively to negotiate with the airlines on our clients' behalf.

While we were gathering and analyzing these statistics, a lot of other agencies were letting it slip past them in the wake of the storm caused by deregulation. Having a central system to capture this information was critical, and it gave us a sustainable competitive advantage.

The reservation center enabled us to share expertise, information, and resources to serve our clients better. At the same time, we were preparing for future growth. Today, we have reservation centers around the world (you will read about our Intellicenters in Chapters 11 and 13).

Planning the structure for rapid growth proved to be a self-fulfilling prophecy for us. Just as most architectural plans include potential extensions, growth plans help a company prepare for expansion. They can also *provide* the opportunity for growth, because it's comforting to potential clients to know a company is ready to handle their business.

Third—Go Big or Go Home
Growth Without Gambling

By 1984, we were by far the strongest regional player in corporate travel management, but then something happened that pushed us over the edge to national status. The Du Pont company awarded Rosenbluth its national travel account. At that time, it was the single largest corporate travel management program in history.

Taking on this account meant we had to go national. This is something we had wanted to do, but we decided it was too risky to speculate in new markets without national recognition. Being awarded this account allowed us to grow into all of Du Pont's major markets because we had the business to warrant it. From there, we acquired new accounts in each of those locations.

To date, we have saved Du Pont more than $500 million; almost half of that in the last five years alone. So it's no surprise that our partnership with Du Pont set off an industry trend for corporations to consolidate their travel accounts on a nationwide basis. And we were positioned as the leader in consolidation. We began to share our expertise and resources with corporation after corporation, consolidating their travel programs. We continued to grow with our clients, entering their major markets. Then we attracted additional business in each of those cities.

Our client-driven approach to growth ensures that our focus remains on our clients, but at the same time, it ensures our expansion. Because every new location exists to serve a client, we take minimal risk in our investment of capital and human resources. This guarantees that we'll be around to serve the clients for whom we've expanded. So, at times being conservative or risk-adverse is, in fact, defining the future.

Critical mass can be important for a company, and achieving it presents its share of hurdles. But we've found that the client-driven approach to growth not only makes better business sense, it usually means better client service.

Fourth—Complete Independence
Breaking Ties that Constrain You

The best relationships are on an even scale. Both partners bring value to the table and have the freedom to maintain their own identity. This seems to be especially true in a company like ours—headstrong and a little unusual.

Our company works best in an environment of complete independence, where our creativity and willingness to take calculated risks are not hampered. As we continued to grow, we quickly discovered we needed to claim independence in our back-room technology in order to serve our clients better than anyone else.

Most companies have some form of front-room and back-room systems. In our industry, travel agencies usually depend on an airline for their systems. The front-room system provides flight schedules, airfares, and entry into the reservations process. The back-room system provides accounting, database, and programming capabilities.

In the front room, we declared our independence in 1983 when we created proprietary software called READOUT that fuses airfare data from all the major airlines into one system (explained in Chapter 10, "Technology as a Tool"). We had all the schedule and pricing information we needed right at our fingertips.

But in the back room, where data is stored and analyzed, independence was another story—and still is, for most agencies. Common practice has long been to utilize a back-room system originating from an airline. But we had to have our own. (This system, too, is explained more fully in Chapter 10.)

Creating our own back-room system was one of the most expensive and most important decisions we ever made. Why was it so expensive? Because these multimillion-dollar back-room systems are subsidized by the airlines for agencies that utilize them. They're either provided for free or leased at a greatly reduced price.

Breaking away from this arrangement meant we would have to build our own system and bear all the costs. Why was this so important? For the very same reason that it was so expensive: The airline subsidy meant dependence upon the airline with which you subscribed, and a certain distance from those with which you didn't subscribe.

We decided that information was the key to effectively and proactively managing our clients' travel programs. We'd only take control of that information and be free to use it to benefit our clients if we built our own back-room system. The following hypothetical example illustrates the value of that independence.

Suppose that a travel agency subscribes to airline *ABC*'s back-room system. A key client has a high volume of travel between two particular cities and could fly either airline *ABC* or airline *XYZ* on that route. The client and the agency decide it would be more advantageous to consolidate that traffic with one airline, with which they can negotiate the strongest arrangement for price discounts and service enhancements. The agency's dependence upon airline *ABC*'s back-room system presents some complications.

Complication #1: In order to bring strength to the bargaining table, the agency and client must have their complete travel history between those routes. In order to do so, they have to ask airline *ABC* for that data. The purpose for it would be clear to the airline. Why would they want to provide that information when they perceive it as being used against them in negotiations?

Complication #2: If they do retrieve the data and airline *XYZ* makes a better offer than airline *ABC*, can the agency ask airline *ABC* to write a program to redirect market share to airline *XYZ* in order to take advantage of the better offer? Sure, they can ask, but do you think that airline *ABC* will put a project high on its priority list that steers business *away* from its own company? Of course not.

When you get your ammunition from the person with whom you're negotiating, you're not in a position of strength. While the airlines are our partners in creating the most highly effective travel management programs for our clients, the negotiating balance is skewed by dependence upon them.

Through independence and three-way partnerships, we can ensure a triple-win outcome for our clients, our suppliers, and our company. Our clients lower their travel costs, our airline partners fill more seats, and we can market our ability to provide these savings to potential clients.

A careful look at levels of dependence upon outside sources is wise. Though partnerships can multiply our capabilities, a level of dependence that holds us back from serving our clients to the best of our ability is dangerous. Independence can be achieved without harm to our partnerships.

Breaking out and claiming our technological independence in the '80s was a milestone, but many more technological breakthroughs have shaped our future since that time. You can read more about them in Chapter 10, on technology.

Fifth—Spanning the Globe
Global Expansion Through Strategic Alliances

It was our track record in managing nationally consolidated travel programs that led to the next logical step for expansion—global. Here too, our approach was and is client-driven. Our multinational clients began to ask us if we could serve them around the world, so we set out to find the best way.

In those early years, we studied the feasibility of opening international offices and compared that with the practicality of learning each individual market from an expert there, and decided the latter was a better approach to begin our global expansion. Though our approach today is very different, at the time, opening our own offices overseas would not have been a good use of capital. We developed the Rosenbluth International Alliance (RIA), which was designed to be flexible enough to take advantage of business opportunities that arose in any part of the world at any time. After extensive research, we formed alliances with what we considered to be the very best travel management firm in each of more than forty countries around the world. What we looked for was a match in philosophy and values, dedication to service, an orientation toward technology, and financial stability.

For a time, we benefited from the strong position each member held in its marketplace and from its knowledge of the local culture, government regulations, suppliers, and business climate. So we were able to concentrate on service. The member agencies around the world benefited from the business we brought to them, and they networked business with each other.

This approach worked fine for a few years, but then we began to see its inherent weaknesses and recognized that we had outgrown our initial strategy. The alliance approach met the basic travel needs of clients traveling abroad, but when we were awarded a piece of truly multinational business, the expectations changed. Our clients wanted our service standards, consolidated information, and leverage with suppliers, worldwide.

One of the most critical conflicts we uncovered was that our clients' preferred suppliers did not always align with those of our RIA partners. We negotiated favorable rates for our clients with key airlines, but the RIA members had their own supplier relationships and didn't want to lose commission deals with those competing carriers.

We needed our global locations to have the sophisticated supplier negotiating skills, reporting tools, and support products and services that we had. The inconsistency of their capabilities surfaced, and we came to understand that an alliance is only as strong as its weakest link. So we set out to redesign our global approach.

First we spent extensive time with our clients to determine their exact global needs and strategies. We then met with key suppliers to fully understand their global goals and challenges. From the knowledge gained, we drafted plans for triple-win opportunities. We outlined our clients' global plans and overlaid them to get a clear picture of where we needed to be. We constructed market-by-market client requirements and combined that information with supplier plans. From that, we created our global implementation plan, and we began the shift from alliances to wholly-owned and joint venture/network partner offices.

As soon as we converted from the RIA to our current approach, service consistency improved, reports were more accurate and timely, and our ability to produce crisp market share movements to support preferred supplier programs produced significant savings for our clients.

We implemented nearly $200 million of business through the RIA, and in 1993, we reimplemented all of the business under our new design. I'm delighted to say that we kept every account and still retain all of that business, to this day. In fact, over 65 percent of our North American clients do business with us multinationally.

As far as the future goes, we continue to evolve our model, knowing that having "epicenters of thought" in key areas around the world, with spokes radiating to peripheral centers, is key. Brick and mortar are not the measurements of a global presence, but rather ideas, knowledge, creativity, and client advocacy. These are what our clients hire us for, not dots on a map. What's crucial is to identify the core markets that are important to our clients and their growth strategies and to determine the best way to do business in each of those locations.

By early 2002 we owned and operated offices in twenty-seven countries and began the process of taking equity ownership in twenty-nine more. The RIA was transformed into our Strategic Markets group and our technological and thought leadership was being deployed around the world. Today, Rosenbluth International has the second largest global presence in the world.

Whatever form business takes on (wholly-owned offices, joint ventures, partners), there are three essential steps to follow. First, determine the critical components of the services and products you supply that require global standardization and enforce those standards rigorously. Second, recognize and honor local and cultural variances and keep in harmony with the local communities in which you wish to do business. Third, be flexible where it does not impact the credibility of your program. Many bright ideas will be generated locally.

With great thinkers spread across the globe, we will always stay a step ahead of the curve for our clients. From local to regional to national to global and, in the future, maybe beyond global, growth is a matter not just of a company's size, but of its service. There are numerous steps in providing outstanding service: finding the right people to provide it, arming them with the training and technology to do their best, and of course, having a service orientation that speaks your company's language.

Critical Decisions

A SUMMARY

∎ Look for opportunities that surround change—in your industry, in legislation, even in your competitors' strategies. Airline deregulation created a world of opportunity for our company.

∎ Develop a growth plan. It not only ensures you'll be ready for expansion, but it may even give you the chance to grow because clients feel comfortable knowing you're ready to serve them. Our plan supports our client-driven approach to growth.

∎ Continually examine your business models to see if you're outgrowing them, as we did our global strategy. Be willing to evolve as needed. Though the challenge is great—the rewards can be greater.

∎ Take a careful look at your levels of dependence upon outside sources. Partnerships are wonderful, but not if they get in the way of serving your clients to their best advantage.

CHAPTER TEN

Technology as a Tool

You can't just give a carpenter a hammer and ask him to build a house. A doctor can't provide treatment to patients with only a stethoscope. Every artisan must have all the right tools at his or her disposal in order to do their very best.

Technology is an essential tool in virtually every business today. There probably isn't anything a computer can do that a person can't. It's people who give computers their intelligence anyway. But the secret is time.

Calculations can be generated, geometric designs drawn, and documents produced, but without computers, what we accomplish today would take an impossible amount of person-hours—resources we can't afford to waste.

Technology allows us to accomplish more in the time we are given and makes otherwise tedious work automatic, thereby freeing our time to create. It's a tremendous tool. But for many, technology is intimidating, cause for insecurity, or perhaps seen as a potential replacement for people. Technology should be used to empower our people.

In his newsletter, *On Achieving Excellence,* Tom Peters said, "Rosenbluth has redefined a mundane business through an astonishing array of proprietary software that helps corporate clients track and manage their costs." In the same article he also writes. "The 'elegant service' is as significant as the software. While beating the Joneses on information technology is essential, failing to implement through people would be a disaster."

Reaching Out and Not Touching Anyone
Learning from a Failed Product

Not all technology products will make the hall of fame. In 1983, we created one we called REACHOUT® and it fizzled. It transmitted air schedules and hotel and car information to clients' PCs. We made significant investments to build the system and we never got a return on our investment.

The problem was that we didn't understand the difficulty our clients had in using the product. The people who developed and tested it were accustomed to using it, but they weren't the ones we developed it for. We blindly supported the product because we believed the marketplace needed it. We learned our lesson, and since that time, nearly twenty years ago, we have put a lot more listening behind the development of our products.

Naturally, we now have a product management team that assesses market requirements and designs our offerings based upon client needs (you'll read more about them in the pages ahead). We have also evolved from building solutions around a single business or client need, to developing universal solutions with configurable parameters to extend their reach to answer similar yet unique requests.

There was a silver lining to the failed product's dark cloud. REACHOUT was a first in our industry, and it served as a platform for the development of a product that allowed our clients to send us travel requests via e-mail, which ultimately evolved into our current on-line booking system, @Rosenbluth.

To develop the right products, we have to keep an ear to the ground to know what's coming, and we have to listen to both our clients and our people. We don't necessarily have to get to the marketplace first with our products, and we don't have to invent all aspects of them in-house. We just have to be the best and to keep a step ahead. At times we take commercially accepted products or concepts and tailor them to meet our needs.

For example, our REACHOUT product evolved into an e-mail booking tool, which we then took to a client server application, and next to an Internet application. However, our system wasn't real-time and couldn't handle complex, multi-destination itineraries or international trips. We wanted a system that could do these things and integrate with all of our other systems. Given time to market and cost to build, we decided to partner with a company with proven technology. We did. The result is @Rosenbluth, and it does everything we envisioned. Not a bad end result from an initially failed product.

To provide a map of our information systems landscape, I'll divide it into three primary areas: the front room, middle room, and back room. I'll discuss selected products of each. While in our case they pertain to travel, what they offer has application to virtually any industry.

THE FRONT ROOM

There are many differences between our technology and that of our competitors, and this becomes clear when we are bidding for an account. In years past, we put most of our emphasis on our front-room investments and capabilities, stemming from our philosophy that getting things right the first time is more efficient, less expensive, and more convenient for our clients. These things remain true, and we continue to invest heavily up front. But as more and more transactions are driven by on-line booking tools, a part of the process is out of our hands, and the need for automated quality control and ticket fulfillment takes on heightened significance (we'll get to that in the middle room).

It's still important to build in customization and quality checks up front, where the reservations are made, whether they be made by our associates or by our customers, on-line. Let's take a look at our key front-room products that give us the power to serve our clients the way we want to.

Delivering Value
The Evolution of a Product to Get the Lowest Fare

In 1983, we created a product called READOUT, which I mentioned briefly, in Chapter 9. We were seeing sometimes hundreds of thousands of airfare changes a day. Each airline had its own reservations system, and while the systems included the flights of every airline, there was lag time in updating information between the systems. If an airline changed its fares, it would update its own system first, and within twenty-four to forty-eight hours those rates would register in the other systems.

We saw that our clients could miss out on the lowest fares because of that delay. So we leased every available system, put them side-by-side, and compared the rates. From that manual process, we created our own private system, meshing the information from all of the systems and listing the airfares in ascending order according to price. For many years, that product enabled our clients to use airfare changes to their advantage.

Today, the airline automation offerings have evolved into Global Distribution Systems (GDSs), which include a centralized database of fares, into which client-negotiated discounts can be loaded. But we don't rely solely on these third-party products, improved though they are. We developed proprietary front-room products to be able to offer more to our clients.

Stress Busters/Service Enhancers
Products that Support People

The reservations process directly impacts the highest number of people in our clients' organizations. It takes place 24 hours a day, 365 days a year, and the process has become increasingly complicated since deregulation of the airlines in the 1970s. Pre-deregulation reservations had a handful of components: typically the name of the caller, name of the traveler, address, phone number, and flight plans.

Today, a single reservation has up to one hundred components, including everything from the basics to frequent flyer numbers, special meal requirements, and sort codes for all types of travel management reports. This complexity makes a higher level of service possible. But it also presents additional opportunities for error. The volume and complexity can place tremendous pressure on our people.

A decade and a half ago, a pair of associates—one from operations and one from technology—were discussing the reservations process and asking themselves, "How can we do this better?" The result was a product that automated a majority of the reservations process, virtually eliminating the opportunity for error and giving our CCAs time to personalize service. The product has evolved over the years into Custom-Res®, our point-of-sale quality assurance product.

There are three key areas to satisfy in any reservation: (1) adhering to the client's company travel policy, because a policy is meaningless if people don't follow it; (2) honoring the personal travel preferences of the individual traveler; and (3) capturing information for client reports. Custom-Res automatically accomplishes these three goals. Since each client's travel policy is programmed into Custom-Res, our CCA knows the client's company will allow the traveler to fly business class to London.

Her seats can be assigned on the aisle, where she wants, her frequent flyer numbers are automatically entered, and she will receive the vegetarian meal she prefers. Meanwhile, all pertinent information is being captured and stored in our system for our client's travel management reports.

This product has saved a significant amount of time. The reservations process is faster and more accurate. The quality is enhanced. The benefits of such a tool speak for themselves. Each company has its own processes that cry out to be automated. Our company benefits from the productivity gains, but the client is the real winner.

Detailed customer profiles can be entered into systems to help a company personalize its service. And its people are elevated from the tedious to the nurturing aspects. Here are a few additional front-room products that support our people and clients.

Res-Monitor®, our proprietary low-fare search engine, continues to search for a lower fare and optimal itineraries up until the day of departure, including specially negotiated fares, alternate flights, and alternate airports.

Res-Check is our post-sale technology that automatically verifies the accuracy of each reservation and ensures that each complies with our company's standards and with the individual client's standards.

RAPID™ identifies preferred carriers to our CCAs at the point-of-sale. After all, specially negotiated fares have no value to our clients if their travelers don't take advantage of them.

Each year, the airline GDSs and our competitors' systems gain ground, mimicking features that our proprietary applications offer. For that reason, we continually look for and develop ways to improve our products and enhance our service.

Taking It to the Next Level
Continually Updating Tools

The Internet has become the new communications platform for our business and for most organizations, so naturally all of our development is focused upon web-based applications. This saves us time and money because we no longer have to install applications at desktops for our clients or our associates.

We have always provided our clients with reporting tools to help them analyze their travel and spending patterns. With web-based reporting tools, we allow our clients and associates to access and run their own reports whenever and however they choose. (Previously this was a client server application, requiring more dependence upon us on a day-to-day basis.) These web-based tools are easier to use, more powerful, and they enable us to add advanced features, more extensive information, and graphics.

Another positive development has been the advancement of customer relationship management (CRM) tools. They allow us to capture additional information about the travelers we serve, beyond the traditional travel data. We use this information to develop applications to enhance our service to those customers. For example, let's say a traveler is making a trip to Paris and we know this is his first trip there. We can offer information that will be helpful to him about customs, currency, ground transportation, restaurants close to his hotel, and so on. The possibilities are limitless.

Our first step was to expand the amount of data we capture. Now, we are working with "push" technology, which allows us to extract information based on certain events and to proactively send information to travelers via e-mail or to their mobile devices. For example, when a flight is rescheduled, we can push an e-mail to affected travelers in an automated way. Until now, when we received word of changes, we manually initiated calls or e-mails. But we are in the process of automating that. Or let's say a major storm is heading to a city. We might want to send word to travelers headed there, and again, this could be done automatically.

We've always generated a great deal of information, and used that information to give our travelers an advantage, but now we can closely target and customize it to match, like a glove, the services we provide with the travelers who need them. In the past, our CCAs would call up information from our systems and send it to travelers. The difference is that today, our systems can actually tell our CCAs something they don't know—provide information that can help them enhance their service. Now that's technology worth its weight.

These CRM tools capture information on our interactions with customers so that anyone can pick up on service. We've always captured travel history, but not interaction history, until now. Other industries, like financial and retail, have used these tools, but they are new to our industry. We are leading a shift in travel management, from a transaction focus to truly a customer focus. This shift promises to heighten the level of service we provide, and it's a shift that any company in any industry can make.

The next evolution of CRM is electronic, or eCRM. These tools integrate newer methods of service delivery, like e-mail, chat, and voice over IP. They allow us to extend our CRM-heightened service outside of the traditional phone call. eCRM tools allow us to respond more efficiently. For example, when sending e-mails to confirm reservations, we can pre-program key words to construct those e-mails, or at least build the framework for the message so our CCAs just have to fill in the details. This not only saves time and improves accuracy, but enables us to capture information on the types of e-mails we receive and what our response levels are. And measurement is the key to continuous improvement.

eCRM tools help us to serve our customer via on-line chat, which is the fastest growing method of service. Our customers simply click on an icon to call up a dialogue box, type in their question, and one of our CCAs responds in near real-time (as opposed to e-mail, which is off-line). Chat is more widely used today by consumers than by businesses, but that is changing. The younger segment of our population is more familiar with chat, and they will push it to the forefront. One of the best things about chat is that it affords the opportunity to multi-task, which is critical today.

In the evolution of technology, e-mail is widely used, chat is growing, and the rising star is voice over IP, an emerging technology that allows you to communicate verbally via the Internet. For example, if you are using an application and you have a question, you can ask that question live via the Internet. It's an amazing tool that we are working with on a fast-track, developing applications for it.

Another emerging technology we are aggressively working with is web collaboration, which allows you to see exactly what another person sees on their PC screen. The benefits of people being able to share the same data at the same time are far-reaching. This technology brings us closer still to a reality of real-time global collaboration. Whatever the next tools are, after voice over IP and web collaboration, we'll be all over them, too.

The Knowledge Economy
Capturing and Sharing Knowledge
Around the World

Knowledge and experience are priceless commodities and have historically not been easy to share across an organization. Now there are solutions to capture those assets and make it possible for people to access the knowledge and experience of their associates, for the benefit of customers. We are busy putting these tools to work, and there are endless applications.

For example, when a customer calls to make travel arrangements to New York City and requests a rental car, we discourage them from renting it and suggest a car service instead. Many of our CCAs know from years of experience that it is cheaper, easier, and more efficient to be driven than to drive and park a car in Manhattan. That piece of knowledge can be shared across our CCA population by training our CCAs to recommend it. But we can go a step further by adding it to our knowledge base and tying it in to our reservations system, so that the knowledge is automatically incorporated into our service.

The next step is to offer our clients direct access to our knowledge base. There has been a rapid movement to self-serve, on-line booking. In 2000, less than 2 percent of our bookings fit that category, but in 2001 that number jumped to nearly 20 percent. These systems are convenient, but they don't offer the knowledge our people have gained over the 100+ years our company has been in business. So we've made it a high priority to link our knowledge base to our web-based booking tools. Thus, we will be able to transform our most important asset—the talent of our people—into something that can be quantified, shared, and grown.

A Two-Way Street
Good Products Aren't Created in a Vacuum

Our technology wizards don't create their products in a vacuum. They are constantly in touch with our clients and associates, seeking input on what they need. For example, when Custom-Res was developed, focus groups of users designed what they wanted it to do, and an evaluation mechanism was incorporated into the product allowing our CCAs to comment to its creators as they used the program. These evaluations led to continual enhancements.

We constantly seek to balance client and market requirements with competitive intelligence and innovation. When we balance all of these components, the gaps, the areas of overlap and the edge become very clear, and that drives our strategy and development.

One of our most sought-after programs is our Diagnostic Consulting, which helps our clients determine what their true needs are. We'll cover this revolutionary program in Chapter 12, "Open Partnerships."

THE MIDDLE ROOM

The middle room serves as a filter process, where we make sure that our clients' needs and requests are fulfilled. Even though our front-room systems ensure accuracy up front, not all client preferences are available at the time of booking, and we can't stop there. We need a system that keeps trying. That's our middle room, and it performs a variety of functions.

Build or Buy?
Seeking the Best Automated Quality Assurance Program

As rapidly as technology evolves, the best solution today can pale beside tomorrow's release. So we're always searching the marketplace with an open mind, seeking the best solution, whether we created it or someone else did. In the middle room, for years we used our own automated quality assurance product, but we have now retired that product and moved to a partnership that ensures that we have the best-in-breed solution.

Its primary feature is automated quality assurance. In addition to double-checking that all the basics of a reservation are correct, it also makes sure that no schedule changes have occurred, and if they have, the system sends a message to our CCAs, to contact their clients with that information. This technology, together with our eCRM tools, will enable us to keep our clients up-to-the-minute on any conditions affecting their travel.

Over 90 percent of the tickets we issue are e-tickets. We e-mail documentation to our clients, and they simply print their receipt and itinerary, and they're on their way. Any changes are e-mailed automatically to them.

Another key function of the middle room is to ensure that the lowest airfare was obtained. If, for example, the lowest fare was sold out at the time the reservation was made, it is automatically wait-listed until that fare becomes available.

The same thing with seats. Everyone has that favorite seat—bulkhead or near an exit, window, or aisle. Nobody wants a middle seat. This can be a big frustration for travelers. The system automatically checks to verify that each client's preferred seat is obtained, and if it's not the client is wait-listed for her special seat until the flight departs.

Our middle room also makes pre-trip travel management information available to clients by extracting it from our database of future itineraries. Our clients use this information for three purposes.

The first is risk management. For instance, companies can pull the records of those planning travel to destinations that have been placed on security alert by the State Department, so they can make alternate plans.

The second is adherence to company travel policy. Information on any arrangements made outside of the client's guidelines can be reviewed by the company's travel administrator and acted upon before the travel takes place.

The third purpose to pull pre-travel information is for negotiations with suppliers for group travel rates. Whenever ten or more passengers from the same company travel on the same carrier to the same destination, they are usually entitled to group rates. But they can only take advantage of it if they know they've reached the required numbers.

In addition to these functions, our middle-room product provides e-ticket tracking, automated ticketing, and profile management (the data for each individual traveler). These are just a few examples of what a middle room can do. It covers a lot of work that, in the past, took a lot of people a great deal of time to do. Automating the quality assurance process can heighten quality, customize service, increase productivity, and strengthen client confidence for any company. It's another tool to hand off stress to a machine so people are free to do what machines can't.

THE BACK ROOM

I mentioned our independence in the back room in Chapter 9 and our strategic leap two decades ago to invest in our own systems and programmers. This gave us freedom to use information in ways it had never been used before in our industry—ways that brought enormous benefit to our clients.

We were limited with the airline system. There were clear-cut boundaries on what we could and couldn't do with a system and programming staff that weren't our own. When a client asked us to do something unique, we often had to say "no," and that got under our skin. We like to at least say "maybe," and usually "yes."

Our people are always eager and proud to tell me about meetings with clients where multiple agencies are represented. Because when the topic gets to technology and the client asks around the room which agency can achieve a certain technological goal the client has set, usually our people are the only ones in the room who unequivocally say "yes." They like that and so do the clients.

Vision
The Nuts and Bolts

We call our back-room system VISION®, and it captures and scrubs data, housing a database of information collected from all of our locations worldwide. The system holds information on all travel activity for more than a year at a time. This data is vital in negotiating with suppliers on behalf of our clients.

Using this information, we can also help our clients direct travel to the most cost-effective alternatives for their company, in terms of carriers, hotels, car rental companies, times of day, and days of week to travel. The system is supported by a twenty-four-hour-a-day, seven-day-a-week operations and engineering staff. And it has backup upon backup, daily off-site storage of information, and a multitiered password system for security.

We have an extensive data warehouse (an enormous database designed to support decision making), storing all of our clients' information. We have integrated this data with our Oracle Enterprise Resource Planning (ERP) system, merging operational and financial data. Among the first industries to integrate their financial, inventory, and accounting information was manufacturing, and it makes sense.

Most companies still have separate systems, but we have benefited profoundly by combining them. Our Oracle ERP system takes a feed from VISION, which allows us to look at the entire picture when we make decisions or projections. The analysis we can derive is more sophisticated and more comprehensive, and therefore significantly more effective.

As we expanded rapidly around the globe, we reached a point where we needed to expand our data warehouse functionality. Accordingly, our information technology group completed an aggressive project to enhance both the content and capabilities for mining data (digging through layers of information to discover trends and opportunities). We now offer our clients the most comprehensive database available, empowering them to further excel in making proactive decisions regarding their travel programs.

Our data warehouse expansion focused on further enhancing our abilities to import and export data from a variety of sources (like suppliers and clients) and further streamlining all of our reporting platforms to one source, including financial and other such reports. The goal was to leverage all of the information we receive and send from a single repository, one that is large enough to accommodate our worldwide growth. I am indebted to the great associates that make up our IT organization.

Our strategy is to provide our clients with the web-based tools to access and analyze their own data. Here are some services currently driven by our warehouse:

VISION Consolidator enables the collection of data from multiple service providers worldwide into a single consolidated source of information.

VISION@Rosenbluth™ is our on-line reporting tool featuring twenty standard reports, which are pre-programmed and published to the web on a pre-determined schedule.

iVISION@Rosenbluth™ enables query-based reporting capabilities via a browser, for our clients whose reporting needs are more dynamic, allowing them to establish their own parameters. They can run reports ad hoc or according to a regular schedule.

Corporate Marriage at Its Best
Integrating Information Systems with Clients

The concept of "corporate marriage" is discussed in Chapter 12, "Open Partnerships." The term applies to a union between a company's people and those of its clients, on a multilevel basis. The same union can take place in technology. Two instances in which we mesh our system with those of our clients are payroll updates and credit card reconciliation.

As far back as 1991, we had a meeting with a very large account in which thirty-four divisions of the company were represented. Each had a totally different structure and set of travel guidelines and reporting requirements, and they wanted us to be familiar with them all and to serve each traveler in each division accordingly. It was a logistical nightmare.

After five hours, we came up with a solution that made life a lot easier and service a lot better. We developed a program with that client to interface with their human resources database, which includes the most current information in all of the areas needed.

Now, in order to access the travel policy, reporting requirements, department number, and a host of other information needed for each traveler, the only thing our CCAs need is the caller's social security number. This lessens the amount of time needed for both the CCA and the client at the point-of-sale and ensures that we are working with up-to-the-minute information. Over the past decade, we have instituted this program with countless clients.

Along the same lines, we interface with our clients' accounting systems to perform corporate credit card reconciliations for their travel expenditures. This saves our clients tremendous amounts of time because it eliminates the need for their people to manually reconcile their statements each month.

We produce reports that indicate charges that matched, credit card charges for which we have no travel record, and travel records for which no charge has been posted to their credit card. The reports serve as accountant and auditor for our clients so their companies don't have to.

Sharing our Capabilities
The Story of a "Make or Break" Product

We have a client in California who awarded 60 percent of its business to our company and the remaining 40 percent to a local agency. This client has very sophisticated technology needs, which the smaller agency is unable to meet. Some ten years ago, we came up with a solution that turned heads in our industry.

We offered to consolidate the smaller agency's travel information with our own, to provide our client comprehensive data on their entire travel account. This was no easy task. First, it's risky to become the gatekeeper for another company's information—travel arrangements we didn't make. Second, it's vital that this data not fall into our own general ledger activity.

We worked it out, and it opened up a world of opportunity in serving clients who choose to contract their business to multiple agencies. Today, we consolidate multiple agency data on a grand scale through our VISION Consolidator, and by charging a transaction fee to the agencies whose data we handle, we have been able to recoup our initial investment.

The Information Broker
Recognizing the Power of Information

Information is power, and we're all information brokers. We just need to recognize it. We need to know which information to capture and how to analyze it. We have to find ways to turn that information into understanding, and ultimately, into benefit for our clients.

Our VISION system is all about providing information to our clients. The reports it generates show savings realized, but more important, they show opportunities for savings that are being missed. This enables us to work with each company to provide a plan of action to take advantage of those opportunities.

There are countless ways companies can use technology to positively impact the lives of their people and clients. The key is to get close enough to their customers to find out how to best support them. The most sophisticated hardware or software won't help a client if it doesn't address his or her particular needs.

People can get carried away with technology and lose sight of the fact that it needs to provide either strategic or financial benefit, in order to be worth the investment. Just because something is technologically possible doesn't mean it will benefit the company. It's imperative that companies prove a business benefit and not just chase after the latest technology.

It's also crucial to look at everything you do, improve it first, and then apply technology to it. A lot of companies make the mistake of just making faster what they already do. A combination of process *and* technology is what yields the greatest benefit.

Translate, Please
Technology Specialists Who Speak English

We have a department of terrific people dedicated to matching the specific technology needs of our clients with solutions. The department, which we call Global Solutions Architecture, assesses both internal and external client needs, documents the business requirements, and sponsors each request to the decision point.

Beyond that, a Product Management Team further enhances the competitive position, ongoing usability, release, planning, and positioning of the product or service. Our Product Development eRoom offers our associates a single source to check on the status of each project.

The beauty of the Global Solutions Architecture team is that they can get to the bottom of real requirements and have a deep understanding of what's behind the products, yet they speak in layman's terms—something I'm always grateful for.

This crew does such a tremendous job of explaining our technology products that once, when a prospective client came to our headquarters for a technology demonstration, she conducted the demonstration herself. The company's travel manager had been learning about our information systems in order to evaluate them against our competitors', and when she brought her selection team in for a final analysis, she jumped up and said she knew our products so well she'd like to demonstrate them to her colleagues. We were awarded the account, and she's a great ambassador for our company.

Every Great Inventor Needs a Lab
Resources for Research and Development

Since our industry doesn't have its own version of an underwriters' lab, many years ago we created an "Automation Lab" where a select group of our technology associates could develop and test new products. The lab took on new proportions in 1996 when we opened The Continuum. It looks like a future center, but is actually a working research and development lab, which demonstrates how technology will affect our work and personal lives in the near and distant future. (We'll talk about this in more detail in Chapter 12, "Open Partnerships.")

Most companies have research and development initiatives, but they don't always set aside the space, people, and capital to make them what they could be—the power to design the future. It's tempting to apply profits entirely to the bottom line, but it's essential to reinvest money in projects that keep your company ahead of the competition. Without that investment, companies will lag behind.

On the Horizon
Progress Never Rests

We have a number of exciting and newly released products. I'll share three with you for which the basis could apply to any business. *Rosenbluth Everywhere* is a comprehensive global corporate travel portal (web "supersite") providing a gateway to a wide variety of travel-related products and services. Tailored to each corporate client, it brings together information and access to products and services in a single place. It offers links to booking tools, on-line itinerary access, customer service information, policies and procedures, helpful information (like weather, maps, travel advisories, news, etc.), and links to additional services. It provides flight status information, a link for expense management, and wireless access.

Rosenbluth Mobile provides a wireless travel solution for our clients who wish to access our services via cell phone, Personal Digital Assistant (PDA), or two-way pager. Mobile customers can receive flight information (including tracking and gate information), car and hotel information, and displays of their itineraries. They can also review cost analyses, make reservations, seat assignments, and airline upgrades, and access information about the destinations they're off to—all over their wireless devices.

Rosenbluth Everywhere was created to make life easier for our clients, bringing a world of choices to them, and Rosenbluth Mobile was designed to make access to that information even more convenient. A portal bringing together information and services from all aspects of your industry, along with offering wireless access to your products and services is a combination that promises to draw your customers closer to your company.

Of course, wireless is just part of a never-ending line of emerging technologies. Whatever the tool, the key is leverage across all delivery platforms, whether it be web, wireless, or any technology that emerges in the future.

Our latest technology offering came as a direct result of the events of 9/11. It is our *Global Security Suite* and addresses the importance of global security issues for travelers and the corporations they represent. It has three components: the first is a database that allows travelers access to a variety of destination information including political conditions, currency, climate, and passport/visa requirements. The second allows chief security officers and travel managers of companies access to our global database that displays a pictorial of the world and information on the number and names of employees that they have traveling in any one particular country (i.e., provides information on each traveler's itinerary). This product allows a company the ability to find their travelers during times of emergency. The third is a push technology product that sends a message to the traveler's PDA, mobile phone, or any other e-mail enabled device to inform them of situations that may impact their scheduled travel plans (i.e., political upheaval, weather, strike). In addition to the services these products offer, a week before the travelers' departure a message is automatically sent to U.S. Embassies and Consulates notifying them of when a U.S. client of ours will be arriving and where they are staying. In a world where all too often political and military unrest can pop up at any moment, companies have a responsibility to know where their people are at all times and to be in a position to contact them immediately. They owe it to their employees and to their respective families.

Backseat Drivers Prohibited
Giving People the Freedom to Create

The freedom to create innovative technology products and services starts at the top and permeates a company. If you put people in a room with a low ceiling and tell them to jump as high as they can, they'll jump to the ceiling, never knowing if they could have jumped higher.

Raise that ceiling far beyond their reach and they have room to strive. Provide them with a trampoline and they will soar higher than humanly possible. Give them a pole to vault with and they'll go even higher.

This is our view of technology. We try to create an environment in which our people can realize their full potential. We provide them with tools that empower them to reach for the stars. And we let them choose the tools, for example, our Sun Solaris hardware and Oracle Database and portal technology, through which our associates have been able to do great things.

We give our team the resources to make things happen quickly. They're not held back by restrictions. They're not enslaved by bureaucracy. They are limited only by their own imaginations and by the capability of the world's technology. That's a lot of space in which to work, and the results have given us a sustainable edge.

To keep ahead of the game, technology experts need to be able to run their own show, but at the same time their companies need to take an interest in what they do. People should work to understand technology so they can fully appreciate it, understand the needs of technology specialists, and talk intelligently with them about their work. To keep abreast of what's happening in technology, I read as much as possible on the subject and I meet with our technology associates frequently to gain a clearer understanding of what they're up to and how they're doing it. But I do try to sit back and let them lead the way.

I was once in a crucial meeting with a prospective client, in which a demonstration of a new technology product, still under development, was being given by one of our associates. At the end of the demonstration, the prospective client asked when the product would be complete, to which our associate replied that she felt it would never be complete.

For a moment, I regretted my backseat approach. Then she proceeded to tell the client that she and her fellow technology associates believed that no matter how much a product is refined and enhanced, there will always be room for improvement. I quickly went from nervous to proud, and the prospective client (now a client) went from confused to impressed.

DACODA
The Ultimate Purchasing Tool for Clients

Since the 1980s, airlines have used sophisticated yield management systems to maximize their revenue. These systems have resulted in pricing so complex, it's nearly impossible for a company to determine the best choices—until DACODA. What in the world is DACODA? It stands for Discount Analysis Containing Optimal Decision Algorithms, and it's our patented yield management system *for clients.* It inversely applies the principles of airline yield management.

DACODA helps clients achieve more savings than they would by just pursuing the lowest fare, because the face value of a ticket is not always what it appears to be. We can determine for each city pair that a client travels between, the true low-cost alternative, considering every factor that can influence the decision.

DACODA takes into account each company's specific objectives, policies, patterns, and needs. It considers complex factors like airline capacity, market presence, contract requirements, specially negotiated fares, fare changes, point-of-sale discounts, back-end discounts, and threshold bonuses. Analyzing these varied factors, the choice becomes clear about which airline contracts to accept and in which proportion, to capture the highest savings.

We offer four levels of DACODA licenses, ranging from a one-time assessment of contract opportunities and insights for maximizing savings, to a monthly analysis of contracts, performance toward goals, traveler compliance, specific recommendations for optimizing savings, scenario analysis for contract optimization, and point-of-sale decision support to help achieve goals. DACODA is integrated with our interactive self-booking tool, @Rosenbluth, so clients can achieve the savings no matter how they choose to book their travel.

Our clients using DACODA have saved up to 20 percent of their total travel spending and about 10 percent from DACODA Car (for car rental program analysis). Next on the horizon are DACODA Hotel and DACODA for meetings.

eCLIPSE
Spinning Off Bright Solutions

In 2001, we launched a new business called eCLIPSE (empowering Customers to Leverage Information through Procurement Solutions Expertise). eCLIPSE combines our patented DACODA system with consulting services in the practice of business travel management and makes this expertise available to any company—beyond our client base.

We looked at the market and at our knowledge and saw an opportunity. Among the Fortune 50 companies, 14 percent are our clients and 18 percent have used DACODA. That leaves more than 80 percent of the companies that could benefit from our patented technology, without making a full change to a new travel management supplier. So we packaged our DACODA decision support system together with our RAPID automated preferred supplier information display; ROCS, our eRFP/RFQ technology; our Agency Incentive Management (AIM) tool, and other products to create a comprehensive, end-to-end procurement solution.

eCLIPSE is a separate entity that helps companies reduce costs, gain greater control, heighten efficiency, and speed processes in the procurement, fulfillment, and reconciliation of travel-related services. eCLIPSE brings objective, scientific solutions to an industry that has relied heavily on subjective, manual analysis. The marketplace benefits by being able to access this unbundled expertise, while our company and its associates benefit from a diversified business and new opportunities. Any company in any industry can and should review what it has to offer that is truly unique and look for ways to market it beyond the traditional.

Happiness: The Ultimate Technology Tool
Special Significance for the People-First Theory

Our credo of happiness in the workplace has a special significance with respect to technology. Without a doubt, technology is making a greater impact than any aspect of business today. It touches virtually every facet of people's lives.

The field of technology is fiercely competitive, and to keep pace with its changes takes special skill that is fervently sought by companies around the world. Attracting and retaining technology talent is a daunting challenge for businesses, above and beyond their ardent search for the right people for their organizations, in general.

Turnover in any company is costly, both financially and emotionally, but perhaps more so in technology. The development of products takes time, and turnover creates delays in the introduction of those products. By the time you've searched for, hired, and trained the person to take over the development of an abandoned product, it's often too late. It's no longer leading edge. Not only do you lose the opportunity, but the initial work on the product becomes a complete waste.

Delays in technological developments can be devastating. Turnover is disruptive. The world competes vigorously for qualified and creative technology specialists, and companies end up in costly global bidding wars.

We feel we've found a solution in our people-first policy. Our technology associates are very much a part of our company, unlike so many companies in which the technology department winds up like an isolated island within an organization. We involve our technology associates in all aspects of our company and seek to have people throughout the company involved in technology. This helps them to develop the *right* products for our associates and our clients. It unites technology with the rest of our company and it goes a long way toward happiness in the workplace.

The Dream Machine
Technology as a Company Hero

Our people cheer on our technology group because the products they design empower us to do a better job, to do things our competitors can't, and to provide our clients with services they never expected. They give us a competitive advantage.

One of their keys to success is the right combination of strategy and speed—taking the time to investigate, plan, and prepare, but working quickly to seize opportunities with narrow windows. They realize technology's strength begins when it is proven as an enabler.

Our technology team earned the nickname "The Dream Machine" because they develop tools for our people that relieve stress and enhance service. That's important in any business. The more steps of a process that can be automated, the better. We have found it critical in our business.

Travelers are demanding. They usually make their plans on short notice, yet the particulars of their trip are really important to them. Often, as soon as everything is confirmed according to the travelers' wishes, their plans change suddenly and the process begins again. It's just a fact of life. It comes with the territory, and our CCAs have to have the nerves of air traffic controllers, while at the same time being able to look for ways to enhance service, making it special.

A lot goes into our service, though you might not realize it when you look at a ticket. Our people work hard to make it happen, and they couldn't do it without the tools that turn the impossible into the possible.

Technology Tips for Your Company to Consider

A SUMMARY

▌ Continually look for methods by which technology can save time in your company, freeing your people to create and to concentrate on the finer, more intangible aspects of service. Automating mundane processes can remove opportunities for error, reduce stress, and improve service. But re-engineer processes before you apply technology. Automating a bad process doesn't work.

▌ Three examples of technology products we employ that may have application to your company are: (1) a front room that automates much of the front-line customer care process; (2) an automated quality assurance program that will heighten accuracy, lower costs, and strengthen the confidence of your clients; and (3) a comprehensive database of customer activity for your use and theirs (and make sure you provide on-line access to them).

▌ The development of technology products—as with all

products, programs, and services—must not take place in a vacuum. Build in evaluation mechanisms that encourage input on the spot, while the users' suggestions are fresh in their minds.

▮ Make sure that you fully understand the business and its needs before you apply technology. The role of the business analyst is critical in this process.

▮ Because the Internet is the world's communications platform, the majority of most companies' technology development should be focused on web-based applications.

▮ Customer Relationship Management (CRM) tools can help organizations capture information about their customer interactions, to help them serve those customers more fully. Additionally, knowledge-sharing technology can help you quantify, share, and grow your organization's knowledge assets. That knowledge can also be shared directly with your customers.

▮ Consider the creation of an automation lab in which products that apply to your industry can be developed, tested, and refined.

▮ Information is power. Capture it and create ways to put it to work for your company and your clients. Companies can never stand still technologically. If you do not have the resources available for your own technology department, team up with a technology supplier who will take you into the future.

▮ Merging operations and financial data will enable you to look at the entire picture when making decisions. An Enterprise Resource Planning (ERP) system tied to your back room can yield sophisticated and comprehensive analysis.

▮ Continually reinvest in technology, both in terms of people and the tools they need to stretch their talents beyond traditional limits. By the way, let *them* choose the tools they need. Be careful, though, to invest in technology only if it provides strategic advantage or the potential for a high return on investment. If it doesn't do one of these two things, don't invest.

▪ Let the experts run their own show, but take the time and make the effort to learn about what they do and how they do it. You will understand their needs more clearly and be able to more fully appreciate what they do. It'll also provide guidance in the technology project priority-setting process.

▪ If you do have your own technology group, be sure to cultivate happiness in their workplace. Turnover in technology is probably more costly than turnover in other departments because of the delays in product development that result.

▪ Don't let your technology department become an island within your organization—involve it in all aspects of the company. That way your technology people will be more satisfied in their work, and they will emerge with a clearer understanding of the needs their products will fill.

CHAPTER ELEVEN

Look Around You

About ten years ago we lost an $80 million account. It was devastating. We didn't see it coming. For years we served the account like a dream, and then all of a sudden our dreams were shattered.

Our associates who serviced that account were taken aback because they believed their service had been outstanding. In fact, the client agreed. But we lost the account nevertheless. You can never be prepared for a loss like that, but we should have at least seen it coming.

Our client was facing the toughest time in the company's history and decided to make a number of major changes. Their choice of a travel partner was one of them.

It seems everyone else recognized their troubles before we did. We were so busy concentrating on providing them with service, we didn't notice that our competitors were circling like sharks. Our service was great, but their highest priority was drastic cost cutting. It's like being all dressed up with no place to go.

We missed the opportunity to adapt our strategy to their changing needs and it cost us dearly. We just didn't see the writing on the wall until it was too late. We'll never know if we could have saved the account with a new approach or not, but we regret not giving ourselves the chance to find out. The account was gone and it was our job to minimize damages.

The first thing we did was to immediately involve all of the people who were impacted by the loss. We met as a team—more than 169 of us—and determined our strategy together. These were some of our best people, in whom we had invested a great deal. We wanted them to remain with the company, but they had to have a client.

In the meantime, we developed a transition plan so that our departing client's service would be uninterrupted by the change. We had served this account faithfully for years and we wanted to uphold our reputation for service. This kept our people who were dedicated to the account active while we pursued new accounts for them to work with.

We accelerated our sales effort and eventually we acquired new business. But what took place in the meantime was crucial to company morale. We kept a list of each of the 169 people affected, and our team of top leaders met every Monday morning to discuss the placement of each person, one by one.

It was critical that each individual be fully utilized in his or her new role. As a company, we couldn't afford to just find something for them to do. We operate on a tight profit margin. And at the same time, it wouldn't have been fair to our people to impose unfulfilling work on them. Of the 169, only eight left our company, most of them to serve the client with its new travel partner.

In the end, we survived. Like most humbling experiences, it taught us a great deal and we emerged stronger. Was what we learned worth an $80 million account? I don't know, but it's certain that we are a better company today. We learned a valuable lesson about paying attention to rumblings in all industries and how they affect our clients. And we strengthened loyalty by showing our people that each individual is important, no matter what obstacles the company faces.

The Food Chain
The Ripple Effects of Corporate Misfortune

Watching your own costs is good business, but it's not enough. You need to keep an eye on the health of companies around you, particularly your clients.

When corporations face economic hardships, when they're faced with slumps in their industry, they're forced to drastically cut expenses. This creates a shock wave up and down the food chain. We can provide the best imaginable service to our clients, but if they have no money to spend, they'll have no choice but to scale back on the business they do with us. When companies cut expenditures, they stop buying computers, office supplies, travel services, and so on. Then their suppliers in each of those industries suffer losses, which leads to cutbacks in their companies. Corporate cuts often involve layoffs, or worse yet, insolvency.

No one escapes these troubles. Even if your own house is in order, if your next door neighbor's house is on fire, yours is in danger, too.

What's the answer? I wish I had a cookbook recipe that would make a company immune to the cyclical effects of a downturn in the economy or in its industry. I don't. But we have learned the value of keeping your eyes open to factors that affect not just your own company or industry but all businesses worldwide. Knowing what problems your customers and potential clients might face puts you in the driver's seat.

Look into the Future
The Importance of Forecasting

Don't look back. Something may be gaining on you.
—Leroy "Satchel" Paige, *Maybe I'll Pitch Forever*

Looking into the future is as important as looking around you. To do so, you have to continually sharpen your ability to think like the marketplace—your clients and competitors. In a way it's like "pirating" the thought processes of those around you. It's an acquired skill that comes with practice.

An admirer once asked Sir Isaac Newton how he was able to make such astonishing discoveries in astronomy. His answer was simply, "By always thinking about them."

We spend a lot of time contemplating the future. When we make a decision, we discuss all the possible outcomes and how they will affect our clients. We debate about what our competitors' next moves will be. When you play the role of another company, its vantage point becomes clearer. By using this process, we've foreseen airline mergers and bankruptcies, personnel changes at the highest levels in corporations, and trends in both our industry and general consumer demand—all well before they came to be.

Nothing is more thrilling than seeing something you've predicted come true, particularly if you've acted on those projections and positioned your clients and your company for a vantage point of strength in that future. This foresight can be reached through the science of deduction, a sort of industrial logic that comes from experience in the marketplace, open-mindedness, and concentration on what waits beyond the horizon.

Listening skills are important and so is the art of observation—studying how individuals or companies have reacted under similar circumstances. Combine the two with "if/then" logic and trends begin to materialize before your eyes, if you become accustomed to watching for them.

One key to discovering trends is open communication within your organization, particularly among your central team charged with initiating strategic development. In our case, our core of vice presidents meets weekly to review intelligence from the field and play out possible scenarios. We try to think like our clients, then as if we were our competitors, and finally prospective clients. This process has given us a clear competitive advantage.

It's rewarding to be on the cutting edge. It's even more fun if, by the time your competitors hear about what you're doing, you're already doing something else.

Forecasting has to be based partly on history and mainly on the ability to recognize ways in which the present can be improved. It's important to be in a position to act quickly. Once you uncover a need you have to be ready to jump. By the time buyers and competitors come to see the need, you'll be the only one properly positioned to fill it.

Successful forecasters understand trends. Whether money managers, meteorologists, or bookies, they're able to spot trends while they're embryonic. We call it "educated anticipation," and it has helped us make some of our most successful decisions.

There's a Reason They Call It a "Brave" New World
The Fears and Rewards of Doing Things Differently

Taking an unorthodox approach can be difficult. Doing things differently sometimes brings on more heat. When you do something the traditionally accepted way and it doesn't work, people tend to say you gave it a good shot. But when you try something unusual and it fails, people often say it's because you went out on a limb. It's important for senior management to give people the security to take intelligent chances, letting them know it's all right to fail if the consequences were well thought out.

We all have natural comfort zones, but beyond them lies a world of new opportunities. It's like the saying, "You can't say anything you don't already know." It's a testimony to listening, because only then do we learn anything. The same goes for our actions. If we insist on always doing things the same way, we can't learn anything new, so we limit our results to what they are today.

A Case Study
Up-Stream

Everyone said the fax machine would put overnight delivery companies out of business. Everyone said the Internet would put travel agencies (along with a lot of other businesses and industries) out of business. It hasn't happened, and it won't for businesses that seek ways to continually add value rather than seek to merely stay in business. One of the key ways to do that is to be completely flexible in everything from which products or services you provide, to how you provide them and whom you provide them to. We'll talk about our shifting role in our traditional business in the next chapter, on part-nerships. Here, we're going to talk about expanding our horizons.

In 2000 we formed our first business venture outside the travel in-dustry when we created Up-Stream, which provides outsourced end-to-end customer services for other companies. Our decision to diversify into customer relationship management made sense. We looked at the things we're good at, and call centers was clearly one.

We built this line of business on existing assets: widely recognized, consistent, award-winning service; extensive experience in network/call center management on a global scale; low-cost call centers (we call them Intellicenters) around the world; a culture that enables us to attract and retain top talent; unique training programs to help ensure our high standards; massive scale and global reach; proven results as a leader in information management; and a 98 percent client retention rate.

The market is there. The Internet has companies scrambling for a customer service solution. As more and more people buy on-line, the need for call centers to support those transactions rises. As the e-marketplace becomes increasingly crowded, success will depend upon providing the ultimate customer experience. Companies are finding that their customers hold them to the same high service stan-dards electronically as with brick-and-mortar based services. Cus-tomer care is becoming the biggest differentiator, yet it's difficult and expensive to do it well.

We decided we would be able to offer the fastest time-to-service with instant access to best-in-class resources. Our Up-Stream cus-tomers' customers can reach us via phone, interactive voice response, i-chat, e-mail, voice over IP, iFAQ, iVideo, fax, or self-help via the web. Every customer contact is captured in a detailed customer profile, from which client companies can generate sales leads, target advertis-ing, guide product development, and improve processes.

According to Jupiter Communications, 90 percent of on-line customers prefer human interaction, yet only 3 percent of major e-commerce sites offer a live-help option. The need is clear, and we think we have a leg up on the competition. Traditional customer service providers are big, slow moving organizations that seem to have a heavy technology focus, with customer service as an afterthought. Web-based customer service start-ups primarily have a dot-com client base and little experience working with Fortune 500 firms. And they seem to operate their centers in higher cost areas than we do.

So, having analyzed the marketplace, our potential competitors, and our own capabilities, we decided to venture into this new line of business. The point of entry that made the most sense was the travel vertical, so we started by working with companies like United Airlines' UAL.com, National Airlines, and US Airways Cargo service. We branched out to other industries from there. Up-Stream employs over 1,200 people operating in seven call centers, and it is growing fast.

Many factors have contributed to Up-Stream's success. One of them was that we treated Up-Stream as a completely separate identity. Companies usually are not willing to take key resources away from their core business and assign them to a new venture, but that's just what we did. We took some of our very best people and put them on a separate floor at our world headquarters. Up-Stream has a core team of forty, including key staff in technology, marketing, finance, human resources, and operations management, in addition to senior leadership.

We believe you can't go into a new venture half-heartedly, fearing risk. You have to launch it as if it were your future. It just might be.

Light-Years Ahead
What Does the Future Hold?

Some popular movies have dealt with going back to the past to correct the present or future, like the *Terminator* and *Back to the Future* movies. The common theme is that what we do today creates tomorrow's world. But since we can't really go back in time, we'd better consider the future effects of what we do today.

What will business be like in 2005, 2010, 2015? You have to think about it and do something about it *now*. Companies will be left behind if they spend all of their time and resources on today, this week, and this year. The lag time between strategy and reality can be lengthy. The only way to ensure success and longevity is to grasp the coming years, plan for them now, and begin implementing those strategies.

It can be better to make a mistake than to delay acting upon an idea out of fear. Ideas become stale when they are shelved, and so does enthusiasm. That doesn't mean we need to make rash decisions. We need to make wise ones *quickly.*

How can a company spare this much time studying the future? Thinking about the future takes no more time than thinking about the present. While some companies might be thinking about this year, others are thinking about next year and two years from now. In three years, while short-term companies are thinking about the current year, companies committed to the future will be thinking about two to three years from that time.

The real challenge is to shift the planning cycle from present to future while succeeding today. The shift requires a certain period of double time, when today and tomorrow must be attended to while planning for the longer term. But once a company shifts gears, it's on track for the future.

Even the most thorough planning doesn't guarantee smooth sailing. Every strategic plan has to be built on flexibility to allow for opportunities that present themselves, as well as unanticipated challenges. People need to be able to modify long-standing strategy on a daily basis and fine-tune it to today's application.

For example, changes in technology take place constantly, and business plans need to adapt with them. However, shaping long-term strategy about which markets to pursue and lines of business to build will prepare you to create opportunities. Plans can be adapted if technology changes.

Plato told a story of his predecessor, the Greek philosopher Thales (c. 640–c. 546 B.C.). It seems he was walking along a road while looking up at the sky, studying the stars, when he fell into a well. A servant girl rescued him and remarked that while he was fascinated with what was in the sky, he failed to see what was under his feet.

While we need to keep tabs on the present, we do have a number of theories about what's in store for us in the future. We're building programs, products, and strategies based upon those forecasts. They include things that hardly seem possible today. But then, decades ago, neither did many of the things we take for granted, such as space travel, personal computers, fax machines, and supersonic travel. The science fiction of today is the reality of tomorrow.

We're living in paradoxical times. People are finding themselves with growing demands on their time. They're watching their lives become more complex. As things become increasingly sophisticated, people will be drawn to the basics. So while the new inventions of the future promise to bring on many positive changes in our world, they'll bring with them a renewed desire for the best things in life— nice people, quality, ethics, and trust. The company of the future will master the skill of blending the best of the old and the new.

Looking Around You and Ahead

A SUMMARY

▌ Be alert to changes all around you, because as unrelated as they may seem, they send ripple effects throughout the food chain. It's particularly critical to keep an eye on the health of your clients.

▌ Sharpen your ability to think like the marketplace, your competitors, and your clients. Listen, observe, use deduction, practice spotting trends, and study their origins.

▌ Hold regular strategy meetings, during which your top leaders review intelligence from the field and play out every possible scenario and its effects on the marketplace and your company.

▌ Be flexible about what products or services you provide and how and to whom you provide them. Be on the lookout for opportunities to venture into new areas where you can add value. These may be keys to your future.

▌ Act *today* for the coming years and decades. There's lag time between concept and reality in developing new products and services. If you spent yesterday planning for today, you can spend today preparing for tomorrow.

CHAPTER TWELVE

Open Partnerships

Dr. David Livingstone, a Scottish medical missionary and explorer, made a trip to central Africa in 1870 and disappeared. Sir Henry Morton Stanley, explorer and journalist for the *New York Herald*, was commissioned by his publisher to find Dr. Livingstone. After an exhaustive eight-month search, Stanley found Dr. Livingstone in Ujiji on November 10, 1871, and uttered his famous words: "Dr. Livingstone, I presume?" The news made headlines around the world. And after this historic meeting the two explored Africa together.

Not all partnerships begin with such flair, but through the years the world has been better because of partnerships that have produced results individuals couldn't have. Take Rodgers and Hammerstein, for instance. Richard Rodgers composed the music; Oscar Hammerstein wrote the lyrics. Together, they brought us such greats as *Oklahoma!* and *South Pacific* in the 1940s, and they're still popular more than half a century later. Partnerships like that don't happen every day. They take a little magic, creativity, and trust.

Look at how we're living these days. Alarm systems in our cars and our homes, people creating fortresses like Fort Knox. But most of us long for those days gone by when we could leave our doors unlocked. Everyone knew their neighbors. Business was done on a handshake.

We still cling to that type of relationship. Sure, we have contracts too, but to us the handshake is more important. Maybe it's because our company is more than one hundred years old and it remembers doing business the old way. Possibly it's because we started as a family business in the business of reuniting families. Or maybe we just forgot to change. But open partnerships are a key to our success.

The climate today far from encourages open partnerships, particularly in our cutthroat industry, which has been marked by razor-thin profit margins, a siege of mergers and acquisitions, business failures, and at times, a lack of professionalism and integrity. However, this environment makes straightforward partnerships more important than ever. Our company may not resemble the storefront business from which it originated, but we've held fast to its turn back principles: trust, honesty, and faithful partnerships.

More can be accomplished when clients and suppliers work together like true partners in a venture. Great things happen when clients look at us as a strategic partner rather than a vendor. Beyond the purchasing of basic products and services lies a world of opportunity to be innovative in defining and filling our clients' needs.

Operating a Nudist Colony
Getting to *Really* Know Your Client

I recently had an important meeting in Germany with some bankers and a senior executive of ours who is based in Europe. Prior to the meeting, I called my associate to find out the appropriate dress code. I'm most comfortable in my jeans and boots, but I was told to absolutely wear a suit and tie, so I complied.

When I showed up at the meeting in jeans and boots, my colleague was horrified, until I explained that on the train I had opened my suit carrier across the five sinks in the men's room, but I failed to notice the infrared devices that activated the water in all five sinks, and drenched my suit completely. So much for protocol.

We and our banker friends had a great laugh about it, and I got to wear my jeans after all. But sometimes we should wear nothing at all.

Fig leaves are banned at our company. We believe there can be nothing that you hide from your clients. It doesn't work anyway: The more you try to hide something, the more curious people become.

Figuratively speaking, we operate a nudist colony where every last nook and cranny is bared to our clients.

We've found that openness is reciprocal. The more candid we are with our clients, the more candid they are with us. The level of trust we build is mutual. It's surprisingly comfortable to operate in this environment, and this honest information exchange enables us to do a better job for our clients.

The openness has to start with the sales process. The more up-front a company is about its capabilities, the better its relationship will be with its clients. Everyone knows what to expect. Nobody has to scramble to make things happen. This creates the right fit for long-term partnerships.

Companies can't overlook the importance of supplier relationships in helping to meet their clients' needs. To manufacturing firms who operate "just in time" inventory systems, it's essential their suppliers provide quality products on the date needed. A zero-inventory system can be very effective, but only if the products are there when they need to be handed off from supplier to buyer.

In our case, we rely upon our airline, hotel, and car rental suppliers to provide the end product—the travel itself. We have to assume responsibility for more than just our portion of the service. We need to make sure that our suppliers are performing for our clients.

Part of our quality process is to involve ourselves from beginning to end of the service process, regardless of where our portion of it officially ends. For example, our Biztravel.com service guarantee covered supplier error, holding us responsible for the entire process.

Any company could benefit from taking a hard look at its suppliers' businesses. If a company can't manufacture its products on time because of late or defective parts from a supplier, it becomes the company's problem, and ultimately, the client's. Excuses don't work.

One for All and All for One
The Importance of the Three-Way Relationship

We need to work in concert with our clients and suppliers in strategic partnerships. The way we see it, all three parties need to know exactly what to expect. Even in the most delicate arena of all—pricing—we take a very candid approach.

Our industry is very dependent on the price of airfares, but we have chosen a different path. The traditional structure pays higher commissions for more expensive tickets, and that goes against every principle we believe in. So years ago, we began to work with our clients and key suppliers to change the compensation structure of our industry. Today, 82 percent of our clients work with us on a service contract basis, with only 18 percent based upon commissions.

In addition to the inherent conflict that commissions create, they are also a short-lived compensation model. Many factors have converged to drive change in our industry. Rising costs have led the airlines to cut and impose a cap on travel agency commissions. The Internet has enabled airlines to bypass traditional agencies. However, global expansion has led to travel becoming the second largest expense after payroll, and companies need help in driving down those costs. They turn to travel management companies to manage and execute supplier contracts, capture worldwide data, and consolidate their purchasing under one umbrella to maximize savings.

We have long taken the position that we are not distribution agents, but rather strategic partners, capable of much more than merely booking airline tickets. Our clients pay us service fees for the value we add. We diagnose our clients' true needs and offer comprehensive services to help manage every facet of the T&E process, including non-traditional areas like telesuites and corporate payment systems.

Our clients choose to compensate us for what we bring to the table. They rely on our expertise in attracting, training, and retaining terrific people who provide them with unparalleled service. They depend on our global systems and proprietary products and services to bring them savings they could only achieve with us.

We pioneered this new economic model because we disliked the inherent conflict the old method posed, and in the end, it strengthened our position for today's environment, where on-line transactions have squeezed distribution agents to the fringe of viability. Are we in danger of this? Not likely. Our value is portable to the web and primed for the future. For example, our patented DACODA product, which helps companies create optimal purchasing strategies by quantifying a wide variety of factors (as explained in Chapter 10), is available at the point-of-sale for agentless booking, integrating with our @Rosenbluth product. And as you read in the last chapter, the demand for our Up-Stream customer relationship management solution underscores just how people-intensive interactive delivery systems are, when they're done right.

We operate on the premise that most wise organizations would rather purchase a less expensive airline ticket through us (because of the knowledge, proprietary products, negotiating power, and service we provide) than a costly one that comes with a rebate from a traditional agency. We have the information that makes such savings possible, and rather than keep it to ourselves, we share it with our clients and help them use it to their advantage.

The key is to share our information with both our clients and our suppliers. We include our clients in our supplier relationships and vice versa. We show our suppliers that we are able to shift business, on behalf of our clients, to whomever provides them with the best rates and services. The suppliers who participate get more business, our clients get significant savings, and we are rewarded with a loyal client base.

Are You Your Client's Customer?
The Importance of Supporting Your Clients

We're all so busy concentrating on providing our clients with the products and services we offer that sometimes we don't see one of the most basic ways to serve our clients—by being their customers.

We have a policy at Rosenbluth International to utilize the products and services of our clients whenever feasible. We manage the travel account of Subaru, so we naturally use their cars for our delivery vehicles. Philips is a client of ours, so we purchase light bulbs and monitors from them. We work with our client, Oracle, for our database and portal. We have Sun Solaris hardware because Sun Microsystems is our client.

We use Kodak films and digital equipment for presentations from our client, Kodak. Because Armstrong is one of our clients, we specify their ceiling tiles in our new construction. CIGNA is a long-time client, and we turn to them for healthcare and the administration of our 401k plan. We purchase our office supplies from Boise Cascade and Staples, our clients, and I drive a Toyota truck because—you guessed it—they're a client. Some of our associates in Germany drive Porsches (a client) but they must have bought them before the airlines reduced commissions in that country.

We insist on Du Pont fiber carpets in our offices, because Du Pont is our client. We don't often have the opportunity to use Binney & Smith's Crayolas at work, but they're our client, too. So when we ask clients and associates to draw what Rosenbluth means to them, that's what we send. Our clients manufacture thousands of products and offer at least as many services, and our people know to use them exclusively, whenever they can.

Not only does it support our clients, it helps us to understand them better. We make it a point to learn their businesses. We research the products they make so we can incorporate them into our everyday use, and in doing so, we're getting to know them from a broader perspective.

Welcome Home
Creating an Open Atmosphere

We feel that our business should be like home to our clients. They are welcome at any time, in any of our locations. After all, we're working for them.

No one who's expecting company keeps a messy house or has empty cupboards. Homes in which people are welcome are always clean and hospitable. Offices should be no different.

I had an eye-opening experience many years ago in one of our locations. I stopped by the office, unannounced, and what I found was an absolute embarrassment. There were half-empty boxes of paper, half-completed reservations on desktops, and resource manuals askew. While it sounds productive, and might possibly have been, the sight really disturbed me.

When you go to the dentist, do you want to see used instruments? When you visit your tax specialist, do you want other people's W-2 forms lying around precariously? When you dine in a restaurant, do you want to sit down to someone else's half-eaten food? You'd never stand for it.

The same goes for travel. It's a very personal business that takes attention to detail. It's not enough just to be organized—you have to *look* organized. Everyone at Rosenbluth International knows this is important to our clients' level of comfort.

What did I do about the chaos in our office? The only thing I felt was right. There were some clients there, and I asked them to leave. I inquired where each was planning to go on their next trip, and provided those trips free of charge, explaining that I had some business to discuss with my associates. I locked the door and had a talk with everyone in that office about the importance of keeping their workplace a home, to which our clients would be drawn and could feel both comfortable and welcome.

Afterward, we straightened up the office together for the rest of the day, making it a place we'd want to go to. That particular site used to be one of my least favorite, but now it ranks up there with the best of them. Not only have they improved the appearance of their surroundings, but when you look good you feel good. Their productivity has been enhanced and I believe they are happier in their work. I know our clients are happier.

Bringing Clients into the Kitchen
No Areas Should Be "Off Limits" to Clients

Have you ever enjoyed a restaurant until you took a look at the kitchen? More often than not, you're truly disgusted when you catch sight of the kitchen and its operations. Rarely are they very clean, and somehow the food loses its appeal when you see it being prepared.

We try to make the journey into our "kitchen" create a stronger impression than a view from the outside. We work hard to come out ahead in comparisons between our kitchen and the others in our industry. We do know that one rule holds true: When we bring a potential client in to inspect the inner workings of our company, we almost always make the sale.

We encourage current and prospective clients to visit our offices, to see what we're up to and to meet our people. It's common on a typical day for clients to be circulating through our offices, visiting with our associates alongside prospective clients. Our people are comfortable with both their work and our customers, so it's never disruptive. It's just one more way to strengthen the bonds we have with our clients.

The Continuum
Interactive Research and Development

Because we know how effective it is when current and prospective clients visit our offices and spend time with our people, we decided in 1996 to create a place within our world headquarters that would draw them in. We designed and developed an interactive research and development lab (described briefly in Chapter 10), where visitors can experiment with the future and help mold it. It's a hands-on lab where we test products and services (our own as well as those outside our industry). Some of the world's leading companies display their newest offers there, and the feedback from our clients helps direct their work.

We made The Continuum a fun place to visit. It features a virtual trip, including a full-scale partial airplane cabin, where visitors can test the latest in first-class seat design and amenities: a "hotel room of the future"; and a rental car simulator. Visitors can experiment with virtual reality and touch the future where telecommunications, computing, consumer electronics, work, and leisure converge.

The Continuum has been so successful (over three hundred companies have visited) that we've opened a second center in London. To keep them fresh, we constantly seek out the latest innovations, and we close the centers each year to update the exhibits, working with our strategic partners who help underwrite the project and provide cutting-edge, interactive displays. The Continuum is a great way to strengthen our partnerships with both our clients and our suppliers.

Corporate Marriage
The Ultimate Client-Supplier Relationship

The ultimate level in partnership is the fusion of talents. We call it "corporate marriage" (as introduced in Chapter 10), and it's the definitive client relationship. What exactly are we talking about? A form of interchange that takes place in an environment of complete trust. An exchange of people.

Technology specialists know information systems. Human resource experts know personnel issues. Operations people know procedure, process, and efficiency. A great deal can be shared across industries. It may be a meeting between counterparts for a day or an associate exchange for a week, a month, or even a year.

These exchanges provide insight into the needs of our clients that can't be attained any other way. The benefits are reciprocal. Our clients who participate in this degree of partnership come to understand more fully the basis from which we work. They understand the objectives we must achieve as a business and the challenges we face in doing so. A walk in each other's shoes builds the platform for true teamwork.

We've learned a great deal from our clients, and I'm proud to say they've learned from us, too. The best part of all is that it becomes almost impossible for competitors to try to snatch away any client with whom we have cultivated this level of partnership. As in a good marriage, the commitment is for the duration. There is no need to hold back, and because of that, things can be accomplished that before were thought to be impossible.

Basic relationships will produce basic results. When partners open up to a new level of trust, they reach a plane of creativity in which together they can re-create the marketplace.

Diagnostics
Cultivating Connoisseur Clients

Educating your clients about your industry and your business is a smart thing to do. For companies that provide excellent products and services, the most knowledgeable clients are the best clients. The reason is simple: The more your clients know about your industry, the more they will be able to appreciate the service you provide. To the less discerning, all products and services look alike, and the full value of what you provide can be missed.

As a way to not only help our clients understand the complexities of our industry, but to also help them mold programs to meet their specific objectives, we developed something we call "diagnostics." Diagnostics is a process through which we uncover each client's unique needs and align our operating model for that client to fulfill those needs.

Like most companies, we used to respond blindly to requests for proposals (RFPs) that came in, expending a lot of energy in the process. But in that "everyone is the same" rat race, clients end up with mediocrity. We now look to go in proactively to companies we think we can help and work with them to diagnose their true needs. *After that process, we decide whether to bid on a piece of business, based upon the fit.*

Think of it like the medical process. When was the last time you were sick, and sent out an RFP calling for the cheapest doctor to help you with what you've decided the treatment should be? Never. You find a doctor or two, with sterling reputations, and you sit with them, discuss your specific symptoms, and come up with a treatment plan, with their expertise.

We do this through our highly detailed diagnostics process, which is also a key part of our business planning process with current clients. There are three major components: (1) benchmarking; (2) DACODA analysis (taking their policies, requirements, goals, business patterns, and culture into account); and (3) a three-year forecast based upon the input gained from the first two components.

The forecast includes a cost analysis, a series of recommended initiatives to take, along with specific steps, potential benefits, areas of opportunity, and likelihood of success. In other words, we show them the potential prize to be gained, exactly how to get there, and how likely it is that they will. This information is invaluable to current and prospective clients and helps us direct our energies toward where we can have the most impact.

The Source
Helping Those Helping Clients

The most carefully outlined plan won't work if those charged with carrying it out don't have the right resources to support their efforts. We used to hear from the field that it was sometimes difficult to reach headquarters, with the pace of things, voicemail, and other typical business frustrations. We no longer hear those complaints . . . since "The Source."

The Source brings together several key support areas that previously were separate and provides "one-stop shopping" for the field. Four key areas make up The Source: (1) business development (sales); (2) implementation (delivering what you sell); (3) automation services (ensuring compliance with plans); and (4) information management (reporting the results to clients).

We brought together these four areas "under one roof," occupying half a floor at our world headquarters. Because this newly united team wanted to work together with no barriers, they designed their workspace to resemble a big living room, complete with comfy chairs and a coffee table, where people frequently meet, including clients. The Source is a hub of electricity, and you can feel it.

No one has their own office, nor do they want to. The leaders of each of the four areas work together constantly, and the leader of The Source sits right out there with them, always being pulled into meetings and having ideas run past her. At first, people were taking bets on how soon she'd request an office, but now they know she won't.

The Source is currently open twelve hours a day, and when someone in the field calls they never reach voicemail. They always get a live person who can help them with whatever they need. Everyone in the field knows they have to turn to one source only, as do our clients. Our clients turn to their general manager, and our general managers turn to The Source. Decisions are made quickly, and everything in The Source is web-accessible in "e-rooms" (for example, proposals, case studies, best practices, etc.).

Once I tested The Source, and they passed with flying colors. I was heading to an important client event after work, which required black tie attire, and I had forgotten my cuff links. I went down to The Source and asked what they could do for me. Within minutes, they found two associates to donate their service pins, and I wore them as cuff links.

No job is too unusual for The Source, and in fact, it has been so successful that a few of our clients have asked us to develop "Sources" for them (to support their field operations), which we are in the process of doing. The concept of one-stop shopping makes more sense today than ever, and we have found a way to provide it that benefits all concerned.

The Three R's
The Best Way to Find Good Partners Is to Be One

We all learned in school the fundamental "three R's" that make up the foundation upon which we learn the rest of our lives. Rosenbluth's three R's are just as fundamental to our success as a company: relationships, reputation, and references. We know these are the factors that draw both associates and clients to our company.

I've talked about relationships, but reputation and references are also crucial. Any company can advertise its service, but what really counts is what clients have to say about it. That's reputation. The secret is to translate reputation into references.

Our clients are our best salespeople. When they do the bragging about us, people listen. Most of our clients are happy to discuss our service with prospective clients. The references they have given have made all the difference in the world to our sales efforts. When we and our clients truly see each other as partners, great things happen.

Framework for Open Partnerships

A SUMMARY

▌ Build open partnerships with your own people, your clients, and the suppliers who affect your ability to provide service to your clients. It's the only way to ensure that all concerned will "buy in" to your company's goals and objectives. Empower them with the information necessary to help you succeed.

∎ Operate your company like a "nudist colony" where you hide nothing from your clients. They will quickly feel comfortable being just as open with you. This straightforward environment has to begin with the sales process and continue through to the end of each transaction, including your suppliers' part in what you do.

∎ Candid partnerships with suppliers are just as important. They make your work possible. Your clients' perception of your service can hinge upon your suppliers' ability to deliver the services and tools you need to get the job done. Bringing your suppliers into the loop is critical.

∎ Make your business a home away from home for your clients. Encourage them to visit often and mingle with your people. It'll deepen your relationship. Make sure that every day in every location, you can be proud to host your clients in your offices.

∎ Bring your clients into the kitchen. Let them in on your strategy, your goals, and objectives. They'll see their role in your long-range plans.

∎ To encourage current and prospective clients to visit your offices and get to know your people, consider creating an attraction to draw them in. Inviting other companies to participate will help you underwrite the venture and add dimension to it. Ours is a working research and development lab that provides clients and suppliers real benefit.

∎ Know the true value of your products and services and sell based on that value. Look hard at your pricing strategy to see if there are any inherent conflicts of interest, and if there are, overcome them. Go for long-term relationships that benefit everyone equitably. That's the way to ensure staying power.

▌ Make it company policy to use the products of your clients and let them know. It increases your people's knowledge about your clients, it helps your clients' sales, and it further cements your relationships.

▌ Consider an exchange program with your clients. Your marketing people should work with theirs, their technology people with yours, and so on. Not only are you sharing ideas and learning new ways of doing things, it'll put your clients out of your competitors' reach.

▌ Diagnosing client needs is far more effective than responding blindly to RFPs. Try developing a process that will help you truly uncover client needs and align your operating model around it.

▌ Clients can only get great service if the field is supported by headquarters. Consider combining key support areas in an easy-to-reach, one-stop shop for the field.

▌ References are essential sales tools and your clients should be your best salespeople. Cultivate your client partnerships and utilize them as references. Continually ensuring client satisfaction will not only help you keep the customers you already have, it'll also reward you with new business.

CHAPTER THIRTEEN

Blazing New Trails

The French classical painter Nicolas Poussin became exasperated when he failed to create the image of foam at the mouth of a spirited horse he had painted. He dashed his sponge against the canvas, and the result was exactly what he had struggled so tediously to produce.

One of the best partnerships we ever forged was a similar case of serendipity. Sometimes an idea just shines for you like a distant light you can't ignore. The concept of our global Intellicenter operations, which began in a sleepy farm town, was one such light, and the benefits to our company have been astounding.

In 1988, we stumbled upon an answer to so many concerns—not just of our company, but of all companies: finding, retaining, and continually motivating the finest people. The answer lies in partnerships between corporations and rural communities. Through ours, we eliminated overtime and temporary work, lowered our operating costs, found an untapped human resource, and branched into new lines of business.

From Cows to Computers
An Offbeat Idea that Changed Our Company

One day in the summer of 1988, my wife and I were discussing the fact that we were expecting rain in Philadelphia for the fifth straight day in a row. Then we got on the subject of a serious drought that was hitting the Midwest, and we wished we could send some of our rain their way.

The next day, my associates and I were talking about what we *could* do to help, and the series of events that followed made a real difference in our company. We decided to open a temporary office in the heart of the drought country to provide employment until the drought subsided.

The saying goes, "Give a man a fish and he eats for a day; teach a man to fish and he has food for life." We decided that rather than contribute to a drought relief fund, we'd offer to teach skills that people could use to lessen their dependence upon farming, in which success is contingent upon Mother Nature's cooperation.

We contacted the U.S. Department of Agriculture to ask which state had been the hardest hit, and the answer was North Dakota. We visited the state and asked which area had been most negatively affected and were told about Linton, a town of about one thousand people. This community was almost totally dependent upon agriculture for its livelihood, and it was here that the drought had been most merciless.

Off we went to Linton. The local economic development group helped us to locate an old tractor implement shop where part of the space was not being utilized. The next day we ran a small "HELP WANTED" ad in the local paper, the *Emmons County Record,* for twenty full-time positions for a three-month period.

From that one mention in the local paper, eighty people showed up the next morning looking for work. So we decided to hire forty part-time people instead of twenty full-time, in order to have a positive impact on more families. We installed computers in our makeshift workspace, brought in a team of trainers, and set up shop.

Everyone in the company was asked to submit ideas for work that could be done in our rural office. We studied the type of work that was being done on an overtime basis or by temporary help. It was almost exclusively data entry and other work that was ideal for our new associates.

We came to rely more and more on that office for all types of work, and we noticed that overtime and temporary help in our offices across the country ceased. The alternative became our Linton associates, and we began to wonder how we ever survived without them.

We faced some skepticism. In our own industry, a lot of people thought we had lost our minds. Even in Linton, at first, people wondered why we were there and what we hoped to gain from it. In the beginning, we didn't expect to gain anything from it, but the benefits began to unfold.

In just the first few weeks, we began to see a pattern of quality work, with no absenteeism and no turnover. The scope of our new associates' work expanded along with their productivity. Morale was high and that office was the epitome of teamwork.

When we opened there, we hadn't expected benefits to our bottom line, but they were unmistakable. Operating costs are notably lower in rural areas, and because the cost of living is so much less than in major metropolitan areas, the salaries are typically lower. You don't see the salary scuffles over highly qualified people that take place in larger cities. Add to that the costs that can be saved by eliminating overtime and temporary work, and you begin to see that doing business in rural communities is a sound alternative.

These are just the *financial* benefits to corporations utilizing rural communities as a viable option for human resources. Companies should consider looking to farm towns to find available quality people. This is still a largely untapped resource.

Forecast: Continued Drought
The Impending Need for Quality People

When the first edition of this book was published in 1992, the hiring market was plentiful and it was jobs that were scarce, not people. At the time, we warned that a human resource crisis was eminent, and that crisis is now upon us. The labor force continues to shrink and the demands of corporations are growing. We'll be feeling the effects far into the future.

The population is aging. Concurrently, the number of people entering the workforce under the age of thirty has decreased since 1980 and is expected to continue to decline well into the millennium. There are concerns over the decline in basic skills our youth possess.

More alternative labor sources are being utilized, and this leaves fewer to call upon in the future. Human resources are the single highest cost item for most corporations. And people make companies what they are. There is no more important corporate concern for the future than finding and keeping great people.

An Unsheathed Weapon
A Human Resource Solution for the Future

For the most part, corporations and rural communities lead separate lives. Sure, we need the products and services that each of us manufactures, but when it comes to business, we don't work as a team. Farmers try to make a living from the land, confronting all the unpredictable forces of nature in the process. Corporations struggle to compete in a fast-moving global arena.

Rural communities offer a wealth of human resources, not just in sheer numbers but in extraordinary quality and work ethic. The ultimate weapon for corporations is a double-barreled gun: high quality with low operating costs. It can be found in rural communities.

On the other side of the fence, bringing work from corporations into rural communities lessens their dependency upon agriculture. This allows people to continue farming, because they are better able to withstand its ups and downs.

I'll Place My Bet on the Farmer
Farming and Business Have More in Common than You May Realize

The celebrated lawyer Clarence Darrow, who was the defense attorney in the historic *Scopes* trial, was once being interviewed for a magazine article on secrets to success. The interviewer said, "Most of the men I've spoken to so far attribute their success to hard work."

Clarence Darrow replied, "I guess that applies to me, too. I was brought up on a farm. One very hot day I was distributing and packing down the hay which a stacker was constantly dumping on top of me. By noon I was completely exhausted. That afternoon I left the farm, never to return, and I haven't done a day of hard work since."

I don't mean to imply that if you don't come from a farm you don't know how to work, but that there are certain parallels between farming and business. The resourcefulness it takes to run a farm at times exceeds that required for a business. Struggling with nature is no easy task. The days are longer than those of a driven corporate executive. A day on the farm normally begins at 5:00 A.M. (but you won't find too many farmers calling it a day at 5:00 P.M.).

Farming is teamwork personified. No one can run a farm alone. The land and animals have to be tended daily. There's no such thing as a weekend, holiday, or sick day on a farm. The only option is to cooperate with friend and neighbor to get the job done. And the quality that goes into the making of the product becomes clear at harvest or cattle auction time.

These solid values are learned at an early age on the farm. Most kids put in a full day's work on their family's farm in the hours before and after school. Contrast this inherent work ethic with the challenges companies face in motivating people and the application of the comparisons between business and farming becomes clear.

A Part of the Family
Planting Permanent Roots in Rural America

As I've discussed, we go through countless interviews each year to find the right people. We search far and wide for the cream of the crop and we've been able to find them, but it takes a lot of hard work. What we've found in rural communities is an abundance of the type of person we look for, and that's rare.

So after just six weeks of temporarily employing people in our makeshift Linton location, we decided to make our rural office a permanent one. We announced our plans during the final session of our company-wide meeting, and the announcement was met with few dry eyes. Every one of our people had been touched by our Linton associates in some way, whether through the quality of their work, their can-do attitude, or their contagious enthusiasm. This was a clear instance of a decision that was good business *and* the right thing to do.

Today we have two hundred full-time associates in that North Dakota office and have since opened four additional North Dakota offices, one in Campbellsville, Kentucky, another in Killarney, Ireland, and elsewhere. Data entry is still a part of their work, but they also take travel reservations, do much of our accounting work, handle our entire customer service operation, and service our Up-Stream line of business (customer relationship management, which you read about in Chapter 11). For example, National Airlines outsources its entire reservation service to us. We handle customer service work for Orbitz, Travelocity, and UAL.com, United Airlines' website. And US Airways Cargo entrusts their entire cargo shipping service to us.

This type of work has taken most of our Intellicenters into a 24/7 environment and offered a new level of job variety for our associates there. We create an atmosphere where people are given the opportunity and encouragement to constantly learn new things. Our associates move throughout their Intellicenter to learn different roles. Each time they develop a new skill, it strengthens our flexibility. We have experienced associates on hand for whatever is called for at any given moment. This type of diversification not only smoothes out the peaks and valleys that any business faces, but it also adds to job security for our associates.

Our Intellicenter network has grown tremendously. A location in Fargo, North Dakota, employs 375 people, and our Dickinson, North Dakota, office staffs up to 380. Both are open 24 hours a day, 7 days a week; serve large corporate accounts, Up-Stream clients, and en route services; and offer web business support. Another center in Williston, North Dakota, employs 120 (with room to grow to 200), and we've now ventured into "satellite" locations (our first is Jamestown, North Dakota, with 75 people) to reach smaller communities, sharing leadership and technology from our larger centers. This enables us to tap into some terrific talent.

Our corporate travel and Up-Stream clients rave about the service in our rural Intellicenters. For example, a station manager in Dallas, for an airline whose reservations we handle, wrote to us, "This is my fourth airline, and the first that contracted out the reservations aspect of the company. By far, your staff is superior to any of them. It never seems to make a difference what it is that I need. I know it's a simple phone call and the answer is always 'Yes, we can do that.' It's refreshing."

Underwear, Underpaid, Underappreciated
Underneath It All: Terrific People

The story of our Intellicenter in Campbellsville, Kentucky, reads like a fairy tale. Campbellsville (population 11,000) was the site, for half a century, of a Fruit Of The Loom underwear plant, which employed over four thousand people. Virtually every family in the community was dependent upon the factory in some way, but then the unthinkable happened . . . Fruit Of The Loom left town. The community was devastated, with no future in sight.

What happened next was a Cinderella story. Amazon.com was growing by quantum leaps and searching for ways to quickly establish service centers to meet demand. They found Campbellsville through sophisticated analysis and opened a distribution center with plans to employ up to one thousand people. That began to put the community back on its feet.

How did we happen upon Campbellsville? One day someone called from the town, who had read about our rural operations. It was the owner of a local travel agency, who tried to talk us into purchasing their company and setting up shop in their community. If we'd used pure logic, like most companies, we would have missed this opportunity. But we let emotion play a key role in how we do things, and we knew instinctively that there was a treasure of human resource waiting for us in Campbellsville.

We did purchase the local agency and turned it into an Intellicenter, expanding to two hundred positions. We think our associates there are terrific, and they feel the same way about our company. An article on the transformation of Campbellsville in the July 2000, issue of *Fast Company* says, "A hallmark of the best new-economy companies is that they appreciate the distinction between labor and talent, between muscle and mind, between present value and potential." We see the vast potential in rural communities and will continue to make them our home.

Sharing the Luck of the Irish
Branching Out to the Global Rural Community

After years of wonderful experiences in rural America, we decided to venture into rural communities abroad to serve our global accounts, and we stumbled across Killarney, in the heart of the southwest Irish countryside. We chose Killarney because the people, values, and service orientation are so similar to those we have found in our U.S. rural locations and because of the technology infrastructure and the high linguistic ability of its people. Killarney has a strong educational system and close proximity of third level colleges. These, together with an abundance of tourism-related services (which strengthen a service orientation), made for the right conditions.

We opened our Killarney Intellicenter in 1998, and today we employ about 100, with plans to add another 150 in the near term. Our associates there provide service in English, French, German, Dutch, Italian, and Spanish to clients from all over Europe. Our technology allows our associates to know where each call is coming from and to answer in the appropriate language. Their skill level and dedication enable them to provide stellar service.

Doing business in rural Ireland is as fascinating to our global clients as doing business in rural America has been to our domestic clients. Once a global travel manager for a large corporate account visited the center with us. It so happened that the All Ireland Football Championships were underway, and Kerry (Killarney's county) was in the finals. The farmer next to our Intellicenter holds a tradition of painting his sheep in the Kerry colors for the championship. Our client was so intrigued that he wanted to capture a picture. It was quite a sight to see him chasing the sheep for a close-up. But then one of the sheep became paparazzi-weary and charged toward him. He stepped back into a barbed wire fence, ripped his beautiful Italian suit, and broke his camera. I guess our service training doesn't work on sheep.

Home on the Range
The Story of a Very Special Place

Happy the man who far from schemes of business, like the early generations of mankind, works his ancestral acres with oxen of his own breeding, from all usury free.

—Horace (65–8 B.C.)

In 1989 we held a strategic planning meeting in Linton (the one I discussed earlier, when I talked about our fence-building exercise). We stayed at a roadside motel, held our meetings in the local electric cooperative building, and instead of playing golf or skiing for recreation, we rode horses and did farm chores. It was the best meeting we ever had.

We found ourselves doing everything as a group, not breaking into foursomes. Everyone felt unrestrained, renewed, creative. We came back a stronger team. Virtually every strategic meeting since then has been held in North Dakota.

From the beginning of time, man worked with the land. Only since the turn of the century have people become disconnected from it. Something natural has been lost in urban life that can be recaptured on a farm.

We decided the experience was worth sharing with other companies, so we bought three thousand acres of rolling prairieland and built a place like no other. We call it "The Rivery," and it's a ranch where companies can hold small meetings in seclusion—one group at a time. We designed The Rivery based on trust. There are no cash registers. We operate on the honor system. Most of our guests leave their doors open. The kitchen and the bar are open twenty-four hours a day, so guests can help themselves to whatever they'd like whenever they want. Accommodations, meals, and many activities are part of the all-inclusive package. Our guests help themselves to any additional activities or amenities and simply notify us afterward. Charges are billed later so our guests don't have to worry about it while they're enjoying their stay.

The Rivery specializes in creating out-of-the-ordinary experiences, like meetings in a one-room schoolhouse or out under the open skies, perched on bales of hay. Our motto is, "Open skies: Open minds." There are rodeos, cattle drives, square dances, and trail rides. It's an unusual blend of rusticity and elegance.

Each day our guests are served afternoon tea, and turn-down service includes freshly baked warm cookies and ice-cold milk. There are no room numbers and there's no check-in or check-out process. Every staff member knows each guest's name.

Our staff is made up of local farmers, trained by the Ritz-Carlton organization in the art of hospitality. Our clients say we've created a place that embodies the spirit of the heartland, and we're proud of that. We've been sending our clients to resorts for a century—why not our own? And what better place to build it than a place that has played such a vital role in our company?

All Around the World
Exploring Rural Opportunities for Your Company

We have received information from literally hundreds of small farm towns across the nation and around the world inviting us to become a part of their communities. When we add new Intellicenter locations, we face tough choices.

There are "Lintons" all across the globe, ripe for partnerships with corporations. The diversity of industry offered to rural areas will save those farming communities. The wealth of affordable, quality human resources will help companies overcome one of today's most daunting challenges—finding enough great people.

Companies have come to realize that so many types of work know no geographical boundaries. When you call a company to order merchandise or speak with a customer service department, do you know or even care where your call is being answered?

It doesn't matter where the call originates. What most people want to know is that their merchandise order or customer service request is being handled expertly and courteously. Companies are beginning to appreciate that, and we've been inundated with calls from corporations interested in what we've done in our rural Intellicenters.

Many of our clients have become interested in the feasibility of such an operation for their own companies because of the work we have done on their behalf in our rural locations. Non-client companies call us about it, too. We have regularly hosted executives from organizations far and wide on visits to our rural offices. We share information on how we establish these offices and put them in touch with people who can help them get started.

A number of companies who have contacted us have opened rural facilities. For example, a large healthcare organization, a hotel reservations company, a telemarketing firm, and a large airline's frequent flyer tracking operation.

Through our initial office in Linton, all of the rural locations we've expanded to, and our introduction of rural and corporate partnerships, we have benefited our clients in an unconventional and unexpected way. And we have picked up a few new clients along the way.

The Rural Route

A SUMMARY

▌ Pursue an idea if you believe in it, no matter how absurd it might seem to the outside world. That's how most revolutionary ideas are born.

▌ Search for pockets of people who fit your company's culture and work ethic. We have found ours in rural communities.

▌ Prepare your company for a continued drought in human resources, perpetuated by a number of factors. The population is growing older; basic skills are declining; more alternative labor sources are being utilized, which all leads to fewer untapped human resources as we continue into the increasingly competitive future.

▌ Consider rural resources as a weapon for global competitiveness. The combination of high quality and reasonable operating costs is hard to beat.

▌ If you are interested in exploring your options in rural communities, our company would be more than happy to help you in any way we can, including providing information we have gained through our experiences and those of the companies we have helped to establish rural operations.

Afterword

A Lot to Digest

I've made some statements in this book that might seem strange to a lot of people, things like "The customer can no longer come first." If you were to look at that statement alone it could be alarming. But when you explain why it works it's as comforting as a hug.

I want to bring it all together, so you can see it as a trail to a different way of doing business—a way that has worked for us and can work for any company that's willing to try it.

First impressions are lasting. Most people spend their first days on a new job filling out forms. But the beginning of a career should be an event to remember. A creative and inspiring orientation program gets everyone in step, instills culture, and builds loyalty—rewards that will repay a company time and again.

Happiness in the workplace is a strategic advantage. Service comes from the heart, and people who feel cared for will care more. Unhappiness results in error, turnover, and other evils. To strengthen happiness you have to measure it—using Crayolas, voicemail, it doesn't matter as long as you gauge it. Finally, companies have to have fun. When was the last time you excelled at something you disliked?

Finding the right people takes a broad view, looking beyond the standard sources of your industry. People should be selected as much for team fit as individual contribution. They should be interviewed not only by their potential leaders, but by those whom they will lead and their peers. The interviewing process should be unusual because you can tell more about a person when his or her guard is down. But above all, look for nice people.

Perpetual training is a secret weapon, because the growth of a company is really just the aggregate of the growth of its people. Broad-based programs that are philosophical in nature are as important as technical training. It all starts with the very first day of work—people should be initiated in the company with an orientation they'll never forget. And training should be offered to everyone throughout their careers.

Service is an attitude, an art, and a process, and we're all in the service business no matter what our industry is. When you're in tune with your clients, you feel service in your gut. That's attitude. Art comes from caring and creativity. And process comes from quality. You have to have the right quality approach for your company because if it's not, process can get in the way of progress.

Culture defines every organization. It's important for companies to capture the concept of what they'd like theirs to say, formalize it, share it with their people, and celebrate it. But the secret to culture is sincerity, for without the actions to go with the words, they're empty.

The birth and nurturing of ideas has to be taken seriously. Innovation will be encouraged in an environment of creativity and freedom. Studying the origin of ideas can spark the process. They can come from the desire to do something better, a problem that needs solving, or from almost anywhere. Ideas need to be protected, but they become stronger when they are tested.

The gardening process has application in the workplace. After all that work finding the right people you need to help keep them that way. Make sure politics doesn't work in your organization. Reward those who are contributing and not only seeking recognition, and reward those who help others succeed. Break down barriers by moving people around and cross-training them. People should be reviewed by those they lead as well as those who lead them.

Inventing the future is a matter of seeking opportunities to capitalize on change and being ready to seize them. Before a company can do that, it must be free of undue dependence upon outside parties and prepared to manage the impending growth.

Technology is a tool that can reduce stress and improve service. It can automate mundane processes, leaving people free to concentrate on the more creative and personal aspects of service. The best technology tools are built based on the input of the people who will use them. This also incorporates the technology group into the company's mainstream.

Look around you and up ahead, because it's not enough to just mind your own company and industry. The health of surrounding industries can have a ripple effect, particularly the industries of clients. But it's just as important to look into the future by thinking like the marketplace. It'll prepare you to proactively serve your clients and to outwit your competitors.

Open partnerships make a higher level of relationship possible with your clients. Your offices should remain welcome homes to them. They should be invited into the kitchen to inspect the ingredients of your product. Your clients should be your best salespeople. And you should be their customer.

Blazing new trails means pursuing what you believe in no matter what anyone else thinks. By locating in a farm town, we discovered a gold mine. The people in rural communities are our answer to the human resource drought. They could be your answer, too.

Now It's Your Turn

The great thing about ideas is that they are works in progress. The more they are tried and adapted, the better they get. The ideas we talked about a decade ago still work, but they've been improved upon over the years to the point where a new book was necessary. Now it's your turn to have a crack at the ideas outlined here.

I know you can adapt them for use in your business, and in doing so, I'm sure you'll refine and improve them. Don't make the mistake we all tend to make of getting swept up with enthusiasm for the message, only to face your desk and put fresh ideas on the back burner while you put out fires.

Take one idea right now, and try it. I dare you to. Begin cleansing your company of what is wrong, and replace it with what is right, humanistic, and competitively essential. You owe it to yourself, your people, your company, and your stakeholders.

A Distance To Go

We're confident in what we believe and secure in sharing it with you. But that doesn't mean we always live up to our expectations. While most of the principles and programs I've discussed here are daily practice, some still remain aspirations. I think it's important to tell you that we're not completely there yet, but we're getting close. I hope that putting these beliefs in writing will help both you and us.

Rosenbluth International
2401 Walnut Street
Philadelphia, PA 19103
www.rosenbluth.com

Epilogue

A Changed World

Just days before we were about to submit the final manuscript of this book to HarperCollins, the horrific events of September 11, 2001, took place. Our company, our people, our families, and our world were to be changed forever. Much happened over the following months that would challenge everything we believed in. Only now can we say that had our company not been built on the beliefs and practices contained in this book, we might not have had a company to write about.

Perhaps I wrote this chapter because it was cathartic, a way for me to deal with the most challenging time I've ever faced as a leader. Perhaps because what you are about to read has never been chronicled before by a chairman of a company. Mostly, I guess, because it's important for other leaders of companies to get an inside view of the emotional roller coaster that at least one corporate leader was willing to share so that others can gain from it.

This is a chapter full of pain and love, fright and delight, life and death, but mostly about the inner thoughts of being the chairman of a $6 billion business that saw its revenue dry up overnight, and how it fought to stay alive after the September 11, 2001, attack on America. It's candid and it's true. Some parts are upsetting and some exhilarating, but for the most part, it's surreal. I am indebted to the associates and clients of Rosenbluth International for their staunch support of our company and the sacrifices they made during that difficult time.

I never let a moment go by without reminding myself how blessed

I am to employ the greatest people in the world, and the work they do on behalf of our clients. The chapter begins on September 11, 2001.

Our Darkest Days

Outside my office sit a number of television screens that monitor world events, financial markets, and other news that might affect our clients or industry. At 8:45 A.M. on September 11, 2001, I witnessed on these screens the tragedy that would begin a series of events unprecedented in our company's and country's history.

Like millions I watched in horror as a commercial jetliner smashed into the World Trade Center. My immediate reaction was to notify our Network Communications Center to begin our process of identifying Rosenbluth International clients that might have been aboard. Eighteen minutes later it happened again. By now, we all instinctively knew we were under terrorist attack. Again it happened, this time at the Pentagon, and then another plane went down in rural Pennsylvania.

Within minutes I received a call from one of our customer care associates that she had received a call from a passenger on board one of the hijacked planes asking her to call his family and tell them he loved them. Moments later I received a list of clients from our database of those on board each of the planes that had been destroyed. By now, my heart was in my stomach, anger was in my heart, and I knew what was about to happen to our company and our associates.

During the next thirty minutes I placed phone calls to the four CEOs of the respective companies that had employees on board each of the airplanes. My heart sunk as I shared the names with each of the companies' leaders. In each case, regardless of their size (most being Fortune 500 companies) the CEOs knew the victims personally.

Following the calls, I knew that the leadership of our company was going to be tested like never before. We also understood that while immediate action was needed for our company, we first had to focus on our associates and the grief and fear that gripped their hearts. Our first task was to evacuate all of our offices in tall buildings throughout the country and to notify all other offices that any associate who felt they needed to take some private time or go home to be with their loved ones should do so. Since the vast majority of our call centers are telephonically linked, we moved client calls around the country without disruption.

A report was handed to me of fifty of our associates who were still in the air traveling to meetings with clients and suppliers. Our people tracked each of these planes until we knew they were safely on the ground somewhere in the United States or Canada. Hours later, all were accounted for and we took a collective sigh of relief.

By the time noon rolled around, our Thought Theatre was turned into an interfaith chapel for all who wanted time to pray. By two in the afternoon the mayor of Philadelphia called for all offices to close, and most of our headquarters staff had gone home to be with their families. Those of us who remained began assessing the situation and putting in place our process of steps to keep our clients informed of airline and airport closures, manning the phones to accommodate our clients' informational requests, and working to get stranded passengers back to their homes. Lingering in the back of our minds was the reality that we were going to operate without any revenue for some time to come, since no one was buying any tickets and the fear of flying was going to become omnipresent.

We left for home that night exhausted but knew that our families and especially our children needed us to be with them, to hug them, and to try and comfort them. By 3 A.M. I could no longer sleep so I headed to the office to contact our European leaders to discuss the impact there of the events in America. Then I set about writing a letter to all of our people. The letter went like this:

Dear Friend:

Yesterday, a tragedy of incalculable human and psychological proportions took place in America. It was a day of death, destruction, and heroic efforts never before seen on the shores of the

United States. Each of us, in our own way, will over time learn to deal with this unconscionable act of terrorism and insensitivity to human life.

By late last night an eerie hush had fallen over our country as family and friends gathered together to grieve and comfort one another. Parents did their best to explain the events of the day to their children and many, like mine, may have spent the night sleeping all together in bed as we tried to comfort the fears of our children. Many associates had friends or acquaintances lost during this horrible attack on the sanctity of our individual and collective psyche and our thoughts and prayers go out to them.

Unfortunately, this may only be the beginning. The United States will assuredly attack the perpetrators of this attack on America, which in return, may cause rise to further reprisals. We must learn to live with this and resolve ourselves to the fact that we now live in a very different world.

It may not be talked about over the airwaves or written in the newspapers, but an unspoken fear now grips many in America, a reaction that is normal and reasonable. But we must, like others in countries less fortunate than ours, overcome this fear and understand that an attack may lie right around the corner and could happen at any moment. During periods of my life, I have lived under these circumstances and know that we can rise above these well-placed fears and live the normal lives our parents and grandparents fought and died for over the past century. It's not easy, but we can't let ourselves be held captive to the fear this attack on our country was designed to create. To give in to fear is to give up. That is not the American way. Franklin D. Roosevelt, a previous American president, put it best when he said, "We have nothing to fear, but fear itself." Having personally lived through terrorist attacks and months of war, no truer words could be spoken. It's up to us to comfort one another, share words of sorrow and compassion, even horror, and then move on. Not to do so is to admit defeat. America is united, our government and military will be resolute with responding with appropriate force, and we will prevail as a nation.

Over the past sixteen hours I have received words of support from associates throughout the world. Each shared their sorrow with all those working in the United States and offered to be of whatever assistance they could. To all our overseas colleagues I say "Thank you."

It has been traditional from the day our country was born that tragedy brings out the best in all of us. Yesterday was no exception. Associates across the country, and indeed the world, fielded calls from frantic and concerned clients and family members inquiring into the fate of their loved ones. Each one of the tens of thousands of calls we received had to be handled with care, sympathy, and facts. Every one of you was a hero yesterday, as you did just that. From the associate in North Dakota who handled with professionalism and grace a call she received from a frantic passenger aboard a hijacked flight asking to please send his devoted love to friends and family members, to the telecommunications and IT departments that kept our lines open and computers running so that communication with clients and one another could take place were heroes. The associates from the Network Operations Center and Corporate Communications group who worked tirelessly throughout the day and night to keep our operations going and our clients and associates informed on a regular basis performed heroically, as well.

The cooperation of offices and centers to move calls around the country as Rosenbluth offices in high-rise buildings were closed was unbelievable. The associates working our database determining which Rosenbluth International clients were aboard the four flights produced the information in record time allowing myself and other leaders to contact corporate leaders to inform them of the loss of their employees, all performed in a fashion we can all be proud of. On a personal note, my executive assistants Paula Coursey and Jen Hand were of incalculable aid in helping me coordinate the activities of the company during this crisis.

There were thousands of other silent heroes throughout the company yesterday and the thanks of associates from around the world go out to you for your efforts with external and internal clients alike. In short, the associates of Rosenbluth International performed at their best during the worst of times.

I'm pleased to report that all fifty Rosenbluth International associates who were traveling on business in the United States have been accounted for, and our associate who works in our office in the World Trade Center was unharmed.

Today, and for many weeks to come, a different type of fear may fall upon our friends throughout the company as the phones stop ringing. It will begin this morning and none of us can predict how long it will last. It will be a time for each of us to be brave and not panic. The American people are a resilient lot, but you must recognize that each traveler is being urged by their spouses, children, and parents not to travel. It's human nature to do so and I'm certain you'd do the same. Only time will tell when people feel comfortable flying again.

The officers and senior leaders of the company will be meeting today to assess and forecast the damage to our company and the effects on us all. We will communicate our plan once we have properly assessed the situation.

Some of you may know that I had prepared a letter for all associates that was to be distributed yesterday sharing with you the tremendous downturn in travel, the effects on the company and associates, and a plan we were about to put in place to deal with it. I have held that letter back as the situation has changed dramatically over the past twenty hours. Your leaders are in receipt of that letter but its contents are now unrealistic given the events of yesterday. You have my assurances that as soon as we agree on a course of action we will notify you immediately. Since conditions are certain to change on a weekly basis our strategies and decisions will most likely change, as well so please bear with us as we do what is best for associates, clients, and the company alike.

I don't want to end this letter without making mention of the hundreds of firefighters, policemen, and policewomen who lost their lives trying to save others at both the World Trade Center and Pentagon. Many of us take their work for granted and rarely take the time to appreciate how often they put themselves in harm's way. They are America's best, selfless and undaunted in their efforts to save lives and protect citizens. When you next see a policeman, policewoman, or firefighter, salute them and let them know you appreciate the line of business they are in and the importance they hold for all of us.

We will get through this as a nation, as a people, and as a company. There's no fooling ourselves that times will get tough for us all as we deal with the ramifications of this national tragedy, but deal with it we will. We are a company made up of people from all races, religions, and nationalities, and that is the strength of Rosenbluth International.

My prayers go out to all of you, wherever you call home, from wherever you may have been born, and whatever your beliefs may be. We are "One World, One Company," give each other a hug today, look out for one another, and take whatever time is necessary throughout the day to collect your thoughts and comfort those who need it.

Warmest regards,

Nal

By 7 A.M. we had established that the senior leadership team would meet every four hours to review our strategies moving forward and the various scenarios to remain viable during this time of crisis. The logistics of these meetings were a nightmare. All planes were grounded and our president was offshore, our CIO was forced to drive back to our Philadelphia headquarters from Los Angeles, our senior vice president of marketing was, likewise, driving back from New Orleans with a divisional vice president, and our vice president of supplier relations was in a car returning to Philadelphia from Chicago.

I have always felt that the three keys to a successful business are speed, emotion, and trust. Never in our company's history were these three ingredients so critical. With airports shut down, business travelers calling in at a record pace to cancel future flights, and companies issuing travel moratoriums every hour, we estimated that we were going to burn cash at a rate of $1.2 million a day. Adding to our concerns was the threat of more violence and the unknown timing or reaction of a U.S. response to the attack on our country. One thing was certain: we could not accurately forecast travel bookings for the immediate future. When coupled with the slim margins of our industry, decisive actions were necessary. We had to construct, communicate, and execute our path forward with our clients, associates, and suppliers on a concurrent basis.

Our conference calls continued over the next few days as our colleagues made their way across the country. I can only imagine the faces of employees at 7-Elevens and Dunkin' Donut stores as they listened to one-sided conversations of travel management executives rolling up numbers and making decisions that would affect thousands of people and tens of millions of dollars. Frustration was a part of every meeting since at least one executive was always out of range or in a poor cell area and couldn't be part of the decision making process. Needless to say, we got through the inconveniences and frustrations and took action on a number of fronts. One of the first was to communicate to our people that a temporary reduction in pay and many changes in policy and practice were necessary. Here is the letter that was so painful to write:

Dear Friend:

Prior to Tuesday's tragedy, I had written you a letter that started out like this:
The first decision corporations make during tough times is to

cut back on travel. Unfortunately, this has a direct effect on our company and industry as many of our clients have reduced travel by up to 60 percent. CEOs and shareholders of publicly held companies have seen their stock prices decline, company values cut in half, and their workforce cut dramatically. This only creates more pressure for them to cut back on travel expenditures.

Associates and leaders alike have all contributed greatly to keeping our company successful during these times. We have been awarded record amounts of new business to offset client cutbacks, however a large percentage of that business will be implemented over the next few months and had little positive effect during the first three quarters of the year. Tough decisions were made during this period to offset most of the revenue decline from reductions in client travel, however more is needed to finish out the year in a manner best suited for associates and the company alike.

Many of you may not be aware that a decision was made by the officer group back in July to not pay merit increases to all company leaders. In addition, a large part of the compensation paid to eligible leaders is tied directly to company performance thresholds. Therefore, unless something dramatic happens during the last four months of 2001, bonuses paid to eligible leaders will be eliminated, which I know will be a huge burden and disappointment. Obviously, like you, leaders had nothing to do with the reduction in travel but are being directly affected nonetheless.

However, these cutbacks in leadership compensation are not enough to cover the results and goals the company must meet for the year. Accordingly, a determination was made that both leaders and associates must be asked to sacrifice further so that we remain the strong company that we are and positioned for future growth and prosperity that will benefit all.

(I went on to spell out the steps we were going to take to cover the reductions in revenue and the sacrifices we were all going to have to make.)

Unfortunately, the events over the past forty-eight hours have caused us to recalibrate our forecasts as airports have closed, companies have put NO TRAVEL *policies in place, and airlines have predicted a passenger drop of at least 40 percent over the next six weeks.*

Accordingly, we have no option other than to reduce compensation to all associates and leaders by 10 percent through the end of the year. This amounts to an approximate annual reduction in pay of 3 percent. If by some miracle travel returns to levels that exceed our expectations and corporate requirements, we will immediately rescind this decision.

We have also implemented other measures to cut costs where possible. We have enforced a company-wide hiring freeze that is effective immediately. In addition, we are now requiring all senior leadership to fly coach domestically unless they get a free ticket or upgrade. All off-site meetings have been canceled, as have training sessions requiring associate travel. If for some emergency reason an off-site group meeting is required, we will do our best to have them paid for by our suppliers just as they have done throughout the year for company sponsored client golf outings, and other corporate events.

Further contributions to cost reduction have been made by the officer and senior leadership groups. I have cut my pay indefinitely by close to 20 percent and will receive no bonus. The rest of the senior leadership group will see also their total compensation reduced dramatically. While travel is something we must do to run a global organization, it is not something we jump at since it takes us away from our families and loved ones. Unfortunately, in addition to the travel policy change I mentioned earlier, leaders are also being asked to take connecting and/or inconvenient routings in order to take advantage of supplier discounts and save the company more money.

Cost reductions alone do not keep a company healthy nor properly position it for the future. Investments still need to be made to ensure we navigate the right path forward. These investments are in the best interests of all associates, although on the surface they might not always seem so. During the 1992 and 1993 recession, we invested in opening offices around the world while cost reductions and cutbacks were made in the United States. At the time, this may have seemed questionable but in hindsight, I'm confident that all would agree with that vision and strategy. This has allowed for our current and future growth. Today, we compete with only one truly global company.

As in 1992 and 1993, similar decisions have been made this year in Up-Stream, Information Technology, and a new line of business to be announced shortly. The Up-Stream decision saved hundreds of jobs, particularly at company Intellicenters, as we diversified our portfolio of business.

Today, we handle the customer service requirements of many airline websites and reservations and cargo needs for others. These calls are producing valuable revenue streams at a time when corporate travel calls are down.

While the current economic conditions will not improve in the short term, I remain extremely bullish and confident in the future. We are growing faster than anyone, are in the process of improving our margins, and are introducing revenue-producing products at a record pace.

I'd like to end this letter by thanking you for the personal sacrifices you are making for the good of the company and our fellow associates. Any cost reduction measures, like those spelled out in this letter, require that officers, leaders, and associates must all, in the true fashion and culture of our company, be treated fairly and proportionately. I believe we have done just that. I am genuinely sorry for any difficulties these decisions will cause you and take personal responsibility for all of these decisions. From my vantage point, I know the long-term benefits for you and your colleagues of these actions. While they will cause all of us some short-term pain, you have my assurances they are the right and fairest means of protecting our continued success during the toughest of economic times. Please feel free to share your

*thoughts with me by e-mailing me at hrosenbluth@rosen
bluth.com.*

Warmest regards,

Nal

Over the next twenty-four hours I received hundreds of e-mails from
associates supporting our company's decisions and some questioning
our reasoning and timing of the letter. I spent the night answering all
of them.

As the days passed, we continued to work around the clock manning phones around the world, getting stranded clients home as airports began to open up, and praying that cancellations would soon
turn to bookings. Unfortunately, that was not to be, and our people
were beginning to worry about their jobs. It was obvious to all that the
measures taken to date were not enough and that more steps needed
to be taken to ensure the viability of our company as the nation and
the world remained glued to their TVs, and not flying on airplanes.

By now we had eliminated as much cost from our company as possible and delayed plans for investments in new technological products and service enhancements until we had a clearer picture of the
future. We all had our own predictions as to when people would again
feel that it was safe to fly, but if what happened to me the next day was
any indication of what was ahead it wouldn't be soon. I felt strongly
that everyone in our company had to sacrifice regardless of where in
the world they worked. Our decision to reduce salaries in the United
States could not, by law, be mandated in Europe or parts of Asia. I
wanted to show solidarity for our U.S. associates, so I decided to fly to
Europe and solicit the aid of our associates on a voluntary basis.

Early in the morning I shared with my family my decision to travel.
My eleven-year-old daughter was in tears, begging me not to leave. My
eight- and nine-year-old boys showed fear on their faces but didn't
voice their concern until later that day. My eighteen-year-old son tried

to keep a stiff upper lip, but I could see through it and eventually he asked me if it was really necessary that I go. I did my best to calm their fears, but I knew in my heart that after the five days of relentless replaying on television of planes crashing into buildings there was nothing I could say that would comfort them.

Two hours before I was to head to the airport I was in my home meeting with our president and our CFO to discuss plans for the next day. My wife came to say good-bye before taking my daughter to her soccer match, and she broke down. My stomach was in knots as I found myself torn between my family and my company. I knew I couldn't let either down. Our meeting ended shortly thereafter and I began to pack for my trip to Europe, all the while unable to reconcile what to do. For the first time in my life a decision didn't come quickly or easily. A few minutes later a colleague came to pick me up for the trip to the airport. I got in the car but couldn't close the door. We sat in my driveway for five minutes without saying a word. My stomach has never failed me but this time the butterflies were heading in all different directions. I knew it was safe to fly, but I also knew that I couldn't put my family through the misery they were experiencing. I sat for a few more minutes and then turned to my associate and said, "We're not going."

I called our president, informed him of my decision, and asked him to contact our vice president of Europe. I headed to my eight-year-old's baseball game, jumped onto the bench, and gave him a hug. Later that day my entire family was together again reflecting on the day's events and talking about the days that lay ahead.

Back at the office, we spent the first three days of the week looking at numbers, talking with clients, and assessing the continued damage to our company. It was becoming increasingly obvious to us all that our actions to date weren't going to be enough. Furloughs were inevitable. Our leaders began the anguishing process of determining who was to go and who was to stay. These decisions were especially tough since we are a company of friends, and everyone's work is valued.

I sat up in bed that night unable to sleep, crushed by guilt as I stared into space. By one in the morning I had enough and decided to head into the office. I knew what lay ahead for many of my friends and colleagues and wanted to write them the letter announcing that furloughs were forthcoming. By 6 A.M. I had finished writing the most difficult letter of my life.

Dear Friend:

Over the next forty-eight hours, the hearts of many dedicated, loyal, and professional friends will be broken when furloughing of associates throughout the company becomes unavoidable.

Today, there exists an emotional crack through the heart of our company. A crack as deep and wide as the one running through America's Liberty Bell, a mere mile from our company headquarters. The beautiful company we have built together has been temporarily torn apart as the result of an act as unconscionable as one can ever imagine. The events of eight days ago have thrown our industry into a state of complete disarray as carriers and agencies furlough hundreds of thousands of people in order to survive until travelers once again feel confident enough to fly. The big unknown is when. Adding to that mystery is whether terrorism will strike again, and what the impact on air travel will be once the United States retaliates. Most airlines project a decrease in air travel by 50 percent over the next six to eight weeks. In other words, we will issue half the tickets we issued prior to September 11. We, too, have based our projections on a similar number. If no further incidents happen, we hope to see signs of a pickup in the near future, as a pent up demand exists for business travel.

The North American furloughs and international organizational reductions being announced on Thursday and Friday will be devastating to the affected individuals, their families, friends, as well as those left behind. By definition, a furlough is a temporary separation of employment with a potential of recall. Those affected can be assured that any questions related to this process will be addressed by their respective HR representative and leader. Since we have every reason to believe that travel will eventually return to normal, our goal is to bring associates back to the company as quickly as possible.

For those not being furloughed, a decision was made by the leadership of the company to put a temporary freeze on the 401k match program. In addition, senior executives have voluntarily followed my lead and have further reduced their salaries by an additional 20 percent.

Words cannot express the grief and heavy hearts that accompany such a decision. In a company where friendships are so deep, the decisions are even more difficult. It will be natural for furloughed associates to feel a sense of resentment toward the company, and those not affected may find themselves with similar emotions, and that is understandable, as well. The pain this event causes has touched all of us deeply and a piece of our heart breaks with every associate that walks out of our doors. The healing process will not begin until we start returning associates to our family of friends.

There will be many heartbreaking stories of associates who are no longer able to be with us. Single mothers, parents with sick children, associates whose spouses may have received a similar notification earlier in the year from their place of work, and so on. These are legitimate and rational emotions. I would expect no less because all of our associates are kind and caring people.

For eight straight days and nights, leadership has worked assiduously attempting to be as fair as humanly possible. This may come as no consolation to you, and that too is reasonable, but I know in my heart that we did everything possible to avoid this and will do everything possible to rectify it as soon as we can.

We have contacted the White House, Office of Management and Budget, and the Department of Transportation asking that the agency community be included in whatever relief package is made available to the airlines. Senators friendly to the company *have spoken directly to the president's Chief of Staff Andrew Card and Secretary of Transportation Norman Mineta on our behalf. We have contacted members of the House and Senate where we have congressmen and congresswomen knowledgeable of our company and have educated them of the situation our industry faces. We have proposed a plan to the airlines to pass through some of the funds should they receive relief from the government, and we have spoken to David Collins, Chairman of ARC (Airline Reporting Corporation), on how to fairly proportion such funds if they become available.*

We have been contacting clients asking them to support us, as we have supported them, during this very difficult period of time when you have all worked long and hard hours on their behalf without any revenue to offset our costs. The companies we have spoken with to date have been very receptive and understand the temporary predicament facing our company and the agency industry at large.

Today, a temporary dark cloud hangs over a good and compassionate company. A company known for giving, not taking away. A company that has never forgotten that its most important asset is the incredible people that we are honored to call our colleagues. Some companies make decisions like this to improve profitability—we have made this decision so that our people will have a place to return to when times improve.

The company will survive, just as we have through four wars, the Cuban Missile Crisis, and the recession of 1991–93. The world once again faces a global recession and the airline and travel industry have been in one already this year. Talks of airline bankruptcies abound, and flights have been cut back by at least 25 percent by most carriers. This, too, will have a negative effect on the entire travel industry.

Companies need our services now more than ever. Airlines have laid off over one hundred thousand employees and are closing many reservation centers throughout the country. We can only ask that you continue to have faith in our company, serve

*our clients and one another, and know that we are doing every-
thing in our power to bring our friends back home.*

*There are no words that can adequately describe how devas-
tated we feel about the decisions shared with you in this letter.
Nor are there words that will help bring comfort to associates related to those decisions. We can only say that there was no other
choice, we exhausted all options available, and how deeply sorry
and saddened we are.*

God Bless our associates, and God Bless America.

Warmest regards,

Nal

Thursday morning came quicker than any other morning I can remember.

Subconsciously, I hoped we could skip directly from Wednesday to
Saturday, but that was not to be. I arrived at work and shared an elevator with an associate who wished me good luck and told me everything would be okay and to keep my head up. By 8 A.M. associates and
leaders at headquarters began receiving visits to their offices by their
leaders notifying them of their furlough. At 8:30 A.M. the associate I
had earlier shared the elevator with came to my office to say good-bye
and thank you. My heart sunk. Somehow I was able to hold back my
tears and wished her well and thanked her for all her contributions to
our company. Soon there was a steady stream of people appearing at
my office and thanking me for all the great years and telling me how
hard the decision to furlough people must have been for me. Imagine
that, associates who had just lost their jobs were in my office trying to
comfort me. I lost it. I hugged them all, cried, and didn't want them to
leave. Eventually we said good-bye and I promised we would do
everything in our power to get them back soon.

Throughout the rest of the morning I received telephone calls from
chairmen and senior executives of airlines sharing their predicament

with me and looking for actions and suggestions to help get our country flying again. From time to time I'd check the stock market, listen to Alan Greenspan address the Senate Banking Committee, and listen for word of any financial aid the government might be considering for the airline community.

I spent much of the afternoon responding to e-mails of associates furloughed or remaining with the company. The outpouring of support from everyone was heartwrenching. Words of encouragement arrived every five minutes. For a few seconds I would feel strengthened and then another associate would arrive at my door to say goodbye and I'd lose it again. Calls started to come in from large call centers in North Dakota saying leaders wanted to work for free to save their team members. Others with secondary incomes asked that they be furloughed in lieu of those without. Directors phoned me with tears in their voices as they relayed how associates voluntarily gave their jobs to colleagues that they knew were in greater financial need than themselves.

Soon the press started calling wondering if I wanted to comment on rumors that Rosenbluth International was furloughing associates. Television stations wanted to bring their film crews in to interview us on the subject. I was beginning to feel like Silly Putty. I wanted desperately to review our call count to see if telephone traffic was picking up, answer e-mails, and give words of comfort to everyone I could reach out to. But I also realized that the press deserved honest feedback too, even though I was emotionally and physically drained and not up for interviews at this critical time. I spoke with a journalist and was glad I did because a lot of false information was circulating and it gave me the opportunity to set things right.

I hadn't realized that lunch and dinner had come and gone and it was approaching 7:00 P.M. We still had a number of hours before we could make the final decision on the number of associates we needed to furlough the next morning. A group of twelve, led by our senior vice president of North America, was huddled in an office as the numbers rolled in. I sat in awe as they made decisions based on fact, anecdotal information, emotion, and dynamic consensus. It was as if I had been transferred back thousands of years and was sitting amongst the "twelve wise men." In this case however, it was four wise men and eight wise women. The combination of professionalism and compassion made me swell with pride as I watched their decision-making process.

By eight o'clock that night the number of associates in our North America business units and headquarters to be furloughed was determined to be more than five hundred. One call remained; it was in reference to the associates working at our large call centers. I would learn the next morning how many we'd have to furlough. I went home to watch the president address the nation, knowing the number was going to come in around three hundred.

I sat exhausted as President Bush shared with the nation what was to be expected in the months ahead. My thoughts swayed back and forth between listening to his remarks and recounting the events of the day. After the speech was over, patriotism stirred in my heart and anxiety over further reductions in airline traffic screeched through my mind. It took four hours, a pan of brownies, and ten cookies before I finally fell asleep.

The next morning I arrived at work knowing one more list of names was soon to arrive. The stock market was poised to have another dreadful day, adding to the worst one-week point drop in history. I tried to calculate what that meant to travel. Two seconds later I gave up and started to concentrate on preparing a letter to our clients thanking them for their support during these trying times. Next I composed a letter for each of our people who were furloughed, and one to all who remained. Some good news started to trickle in as countries around the world agreed to release letters of credit freeing up some much needed cash. A few of our clients agreed to advance us our management fees for the next month, or two, while others agreed to alter our contractual arrangements. I felt like jumping through the phone lines and hugging each and every one of them since I knew the lengths many of them had gone to internally to get approval to do so.

This was a true testimony to the service and value our people and company have brought to them over the years. It was a remarkable show of partnership on the part of our valued clients.

I sat silent and reflected on how blessed we are with the best associates and clients a company could ever dream of having. Many of our leaders, who had the unfortunate task of delivering the difficult news to associates, did so for the first time in their careers. How difficult it must have been for them. I spent time with our vice president of human resources who recounted to me how, time after time, our people who were furloughed reached out to their leaders to wipe away their tears and wish them luck for the times ahead.

By early afternoon on Friday I received the final number of associates affected at our large Intellicenters in North America. The stories emanating from North Dakota, Kentucky, Delaware, Pennsylvania, and Arizona echoed those of offices and headquarters around the world. One center particularly affected took a group picture to send me along with their thanks. When I heard that I lost my equilibrium and had to sit down. Another center took up a collection for those furloughed to soften the blow until they could be called back. The human emotion shared between associates was a beacon of light in the midst of a storm. A beacon that would form the basis of our new beginning.

On Monday morning I sent out the following letter:

Dear Friend:

A new week is upon us and some of you may see an empty desk or workstation nearby. I share the grief you are experiencing and know that associates and leaders around the world feel the same. The outpouring of love and compassion amongst associates last week was unimaginable.

Leaders asked to be furloughed rather than their people. Associates said, "Take me, I can afford it but my friend can't." Scores of associates volunteered to work for free to save others from furloughs, and we all shed a tear.

Furloughed associates comforted their leaders who broke down as they gave them the bad news. I received e-mails of support, encouragement, and thanks for their time at the company from affected associates, and we all shed a tear.

People volunteered to cut back their time so others could work part-time, leaders voluntarily cut their pay back even further, and we all shed a tear.

What a remarkable group of people we are. What a remarkable group of people we must work hard to bring back. My love and affection for all of you is inestimable. The emotional trauma of last week drained us all and sapped the energy from the bodies of an amazing bunch of associates and leaders.

Today our flower has lost some of its petals; we must move forward without them and grow new ones as the weeks go by. Before the first snow many of the petals will have returned and by springtime a new garden will bloom. We are a different company today, stronger and financially prepared to weather the effects of the insane events of September 11, 2001, but a company that will take time to recover from the emotions of the past week.

The dreams of many have been put on hold; we must stay together, work even harder, so that we can return those dreams quickly to those who have left the company. Sacrifices have been many, but few with complaint. We must try and look forward now, knowing that a new journey has begun and a new industry is forming.

Many airlines and travel companies will be forced to close their doors in the coming weeks. Our prayers should be with them, too. A new paradigm is about to unfold in travel and we will lead it. The outcome, if adopted, will benefit airlines, corporations, and travel management companies, as well.

Our clients have been great through this period of industry crisis and we owe a great debt of gratitude to them. They have sup-

ported us with new contractual arrangements and have kept our associates at the forefront of their minds throughout our discussions. We are truly blessed with compassionate people and clientele. This is not by accident. It has been your dedication to their needs and policy protection that was at the forefront of their decision making to support you and our company during this period of travel uncertainty. They deserve our best, and I know you will deliver it in our customary fashion.

The airlines have just received an aid package from the federal government. I doubt if any was earmarked for us, but that's life and we'll go on. A strong airline industry is critical for our country, our clients, and us. Let's be happy that at least some part of our industry got some aid.

It's time to move forward now. We will create our own breeze behind our sail. Our company is strong, our leadership is steadfast, and you are our strength and inspiration. The future is ours to take; we must walk in lockstep to grab it for our clients, our suppliers, and ourselves.

With all my love and gratitude,

Nat

As the weeks went by travel started to pick up again. It was nowhere near its previous levels, which were dismal to start with, since we had been in an economic slowdown for over a year. But it was a start. Corporate America knew it had to lift itself up and get moving again. The question that remained was how fast? Only time would tell.

Fighting Back

Over the course of the next few weeks bookings began to trickle back. The airlines cut their flights by more than 20 percent and travel became even more inconvenient than it had already been. Security was beefed up at airports and a sense of renewed calm was beginning to set in with the traveling public.

Our leadership and associates continued to work under extreme conditions, which were only exacerbated by the reduction in the number of people at our company. Our senior accountant at Arthur Andersen commented to our CFO that he had never seen a company act as quickly to shore things up and create financial stability as had Rosenbluth International. Once again, a company-wide effort that was quick, decisive, and emotionally painful. Speed, emotion, and trust ruled the day. E-mails continued to trickle in from furloughed associates wishing us well and expressing gratitude for the times at our company. We still consider our friends part of the company so we decided that all company correspondence to associates would continue to be e-mailed to them, as well. Our human resources organization was quick to get everyone's home e-mail addresses loaded into our system.

Our officer group continued to work quickly and quietly on scenario planning to see if there were opportunities that our company could take advantage of during this period of industry chaos and confusion. A few thoughts came to mind and discussions with our investment banking firm were held to gain their insight and input.

As the days went on I became a bit peeved that the agency community was providing 80 percent of all the reservations and ticket fulfillment for the airlines and was for all intents and purposes providing an outsource of these functions to the airlines at almost no cost. The agency industry was, in fact, the only viable distribution channel for the airlines and while they received federal aid, none was passed through to those of us providing these services for them.

It was obvious to me that it didn't matter if the airlines had cash, fuel, planes, or runways at their disposal. If they had no process for people to make reservations, the airlines industry would come to a halt. By this point many airlines had laid off a good percentage of their workforce and had closed innumerable reservations centers. The agency industry employs three hundred thousand skilled reservationists, who handle 80 percent of all airline bookings. Without them travel would gridlock, as corporations would have no viable outlet to handle reservations, information, and ticketing. We service the three largest banks in the world, numerous Wall Street brokerage houses, the largest technology, pharmaceutical, and manufacturing companies in the world, as well as many other corporations critical to commerce. I was beginning to imagine what it would be like for them if they couldn't conduct business as a result of airlines being grounded with no outlet for reservations and tickets. I decided it was time to go to Washington, D.C., and stand up for our industry and its importance.

I arrived on Capitol Hill at 9:15 A.M. and returned to Philadelphia nine hours later. I visited privately with fifteen United States senators, three congressmen, and the Chaplain of the Senate. Three weeks earlier I would have skipped the senators and congressmen and spent the whole day with the Chaplain figuring that an act of God would be better than an act of Congress. However, on that day I felt invigorated, impassioned, and enthusiastic about my mission. As close as Washington is to Philadelphia, the only times I had been there in years was for the Million Mom March and my daughter Jessica's soccer tournament.

Little did I know how much walking I was going to do that day. Worse yet, I was wearing tied shoes for the first time in three years, since my dog Dexter had recently eaten the tassel off one of my loafers. By three in the afternoon my heels were bleeding, since for some reason, my feet had gained one size since I had last worn these shoes a year earlier. I spent the majority of my time with each congressional member and their respective staffs educating them on the importance of the industry rather than our company's interests. It wasn't that our industry doesn't have a representative association. It does, but it just seemed like no one else besides them was articulating the value proposition of the agency world to Congress. Someone needed to step forward and take charge. I left Washington with bleeding feet, while hoping that Congress had a bleeding heart. I was confident that was the case, as each senator and congressman I met with was very supportive of my suggestions and asked that I provide them with statistics and processes that would be helpful in crafting legislation. I made a few calls to ASTA, our industry trade association, to make certain that our efforts were aligned as we moved forward.

The next morning I received the first rough draft of a senate bill resulting from my visit. It was an exhilarating experience to see how quickly things can move when the private and public sector fully understand issues critical to our nation and are prepared to work together in our nation's best interest. By noon I had received another call from Washington, from a different legislator, looking at constructing a similar bill, but with a few changes. Things were moving, but it was becoming apparent that the White House was going to try to take over the legislation, and speed was of the essence. My colleagues and I worked quickly to craft remarks, which urgently needed to be faxed to the Senate. Within hours our letter was on its way to Washington.

I went home that night feeling rejuvenated as a new report from our finance department showed that our cash position had improved dramatically and that airline bookings were up a few points over the previous few days. I chomped down a cheese steak, or two, watched Barry Bonds hit his seventieth homer, and fell asleep.

Friday morning arrived with news that an individual in Florida had contracted anthrax. Some news outlets were reporting it as an epidemic while others said it was only that one individual. I prayed for the person's recovery and that it be an isolated incident. As the day went on airlines began to announce fare sales to stimulate traffic and state governments began deploying National Guard troops to help with airport security. I was glad to see those actions take place.

We held another officer meeting to review how the company was performing and to go over any additional steps and strategies we needed to put in place. It was a pleasant meeting and spirits were rising as each executive reported on their respective areas of responsibility. The best news was that we had begun to bring back quite a few furloughed associates, and if transaction trends kept climbing we could continue the process of bringing more people back home.

By mid-afternoon I began thinking about my oldest son Jeffrey's homecoming football game that night, that he was their quarterback, and the fact that he was playing with a broken finger on his left hand and a cartilage tear in his right shoulder. I gleaned additional strength and inspiration from the leadership he was exhibiting by not succumbing to pain, but rather gutting it out so as to not let his team or school down. I hoped I was doing as well leading our company through similar tough times. One thing I knew for sure, we were both surrounded by the best teammates one could ever wish for. The phone rang; it was the Senate Commerce Committee inviting me to come testify the following Friday on behalf of our industry at their sub-committee hearings. My thoughts returned to my son Jeff knowing that neither of us could afford to fumble the ball this Friday, or next.

The Recovery

By Thursday morning I was putting the finishing touches on the written testimony I was going to present to the Senate. It was required in their respective offices prior to my oral testimony the next morning so I was working at breakneck speed. We have neither a government affairs office nor any lobbyists that work on our behalf. The task of gathering information and statistics and the preparation of my remarks fell on me and our manager of corporate communications. Neither of us had any experience in this area so while my colleague worked diligently to familiarize herself on the procedures and nuances of Congress, I tuned into NBC's *The West Wing* television series to get a better understanding of the goings-on in Washington.

Business was picking up slowly and the results of recalibrating our company to a softer demand for air travel had put us in good shape barring any further incidents. I now found myself going to Washington to fight on behalf of our industry, which was still reeling from the after-effects of September 11, 2001. It was my job to help get twenty-nine thousand travel agencies back on their feet and to help save hundreds of thousands of jobs. The magnitude of the situation was just beginning to hit me.

My wife Renee and I arrived in Washington the night before my testimony and spent the evening at the CNBC studio as guests of our friend Chris Matthews. We sat in on a segment of *Hardball with Chris Matthews*, three hours after the Justice Department had issued a warning that a terrorist attack was imminent within a few days, and the chances of it happening were 100 percent. One of Chris' guests that evening was an expert on anthrax, which had just broken out in Florida. Little did I know that it was just the beginning of a very emotional four days. After his show, the president held a news conference to try and explain the reasons for the Justice Department warning and to try and calm down the citizens of America as much as possible. We watched the news conference together and then he held an impromptu special with Margaret Carlson of *Time* magazine and David Gergen of *U.S. News & World Report*. Chris asked them each what they felt would be the response of the American people to the latest scare. Both said they felt everyone would be staying close to home. During a break Chris looked over to me and I said, "Well, there go a thousand more cancellations." Sure enough, our statistics the next day proved that out.

We left the studios and headed for the hotel to get some rest before testifying the next morning. Since it was now ten at night and we hadn't eaten since noon, Renee wanted to grab a bite to eat when we arrived at the hotel. I was debating between a vodka martini, a whisky and coke, red or white wine, or simply three shots of anything the bartender felt inclined to push my way.

We went to sleep watching one network after another replay the warnings of imminent terrorist attacks on America. All the news began to blend together into a haze of similar information and I fell asleep with the remote control firmly imbedded in my hand.

Morning came early and we headed for Capitol Hill. I felt calm and collected and ready for anything any senator could throw my way. At 9:25 A.M. we entered the hearing room and took our seats. Senator Hillary Clinton testified first on the plight of New York and encouraged everyone to visit her home state. Bill Marriott went next and educated everyone on the state of the hotel industry and encouraged Congress to pass a stimulus bill that would get people traveling again.

I was up next and the heat of the camera lights was beginning to take its toll on me. The last thing I needed was to present my testimony while creating a moat around me from excessive perspiration. Somehow I got through my oral testimony while remaining remarkably dry. I spelled out the critical role the agency community played as the airlines' distribution system. I went on to say that without it the airlines would again be grounded and looking for further government aid to establish a distribution system because they are dependent on agencies as their primary distribution channel. I explained that the airlines had just laid off over a hundred thousand people, closed scores of reservation centers, and that there was simply no other infrastructure for corporations and the public to make reservations and receive tickets.

At the behest of the American Society of Travel Agents, I asked the Senate for a $364 million grant, as well as my original request for government-backed loan guarantees, which I felt were key for most agencies to survive. Following the testimony of three other industry experts representing the car rental, cruise industry, and hotel workers union, it came time for the senators to ask questions. The first, Senator Fitzgerald from Illinois, looked me square in the eye and proclaimed that he was the only dissenting vote on the airline relief package and recounted how he knew it wouldn't end there. He proclaimed that the airlines had mounted a huge lobbying effort and that the result of the airline bail-out program was just going to benefit the shareholders of the airlines as well as the executives running them.

I felt like jumping across the witness table and tackling the dude. I held my cool and waited for the proper moment to respond. Ten minutes later I got my chance and made an impassioned plea for everyone to understand that it didn't matter if the airlines got their package, which I agreed they should, if there wasn't a means for the public to make reservations and receive tickets. The government program would be for naught. I mentioned that our industry had only one lobbyist, that all but two agencies were privately held family businesses and didn't have shareholders, and that I was a rookie on Capitol Hill representing thirty thousand agencies. I went on to state that without an immediate infusion of cash, most agencies would not survive the end of the year. I explained that if that were the case, the airlines lacking a means to distribute their services would be grounded, and corporate America would be severely limited in its ability to conduct business. Commerce in America would fall prey to the terrorist attacks of September 11, 2001.

Fortunately, Senator Fitzgerald appeared to be in the minority. I felt confident that I gave it my best shot and had gained a tremendous amount of support in Congress during that week. Final legislation was going to be crafted starting on Monday, so Renee and I left for Pennsylvania Station to head back to Philadelphia, for what I thought would be a relaxing two days.

I left the house Sunday afternoon to watch my daughter's soccer game and then headed to the airport with my executive assistant for a flight to San Francisco to visit clients and associates. Before leaving I received a call that Levi Jangula, the son of two of our associates from Linton, North Dakota, had contracted meningitis and was in the hospital in Bismarck. I called the hospital only to find out that his lungs had collapsed, his heart was failing, and that things were looking grim. I told Levi's mom to get an air ambulance to take him to Fargo, Minneapolis, or Rochester, Minnesota, if she felt they couldn't perform the necessary treatments in Bismarck. I promised to call from the airport to check in. When I called I found out that he was to be airlifted to Rochester, Minnesota.

We immediately canceled our flight to San Francisco and headed for St. Mary's Hospital in Rochester. My assistant jumped into action coordinating flight options with our twenty-four hour en-route service while I scurried around the airport looking for any flights headed to Minneapolis or Chicago. We were now beginning to become prey to the events of the past few weeks. Airlines had cut their service dramatically and all flights to both cities were sold out. If we took a later flight we would be stuck in either Minneapolis or Chicago since the last bank of flights to Rochester had fallen victim to the cutbacks.

We were able to outsmart the system and got two seats to Rochester through Chicago, but now we had the problem of having to go to the ticket counter, which was swarmed by hundreds of people, in order to purchase tickets from a new airline. The security lines were now taking fifteen minutes to get through and the flight to Chicago was in twenty minutes.

Quick thinking on my assistant's part prompted us to go to the American Airlines Admiral Club where they were able to accommodate us and help us with our arrangements. A new problem arose as the flight to Chicago was delayed an hour and a half and we would have three minutes to connect to the Rochester flight once we arrived. We were scheduled to be twelve gates apart, but my assistant is an adept sprinter, so our plan was for her to run to the connecting flight while I carried all four bags like a pack mule. If we missed it we were prepared to drive from Chicago to Rochester. We made the flight with thirty seconds to spare.

I couldn't get the image of Levi Jangula off my mind. Levi is the son of Sharon and Larry Jangula. Sharon was the first person we had ever hired in North Dakota. They live on a farm ten miles from the small town of Linton, population 1,000. Larry not only works his farm but also works out at The Rivery, our executive retreat on the banks of the Missouri River. Sharon, after opening our data center in Linton back in 1988, had since moved on to manage The Rivery, where she and Larry drive seventy miles round-trip each day to work. I've known Levi since he was nine years old and have watched him grow from a child to an adult. My heart was pumping with anxiety and adrenaline on the way to Rochester. I prayed that his would be pumping by the time we got there, as well.

We arrived at the hospital at 10:30 on Sunday night. In the waiting room his aunt told us that he was at risk of a heart attack at any time, but they had him resting and were administering antibiotics and other fluids, while pumping air into his lungs. I worried about how Larry and Sharon would be as I walked toward Levi's room. Sharon had flown on the air ambulance with Levi while Larry drove nine hours to leave room for the paramedics on board the flight.

I was happy to enter Levi's room but was concerned with what I saw. Levi had more wires and cables wrapped around him than you'd find in a computer room. He had sophisticated monitors checking every vital sign and bells were ringing every two minutes indicating that something was not quite right. Sharon and Larry were hanging over his bed trying to comfort him as much as possible. They had told him he was going to have heart surgery in two days to repair or replace a valve once the infection was in check. The doctor also conveyed to everyone that if he deteriorated dramatically before that, they would go in and perform the surgery on an emergency basis.

My heart went out to the family while it slowly sank into my stomach. Here was a twenty-year-old stud grasping for his life, while at the same time appearing as if he had just left his mother's womb. It was a surreal scene. He looked so helpless; his parents kept touching him, giving him cold compresses and ice chips while trying to get apple juice into him through a straw. It was as touching as it was chilling.

I loved the Jangula family and couldn't get them off my mind as I headed back to the hotel for the night. After reaching my room I turned on the news to see what had happened during the day and then did something I hadn't done for weeks. I turned it right off. Life had been brought back into perspective at the hospital. That night I wasn't interested in the Taliban, anthrax, or airline load factors. Watching the love of parents for their son, trying to instill him with hope while knowing they were going through the ultimate anguish of being able to do little more than placing their son at the mercy of a medical staff and their faith in God. It was a scene that will indelibly be at the forefront of my mind for years to come.

The next morning we arrived back at the hospital and entered the room just as the heart surgeon was explaining that he didn't want to wait any longer and was going to perform heart surgery within twenty-four hours. The infection in his heart had eaten away at the muscle surrounding it, the most crucial valve had burst and was not functioning, and they didn't have time to wait for the infection to leave his kidneys and liver. Then came the part I knew the doctor had to convey. Levi's chance of not surviving surgery was 10–15 percent. His chance of living without the surgery was zero. Once again, my heart found itself conjoined with my stomach and I thought I was going to be sick.

I took care of Sharon and Larry's hotel expenses for their stay in Rochester and recognized I could be of little further help, so we headed to the airport for the flight back to Philadelphia. I spoke to my wife and told her about the chances Levi was given and she helped me to feel better saying that it could have been fifty-fifty, and that would be a lot worse. I've seen a lot of people do some pretty interesting things with statistics, but these were plain and simple. Renee's words of encouragement brought some color back into my face.

The ride to the airport took fifteen minutes. While waiting for the flight I called Senator Dorgan, my friend and the chair of the hearings, and he told me that he felt my testimony had gone well, but that there wasn't much of an appetite in Congress for grants, so he was working on a loan package, which he felt had a better chance. We agreed to stay in touch over the next few days. My next call went to Senator Conrad's office where they were working closely with Senator Inouye to get legislation out as fast as possible. By now I was beginning to settle back into the routine of work and was waxing and waning between exhilaration and exhaustion. I picked up *The Wall Street Journal* at the airport only to read the headline in Section C outlining how banks were not touching anything with a travel tag attached to it. Now the loans for the industry were more important than ever.

I called the office and was made aware of massive schedule changes taking place at major carriers. The carriers asked us to notify all passengers affected, since they didn't have the resources to do it themselves. More work; no pay. If only Congress could really see how the industry truly worked. Airlines get the bailouts and send the work and costs to the agency community. Now I was beginning to make the emotional transition from acting on behalf of an industry in need, to sheer anger and disgust. I knew I had to funnel those emotions in a positive direction making me even more bold and passionate about getting the government to help the agency community.

Levi Jangula was in the operating room for nine hours as he underwent open-heart surgery. I spoke to his mother Sharon while she and Larry awaited his return from surgery. They had just heard from the doctor that the surgery went well and that they were able to repair his heart rather than inserting a new valve. While he certainly was not out of danger he had passed the first hurdle in fine shape. I fell asleep knowing that at least one member of the company family was on the road to recovery.

The next morning we held a meeting of the executive team of Rosenbluth International to review our current financial status and what it looked like going forward. Business was improving as more people took to the skies. That, coupled with the actions we had taken five weeks earlier, proved that we were continuing to make progress, and in fact, were well ahead of post-September 11, 2001, projections. During the meeting I received a call from Senator Dorgan's office informing me that legislation was going to be introduced later in the day, and that it would contain the loan grant guarantees I was pushing for.

Leaving no stone unturned I agreed to appear that evening on CNN's *Moneyline* with Lou Dobbs, to further my message that without a vibrant agency community, airlines would be grounded and commerce in the United States would take another direct hit. By now I had met with *The New York Times*, *The Wall Street Journal*, and the Associated Press to provide them with background on the subject.

On the way to work the next morning, I called St. Mary's Hospital in Rochester, Minnesota, to check on Levi's condition. Levi continued to recover but like most situations he had a setback, or two. His heart, lungs, liver, and other vital organs were functioning well, but the infection had not left his shoulders, knees, or other joints, and another operation was needed to address that. It would take place later in the day.

I was beginning to believe that Levi's recovery and that of the travel industry were on a parallel course as the House and Senate were evacuated due to an anthrax attack. Our bill would probably be delayed until Congress returned the following week. I called the American Society of Travel Agents to give them an update on where things stood and promised to inform them on events as they unfolded.

I held a meeting with our president, along with our chief financial officer, to project the final three months of the year. It was an upbeat meeting as it became apparent that we were not only out of the woods, but we were financially as strong as ever and poised to bust out in 2002. I made the decision that effective January 1, 2002, all pay cuts would be rescinded around the world and that as business began to pick up we would recall as many associates as possible. In fact, we had already been able to recall more than one hundred people. As they returned to work they were greeted by the following letter:

Dear Friend:

I can't begin to tell you how happy we all are that you have returned to our company. Your friends have missed you and they join me in my delight at welcoming you back. I can only begin to imagine how difficult it must have been for you during your absence and I know it gives your fellow associates great joy to see you back with us all.

Your friends have worked especially hard while you were away, but I know in their hearts it was with the knowledge that their hard work would hopefully make it possible for you to return at the earliest possible moment. We are focused on moving forward as a Company, and your return takes us another step in that direction.

Welcome back!

Nal

The Senate remained in session although all of their offices had been evacuated. I received another fax copy of the draft legislation from Washington but had a tough time getting in touch with anyone to go over it. I knew they wanted to get it introduced to the full Senate that day and was anxious to comment on it to make certain that all travel agencies got a fair shake. There was nothing more to do than wait.

I spoke to Levi's mom and she went over the procedures for his surgery, which was to take place at 11:00 A.M. It was the last step needed for his full recovery. I was hoping to receive a call by the time he was out of surgery that our bill was ready to head to the president so that a full recovery for our industry was under way, as well.

I received the call at 10:45 A.M. Following our discussion I was informed that since everyone in Congress was working from home or makeshift offices somewhere in Washington, the bill could not be completed until Monday. I was now confident that I had done all that was possible for our industry and that the proposed legislation would be positively received by our government.

The following week, *The American Travel Industry Stabilization Act*, S.R. 1578, was introduced to Congress. I left work that day knowing that Rosenbluth International had recovered, Levi was on his way to recovery, and that by next week the travel industry would be on the road to recovery, as well.

As the weeks passed, Levi returned home following his surgery and was well on his way to becoming the stud he previously was. Rosenbluth International remarkably turned a profit for the quarter, and subsequently for the remainder of the year. Swissair and Sabena Airlines, National and Alamo rental car agencies filed for bankruptcy, an American Airlines flight went down in New York City, airline analysts were taking odds on which U.S. carriers would fail first, and our Senate bill was stalled in Congress as partisanship ruled the day.

I will never forget the year 2001. It was a year of laughter and pain, loss and sorrow, tears and tranquility. If Noah Webster were still alive he'd have to rewrite the definition of *normal*. I wrote one last letter to associates in an attempt to bring events into perspective.

Dear Friend:

*It has been about four weeks since I last formally communi-
cated with you. A lot has happened in that time frame, and I
wanted to share with you my perspective on the industry, the
company, and some preliminary decisions we have made as a result of the above.*

*It should come as no surprise that all sectors of the travel in-
dustry continue to be extremely weak. This is a direct result of the
effects of September 11, 2001, and a weakening world economy.
The United States has slipped into a recession and Europe is not
far behind. Asia has yet to rebound from a depressed economy
that has lasted years. On top of all this, the United States and the
United Kingdom are at war with the Taliban and Al Qaeda
forces in Afghanistan, and other countries in which Rosenbluth
International has offices are part of the coalition against worldwide terrorism.*

*All of this has resulted in an unprecedented decline in world-
wide travel. If someone were to paint a worst-case scenario for the
travel industry, it would look like the world today. This of course
is the landscape upon which we must compete, but it is also the
landscape upon which we plan to prosper. Your leadership has
undertaken a number of initiatives to strengthen our company
during these difficult times, rather than fall prey to them.*

*We have taken a leadership role in government and in reshap-
ing the broken airline distribution system worldwide. We have
initiated a four-part public series on what is wrong with the industry and how to fix it. We have our own house in order and
now it is time to help our neighbors fix theirs. Whether they are
accepting of our help is yet to be seen, however, some company
needs to take a leadership role in travel and tell it like it is, and
we have decided that company is Rosenbluth International.*

*As to our own company strategies, we have continued to see
growth in Up-Stream, the outsource customer services arm of*

Rosenbluth International, and we recently launched eCLIPSE, an e-procurement division targeting the travel industry as a whole. Our core business of travel management continues to win new business and our pipeline for new sales is strong and growing stronger by the day.

Unfortunately, transactions continue to be down from a year ago and international bookings are far below anyone's expectations. If you simply look at the difficulties of carriers that fly the Atlantic and Pacific you can see just how bad things are. It is the consensus of most that traffic won't pick up from current levels for at least nine months and may take up to eighteen to get back to 2000 levels. I attribute 25 percent of this to fear of flying and 75 percent to worldwide economic conditions. It is estimated that 9 million people worldwide will lose their jobs in the travel industry in 2002.

While the macro view is somewhat dismal, every day I become more and more confident that our path forward is the right one. We have recalibrated our company to be effective in this new environment and, at the moment and barring any unforeseen future incidents, we are comfortable with our cost structure. Last week I attended a meeting with one hundred of the country's top CEOs. Many of the most admired (Michael Dell, CEO of Dell Computers; Charles Holliday, Chairman and CEO of Du Pont; and Richard Brown, Chairman of the Board and CEO of EDS) laid out actions that others should immediately take to respond to the economic crisis we are now in. I am pleased to say that we had already completed each of the suggested actions months ago, far in advance of the most admired companies in America.

Along that line, technology investments and process reengineering will continue to be made in areas that benefit our company and client productivity, making life easier for all. We will also invest in areas of technology surrounding new global security initiatives for our clients, enhancing our global warehouse and global reporting tools, our web portal and global data network. It is times like this that strong companies move forward and create order out of chaos and instill competitive advantages for themselves and their clientele. The results of these investments will improve margins, decrease client costs, add more value to our offerings, and ultimately find its way into better remuneration for you, our associates.

I am extremely happy to announce that we have successfully brought more than two hundred furloughed associates back home and look to continue to do so as demand for our services picks up. I am also pleased to announce that unless something else dramatic befalls our industry in the upcoming six weeks, that effective January 2002, we plan to reinstate salaries to levels prior to September 2001. While these are the intentions of the senior management of our company, we can only effect what is within our control.

I felt it appropriate to communicate our decision as quickly as possible, and yet I must caution everyone again, that there still remains too much uncertainty in the marketplace to make this an absolute promise. As we near the end of the year, the marketplace will have as much to say about our compensation decisions, as will the officers of Rosenbluth International.

To the best of my knowledge, we will be the first company in travel to embark on returning salaries to previous levels. This is a highly risky decision in light of the ongoing "high state of alert" announcements that seem to come every two weeks. However, I wanted all of you to know what our current thinking is. While my hope is that things will remain stable, I must point out again that if conditions deteriorate for any reason I may have to rescind this decision, but I have no intention of doing so at this time.

All of you have been extremely diligent in your work and our company is grateful to you. We now live in an abnormal world, both emotionally and economically. Rosenbluth International will continue to do all possible to bring back some normalcy to your life, although I must admit I no longer know the definition of normal.

Feel free to e-mail me your thoughts at hrosenbluth@rosen bluth.com.

Kindest regards,

The year 2001 turned out to be another profitable year as we made more money than all the world's airlines combined (although that's not saying much). Our people were returning home to work, and our business was growing throughout the world.

As we entered 2002 we happily reinstated salary levels back to pre-9/11 levels and had recalled over 70 percent of furloughed associates. Through anonymous monetary gifts from our senior leadership, we were able to lessen the burden of those on furlough that had come under extreme financial burden. The company was back in the saddle again and financially stronger than at any time in our 110 year history. Had it not been for the culture of our company and the relentless hard work of our people, this would not have been the case.

The company continued to pick up speed throughout the year. We signed a joint venture agreement in Beijing making Rosenbluth International one of the largest travel companies in China with offices in twenty-seven provinces and fifty-one cities. Up-Stream, the customer relationship management division of Rosenbluth International, signed a joint venture agreement with a company from India, placing us firmly in the worldwide call center management business with entrée into the financial services arena. eCLIPSE got off to a roaring start as our new e-procurement line of business was positively accepted by our clients, suppliers, and competitors alike.

Eight months have passed since I first started this chapter. It has been the most exhilarating business period of my life. I couldn't have led our company through these tumultuous times without the comfort, care, resilience, and concern of our entire associate and leadership base. Our clients have seen us give it our all and our people have taken pleasure in doing so. I will once again attempt to submit this book to HarperCollins and hope that there isn't an unforeseen world event around the corner requiring me to stop the presses and return to write this chapter yet again.

Exciting times lie ahead for Rosenbluth International. Our industry is about to change, and we are the ones leading it.

Notes

Chapter 2, page 10. Nancy K. Austin, "Wacky Management Ideas That Work," *Working Woman*, November 1991.

Chapter 3, page 33. Hal F. Rosenbluth and Diane McFerrin Peters, *Care to Compete?*, Reading, Mass.: Perseus Books, 1998.

Chapter 5, pages 80–82. Hal F. Rosenbluth and Diane McFerrin Peters, *Care to Compete?*, Reading, Mass.: Perseus Books, 1998.

Chapter 6, page 103. Richard Borden, *Public Speaking as Listeners Like It!*, New York: Harper & Brothers, 1935.

Chapter 6, page 104. Robert Frost, "The Road Not Taken," in *Mountain Interval*, New York: Henry Holt & Company, 1916.

Chapter 7, page 116. Adapted and reprinted by permission from *The American Heritage Dictionary of the English Language*, copyright © 1981 by Houghton Mifflin Company.

Chapter 8, page 132. Excerpt from *The Little Prince* by Antoine de Saint-Exupéry, copyright © 1971 by Harcourt Brace Jovanovich, Inc., reprinted by permission of the author.

Chapter 8, page 133. Michael Hammer, "Reengineering Work: Don't Automate, Obliterate," *Harvard Business Review*, July–August 1990.

Chapter 10, page 157. Tom Peters, *On Achieving Excellence*, copyright © 1988 by TPG Communications. All rights reserved. Reprinted with permission.

Bibliography

Arnold, Thurman. *Fair Fights and Foul: A Dissenting Lawyer's Life.* Orlando, Fla.: Harcourt Brace Jovanovich, 1965.

Austin, Nancy K. "Wacky Management Ideas That Work," *Working Woman*, November 1991.

Bartlett, John. *Bartlett's Familiar Quotations.* Boston: Little, Brown and Company, 1980.

Borden, Richard. *Speaking as Listeners Like It!* New York: Harper & Brothers, 1935.

Fadiman, Clifton. *The Little, Brown Book of Anecdotes.* Boston: Little, Brown and Company, 1985.

Frost, Robert. "The Road Not Taken," in *Mountain Interval.* New York: Henry Holt & Company, 1916.

Hammer, Michael. "Reengineering Work: Don't Automate, Obliterate." *Harvard Business Review*, July–August 1990.

Lipman, David. *Maybe I'll Pitch Forever.* New York: Bantam, Doubleday, Dell, 1961.

Packer, Arnold, and William Johnston. *Workforce 2000.* Indianapolis, Ind.: Hudson Institute, 1987.

Peters, Tom. *On Achieving Excellence.* Palo Alto, Calif.: TPG Communications, December 1988.

Rosenbluth, Hal, and Diane McFerrin Peters. *Care to Compete?* Reading, Mass.: Perseus Books, 1998.

Saint-Exupéry, Antoine de. *The Little Prince.* Orlando, Fla.: Harcourt Brace Jovanovich, 1971.

Index

AAP (Associate Assistance
    Program), 19
accessibility, 10–11, 189, 204–6
accordion-style management,
    140–43
account, loss of, 184–93
    effects on company morale of,
        185
    as humbling experience, 185
    and importance of forecasting,
        186–88
    ripple effects of, 185–86, 223
    strategy for dealing with, 184–85
    transition plan for, 185
    unorthodox approach to, 188
accountability, 135
adaptability, 48
advancement, routes to, 129–30
afternoon tea, 4–5
Agency Incentive Management
    (AIM), 179
agentless booking, 198
airline industry:
    airline subsidies and control in,
        151–52
    back-room systems in, 151–53
    commissions in, 197
    compensation structure in, 197
    deregulation of, xiii, 147–49
    federal relief package for, 239–40,
        246, 247–48, 256
    front-room systems in, 151
    group travel rates in, 168

lowest fares in, 167, 197
on-line booking system in, 158
reservation center for, 149
reservations process in, 160–62,
    214
security issues in, 249, 261
and September 11 attacks, 230,
    231–34, 236, 238–41, 246–48,
    250, 252, 259, 260–61
slumps in, 185–86
travel as product of, 196
Ambassador's Council, 13–14
American Society of Travel Agents,
    252
Amtrak creativity train, 116
applicants, attracting, 36–38
Arnold, Bill, 10–11
arrogance, annihilation of, 49–50
art, 74, 78–82
Ask Us Anything, 13, 15–17
assessment, 32–33
    Engagement Study, 44–45
    in exit interviews, 45–46
    feedback in, 137
    of happiness, 13–14
    in hiring process, 41–42
    Leader Review by Direct Reports,
        134–36
    performance appraisals, 131
    of quality, 89–91
    of retention rates, 43–46
    30–60–90 day review, 44, 45–46
assignments, short-term, 112

Associate Appreciation Month, 37, 109–10
Associate Assistance Program (AAP), 19
Associate of the Day, 11–12
Associate Opinion Poll, 15
Associate Referral Program, 37
associates:
    Ask Us Anything, 15–17
    assessment of, 32–33
    building confidence in, 143
    customer care (CCA), 34–35
    diverse backgrounds of, 38–40
    drawings by, 7–8
    familiarization trips for, 21–22
    furloughs of, 20
    jeans days for, 21
    lifestyles of, 17–18
    Operation SAFE for, 19–20
    orientation of, 3–6, 64
    promotion from within, 37–38, 142
    retention of, 42–43
    selection, 31–36
    suggestions from, 16
    tea served to, 4–5
    use of term, 99, 101
    watching contributions of, 130–31
    see also people
@Rosenbluth, 158, 159, 198
attitude, 74, 75–78, 98, 99, 101
attrition, natural, 136
audits, third-party, 91
August, as Associate Appreciation Month, 109–10
Austin, Nancy, 10–11
automated quality assurance, 166–68
Automation Lab, 174
automation services, 205

backgrounds, diversity of, 38–40
back-room systems, 151–53, 168–81

Bahrain, Kanoo Travel in, 81–82
Baldrige Award, 85
Beanie Baby salmons, 104–5
benchmarking, 204
Biztravel.com, 40–41, 92–94, 196
Biztravel Guarantee, 92
blazing new trails, 223
"blue teams" (focus groups), 139–40
bottom line, 101–2
Brandeis, Louis, 126
Bravo Zulu (Federal Express recognition program), 109
Brown, Richard, 261
"buck stops with me," 98
budgets, cuts in, 140–41
bureaucracy, ideas stifled in, 117–18
Bush, George W., 243, 251
busied in/busied out, 76–78
"Business and Financial Training" program, 61–62
business casual, 21
business development, 204, 205
business model, zero-based, 132
business units, changes in, 133

cafeteria, 105
Campbellsville, Kentucky, 214, 215–16
Card, Andrew, 240
Career Enhancement Guide (CEG), 35
Carlson, Margaret, 251
Carlyle, Thomas, 97
Carnegie, Andrew, 56
Casa de Botín, Madrid, 117
Centennial Medical Center, Nashville, 10–11
change:
    adaptability for, 48
    in corporate culture, xi–xv, 133
    inventing the future, 145, 222–23
    learning through, 66–68
    mental flexibility for, 47

and movement, 137–38
turning points of, xiv–xv, 150, 264
chat, on-line, 164
Chevron, in Kuwait, 81–82
China, Rosenbluth presence in, 263
Chutes and Ladders, 111, 129–30
clients:
    automated quality assurance for, 167
    bringing into the kitchen, 201
    capturing information for reports to, 161
    commissions from, 197
    company travel policies of, 161, 167
    as connoisseurs, 203–4
    growth driven by, 123–24, 150
    information provided to, 163, 165, 167, 198
    integrating information systems with, 170–71
    mobile, 175
    as our best salespeople, 206
    partnerships with, see partnerships
    reporting tools for, 161, 162
    September 11 support from, 243–44, 245–46
    service contracts with, 197
    supporting our own, 199
    understanding, 100–101
    vantage point of, 187
    welcome to, 200–201
Clinton, Hillary, 251–52
coaching, 65–66
code of ethics, 103–4
cohesiveness, 138–39
Coleridge, Samuel Taylor, 21
Collins, David, 240
commissions, 197
commitment, 101

communication:
    Ask Us Anything, 15–17
    in company-wide meetings, 111–12
    of corporate culture, 102
    e-mail, 17
    feedback, 15–17
    Internet platform for, 162
    methods of, 189
    open, 187
    Quick Connections, 17
    in retention, 43
    on September 11 events, 229, 232
    sharing ideas, 126
    telephone, 99, 108
    The Source for, 204–6
    Town Hall Meetings, 16–17
    voicemail, 15, 204–5
communities, rural, see rural communities
community:
    local and cultural variances in, 155
    service to, 120
    social responsibility in, 120
company-wide meetings, 111–12
compartments, dismantling, 138–39, 142
compensation structure, 197, 262
competency profiles, 35
compliance, 205
confidence, building, 100, 143
Confucius, 76
conscience, social responsibility, 120
consistency, 103–4
continuous improvement, 85
Continuum, The, 106, 174, 201–2
control, of information, 152
core competencies, 35
core markets, identification of, 155
corporate colors, 98

corporate culture, 97–114, 222
  Associate Appreciation Month,
    109–10
  bottom line for, 101–2
  capturing of, 98–99
  change in, xi–xv, 133
  communicating, 102
  company mascot, 98, 104–5
  in company-wide meetings,
    111–12
  elegant service as, 99
  entrepreneurial, 133
  fun in, 106–8
  global professional development
    plan, 112
  inverted pyramid in, 98
  open, 48
  pentimento in, 100–101
  people at forefront of, 97
  personality of, 105
  recognition programs, 109
  Service Day, 113
  sincerity in, 100, 103–4
  summary, 113–14
  unique environment for, 105–6
  Volunteer Days, 110
Corporate Leadership Council, 44
corporate library, 105
corporate marriage, 170, 202–3
corporate mascot, 98, 104–5
*Corporate Operations Standards
  Manual*, 61
corporate travel:
  consolidated nationwide, 150
  as controllable expense, 148
  cutbacks in, 140–41, 232
  deregulation effects on, 148
  global portal of, 174–75
  reservation center for, 149
  Rosenbluth as pioneers in,
    xiii–xiv, xvi, 148
cost analysis, 204
cost-saving ideas, 143
Coursey, Paula, 229

creativity:
  discontinuous thinking, 133
  environment for, 116–19
  epicenters of thought, 155
  freedom for, 176–77
  and ideas, *see* ideas
  in problem solving, 123–24
  setting the stage for, 105–6
  in system design, 121
creativity train, 116
credit card reconciliation, 170, 171
critical decisions, 156
critical mass, 150
criticism, constructive, 135
cross-pollination, 139–40, 142
culture, *see* corporate culture
curiosity, ideas resulting from, 116
customer care associates (CCAs),
  34–35
  Performance Incentive Plan for,
    88–89
  in rural communities, 209–11
  training programs for, 64–65
  see also associates
customer relationship management
  (CRM) tools, 163–64
  DACODA, 177–78, 204
  Up-Stream, 189–90, 198
customer service:
  in Intellicenters, 89
  in rural communities, 214
customization, 159
Custom-Res point-of-sale software,
  121, 161, 166
cutbacks:
  budget, 140–41
  ripple effects of, 185–86
  and sales efforts, 141–42

DACODA, 177–78, 204
  and @Rosenbluth, 178, 198
  and agentless booking, 198
  and eCLIPSE, 178–79
  and mytravelbid.com, 122

Darrow, Clarence, 212–13
data, mining, 169
data entry assignments, 210, 214
data warehouse, 169–70
Decathlon (learning extravaganza), 107–8
decisions, critical, 156
deduction, science of, 187
Dell, Michael, 261
demotion, routes to, 129–30
departments, as natural barriers, 138–39
dependability, 103–4
dependency, elimination of, 153
deregulation, xiii, 147–49
detail, attention to, 200
Diagnostic Consulting, 166
diagnostics, 203–4
Dickinson, North Dakota, 214
dinosaurs, avoiding, 137–38
discontinuous thinking, 133
Disney Company, 106–7
diversity, 38–40
Dobbs, Lou, 257
Doctor, The (film), 73
downsizing, 136–37, 141
Dream Machine, The, 180–81
dress, business casual, 21
Du Pont Corporation, 150

eCLIPSE, 178–79, 261, 263
e-commerce, 40–42, 189
eCRM tools, 163–64, 167
ego-buster exercises, 49
egotists, 46–47
Eighth Air Force, 77
electronic marketplace, 122
elegance, definition of, 99
elegant language, 99, 100, 102
elegant service, 99
  achieving excellence via, 157
  creation of, 5–6

e-mail:
  booking via, 159
  Quick Connections, 17
  service delivery via, 164
  wide use of, 164
"emotional commerce," 40–42
employees:
  avoiding the word, 99
  see also associates
Engagement Study, 44–45
entrepreneurial spirit,
    encouragement of, 118, 133
epicenters of thought, 155
epilogue, 225–64
eRFP/RFQ technology, 179, 204
e-rooms, 205
ERP (Oracle Enterprise Resource
    Planning) system, 169
errors, learning from, 23–25
ethics, code of, 103–4
e-tickets, 167, 168
excess baggage, elimination of, 137, 142
executive assessments, 32–33
executive commitment, 43
executive ranch, 107
exit interviews, 45–46
expansion:
  global, 153–56
  planning for, 149
expectations, exceeding, 99
external pressure, 140–41

face-to-face meetings, 111–12
fairness, 43
faith, 195
familiarization trips (FAMs), 21–22
"family responsibility" policy, 140
Fargo, North Dakota, 214
Fast Company, 216
Federal Express, 109
feedback, 15–17, 137
fence-building project, 49–50, 217
"Fifties Day," 107

fig leaves, lack of, 195–96
flexibility:
    in accordion-style management,
        141–43
    in cross-pollination, 140
    in globalization, 155
    in learning, 56–57
    mental, 47–48
    need for, 188
    in retention, 43
    in rural communities, 214
FOCOS (Fundamentals of
    Corporate Operational
    Standards), 61
focus groups, 139–40, 166
Ford, Henry, 117
forecasting, 186–88, 204, 223
Fortune, 36
Forum on Workforce Engagement,
    44
foster leaders, 112
foundation, building happiness
    into, 25–26
"free agent" attitude, 42
freeloaders, 47
front-room systems, 151, 159–66
Frost, Robert, 104
"Full-Contact Poker," 108
fun:
    as measurement of success, 106–8
    as official strategy, 108, 221
"Fundamentals of Corporate
    Operational Standards"
    (FOCOS), 61
future:
    critical decisions for, 156
    on cutting edge of, 187
    deregulation, 147–49
    forecasting, 186–88, 204, 223
    global expansion, 153–56
    growth without gambling, 150
    independence, 151–53
    inventing, 145, 222–23
    preparing now for, 190–92

reshaping for growth, 149
    summary, 156
    theories about, 192

gardening process, 128–44, 222
    accordion-style management,
        140–41
    Chutes and Ladders, 129–30
    cross-pollination, 139–40
    dismantling compartments,
        138–39, 142
    flexibility, 141–43
    leader reviews, 134–36
    lipomanagement, 136–37
    movement and change, 137–38
    summary, 143–44
    watching associates'
        contributions, 130–31
    weeding out, 128–29
    zero-based business, 132–33
"Gathering, The" (library), 105
Gergen, David, 251
germination, of ideas, 125–26
Global Distribution Systems (GDS),
    160, 162
global expansion, 153–56
global implementation plan, 154
Global Professional Development
    Program, 112
Global Security Suite, 175–76, 261
Global Solutions Architecture,
    173–74
global standardization, 155
grandstanding, elimination of,
    130–31
"Green Vegetables" exercise, 49
group travel rates, 168
growth:
    client-driven, 123–24, 150
    globalization, 153–56
    going national, 150
    planning for, 149
    without gambling, 150
Gulf War, 81–82, 143

Hammerstein, Oscar, 194
Hand, Jen, 229
handshake relationships, 194
happiness, 7–27, 221
    accessible leadership, 10–11
    Ambassador's Council, 13–14
    Ask Us Anything, 13, 15–17
    Associate Assistance Program,
        19
    Associate of the Day, 11–12
    Associate Opinion Poll, 15
    barometer of, 14
    as culture, *see* corporate culture
    familiarization trips, 21–22
    foundation of, 25–26
    jeans days, 21
    learning from mistakes, 23–25
    and lifestyle, 17–18
    measurement of, 13–14
    of middle-level leaders, 12–13
    Operation SAFE, 19–20
    people-first philosophy, 9–10
    Quick Connections, 17
    scrapbooks, 22
    summary, 26–27, 113–14
    Town Hall Meetings, 16–17
    as ultimate technology tool,
        179–80
    work-life rhythm, 18–19
    WorldWide Leaders Meeting,
        13
harmony, with local community,
    155
Harvard Business Review, 133
Hemingway, Ernest, 116–17
hiring process:
    assessment in, 41–42
    attracting applicants, 36–38
    speed in, 41
    as team building, 41
holistic approach, 18–19
Holliday, Charles, 261
honesty, 195
Horace, 217

*100 Best Companies to Work for in
    America, The* (Levering and
    Moskowitz), 36, 53

ideas, 115–27, 222
    creating an environment for,
        116–19
    creating through self-
        improvement, 121
    curiosity leading to, 116
    definitions of, 116
    epicenters of thought, 155
    filling market need, 121–22
    freedom for creating, 176–77
    generating, 124–25
    germinating, 125–26
    innovating through social
        responsibility, 120
    local generation of, 155
    problem solving, 123–24
    sharing of, 126
    sources of, 119–20
    summary, 126–27
    in system design, 121
    testing, 125–26
    wider focus of, 124–25
    as works in progress, 223
if/then logic, 187
implementation, 205
incentive awards program, 88–89
incentives, financial, 101
independence, 151–53, 168
India, Rosenbluth presence in,
    263
Individual Development Plans,
    56–57
individual traveler, personal
    preferences of, 161
infinity, illustration of, 95
information:
    for client reports, 161
    control of, 152
    generation of, 163
    in knowledge economy, 165

information (*cont.*)
    management of, 148, 205
    on market share movements, 155
    power of, 172–73
    provided to clients, 163, 165,
        167, 198
    provided to suppliers, 198
information systems:
    back room, 168–81
    front room, 159–66
    integrating with clients, 170–71
    middle room, 166–68
initiatives, recommended, 204
innovation, *see* ideas
inspiration, sources of, 117
Intellicenters, 89, 149, 189, 214–15
interaction, learning through, 54
Internet:
    as communication platform, 162
    market support needed for, 189
    voice over IP, 164
    web-based client reports on, 162
    web collaboration, 164
interviewing techniques, 31–32
inventing the future, 145, 222–23
inverted pyramid management
      style, 98
Investors in People award, 36
iVISION @Rosenbluth, 170

Jacob, Max, 100
Jamestown, North Dakota, 215
Jangula, Levi, 253–57, 259
Jangula, Sharon and Larry, 254–57
jeans days, 21
job analysis, 34
job description, and performance
      appraisal, 131
job fairs, 38
job-hopping, 42
job market, attracting applicants in,
    36–38
job postings, internal, 37–38
Jupiter Communications, 189

Kanoo Travel, 81–82
karaoke session, 107
key functional areas, 133
Killarney, Ireland, 214, 216–17
"Kindergarten Principle, The,"
    54–55, 107
knowledge economy, 165
Kuwait, Chevron in, 81–82

labor force, shrinking, 211–12
language, elegant, 99, 100, 102
layoffs:
    avoidance of, 141
    lipomanagement vs., 136–37
    temporary furloughs, 20, 237–46
Leader Review by Direct Reports,
    134–36
leaders, corporate:
    accessibility of, 10–11
    assessments of, 32–33
    and Associate of the Day, 11–12
    evaluations of, 134–36
    foster, 112
    hiring requests reviewed by, 142
    in learning, 56–57
    middle-level, 12–13
    monetary gifts from, 263
    Pre-Leadership program, 60
    requests for visits from, 16
    selecting, 31
    September 11 testing of, 226–27,
      231, 247
    skill categories of, 135
    Team Leader Training, 60–61
    tea served by, 4–5
    "Walk in My Shoes" program of,
      119
"Leadership at Rosenbluth," 62
"Leadership Development"
    program, 62–64
learning, 53–72
    broad-based, 54–55
    by challenge, 66–68
    coaching, 65–66

extravaganzas of, 107–8
fluid, 56–57
as fun, 107
Global Professional Development
    Program, 112
investment in, 69–70
kindergarten principle of, 54–55,
    107
leader in, 56–57
Lunchtime Learning, 58–59
from mistakes, 23–25, 158
on-line, 68
perpetual, 222
philosophical training programs,
    55–56
from product failure, 158–59
seminars, 57–59
summary, 70–72
technical training, 64–65
through interaction, 54
trainers for, 68–69
training sampler, 59–64
Transitional Learning Center,
    66
Learning and Development team,
    68
Levering, Robert, 36
library, corporate, 105
lifestyles, 17–19
Linton, North Dakota, 210–11, 214,
    217, 219
lipomanagement, 136–37
listening skills, 187, 188
"Live the Spirit," 98–99, 103
Livingstone, David, 194
Lunchtime Learning, 58–59

Malcolm Baldrige National Quality
    Award, 85
management style:
    accordion, 140–43
    inverted pyramid, 98
    lipomanagement, 136–37
    Santa Claus, 130–31

marginal performance, elimination
    of, 136–37
marketing, 204
market need:
    filling, 121–22
    global, 154
markets, core, 155
Marriott, Bill, 252
mascot (salmon), 98, 104–5
Matthews, Chris, 251
Measurement, see assessment
Memphis Belle (bomber), 77
mental safety net, 75–76
merit increases, 131
merit promotions, 136
Middle East, Kanoo Travel in, 81–82
middle-level leaders, 12–13
middle-room systems, 166–68
Mineta, Norman, 240
mission statement, 98, 102
mistakes:
    costs of, 34
    learning from, 23–25, 158
    success built from, 75
Monet, Claude, 117
morale boosters, 111
Moskowitz, Milton, 36
movement:
    and change, 137–38
    in cross-pollination, 139–40
    of resources, 142
multinationals, 153
muses, encouragement of, 117
musical chairs, 108
mytravelbid.com, 122

National Airlines, 190, 214
network/call center management,
    189
Network Operations Center, 106,
    229
New Associate Follow-Up
    Questionnaire, 46
Newton, Sir Isaac, 186

nonproductive programs,
    elimination of, 136
North Dakota:
    Intellicenters in, *see* rural
        communities
    September 11 support from, 242
    strategic meetings in, 217–18
    "The Rivery" in, 218
nudist colony, 195–96

objectives, zero-based, 132
observation, art of, 187
officers, afternoon tea served by, 4–5
office scrapbooks, 22
Olympiad (learning extravaganza),
    107
On Achieving Excellence (Peters), 157
"One World, One Company," 231
on-line booking system, 158
on-line chat, 164
on-line learning, 68
open communication, 187
open culture, 48
open meeting policy, 106
open partnerships, 194–208, 223
    accessibility in, 204–6
    client visits in, 201
    corporate marriage as, 170, 202–3
    diagnostics in, 203–4
    neat office in, 200–201
    nudism in, 195–96
    reciprocity in, 196
    summary, 206–8
    supporting your clients, 199
    three R's in, 206
    three-way, 197–98
    at world headquarters, 201–2
"Open skies: Open minds," 218
Operation Brain Storm, 143
Operation SAFE, 19–20
Oracle Database, 176
Oracle Enterprise Resource Planning
    (ERP) system, 169
organizational chart, flat, 18

orientation:
    core, 5
    first impressions in, 221
    for new associates, 3–6, 64
    summary, 6

Paige, Leroy "Satchel," 186
partnerships:
    balanced, 151
    dependency in, 153
    faithful, 195
    open, 170, 194–208, 223
    people exchange in, 202–3
    RIA, 153, 154, 155
    three-way, 152–53, 197–98
    trust in, 195, 202
pay freeze, 143
payroll updates, 170
"Peace, Love, and Presentations,"
    108
Pentagon, Washington, 231
pentimento, 100–101
people, 28–52, 221–22
    attracting, 36–38
    bad fit of companies and, 34
    best, 30–31
    commitment of, 101
    as competitive measure, 21–23
    depth of, 101
    diverse backgrounds of, 38–40
    eliminating arrogance in, 49–50
    in emotional commerce, 40–42
    exchange of, 202–3
    in farm communities, *see* rural
        communities
    focus on, 9–10, 36, 97, 179–80
    giving space to, 74–76
    interviewing of, 31–32
    matching with their stories, 110
    nice, 28–29
    nurturing of, 42–43
    ongoing need for, 211–12
    and open culture, 48
    personality types to avoid, 46–48

power of, 1
retention of, 42–46, 142
at Rosenbluth, *see* associates
selecting, 31–36
summary, 51–52
temporary help, 123–24
true colors of, 100
watching contributions of,
    130–31
weeding out, 128–29
pep rallies, 108
"Perception vs. Reality," 58
perfection, as goal, 94
performance appraisal system, 131
Performance Incentive Plan, 88–89
performance measurements,
    objective, 131
perpetual learning, 222
Personal Digital Assistant (PDA),
    175
personality, in corporate culture,
    105
personality types, 46–48
Peters, Tom, 113, 157
philosophical training, 55–56
Plato, 191
political animals, 46
politics, elimination of, 130–31,
    136
pomposity, conquering, 49–50
population, aging, 211–12
positioning, 131
Poussin, Nicolas, 209
Pre-Leadership program, 60
problem solving, 123–24
process, 74, 82–95
    assessment in, 89–91
    building a quality program,
        86–88
    building in quality, 82–83
    continuous improvement, 85
    guaranteeing service, 92–94
    incentive program, 88–89
    infinity in, 95

perfection as goal in, 94
quality control, 83
quality research lab, 84–85
summary, 95–96
tailoring a quality program, 84
Product Development eRoom, 173
productivity, 131, 141, 201
product management team, 158
profile creation process, 34
promotion from within, 37–38,
    68–69, 142
proprietary software, 151, 157, 162
"push" technology, 163

quality, 82–88
    automated assurance, 166–68
    Baldrige Award of, 85
    building a program of, 86–88
    continuous improvement for, 85
    description of, 87
    involvement in, 196
    measurement of, 89–91
    research lab, 84–85
    rewards for, 88–89
    tailoring a program of, 84
    third-party audits of, 91
    training for, 86
    up front, 82–83
    video-wall statistics of, 106
quality champions, 87
quality control, 83
quality of life, 101, 105
quality team, 86
Quick Connections, 17

RAPID, 162, 179
REACHOUT, 158–59
READOUT, 151, 160
reciprocity, 196
recognition systems, 109, 129
recruitment, 34, 41
re-engineering, 133
referrals, 37, 206
relationships, 206

relaxation exercise, 64
remote control, uses for, 128
"Renew for the New Year" program,
    118–19
reputation, 101, 206
Res-Check, 162
research, in quality lab, 84–85
research and development lab, 174
reservation center, 149
reservations process, 160–62, 214
    client travel policy, 161
    individual travel preferences, 161
    information for client reports,
        161
reserve corps, 123–24
Res-Monitor, 162
resources:
    movement of, 142
    sharing of, 138–39
retention, 42–46
    assessment of, 43–46
    communication and, 43
    Engagement Study, 44–45
    fairness in, 43
    flexibility in, 43
    promotion from within, 37–38,
        142
    30–60–90 day reviews, 44, 45–46
right stuff, selecting, 33–36
risk management, 167
Ritz-Carlton hotels, 102, 218
Riverplace (world headquarters),
    106
Rivery, The, 218
rock-climbing events, 108
ROCS, 179
Rodgers, Richard, 194
role models:
    negative, xii–xiii
    positive, 129
Roosevelt, Franklin D., 228
Rosenbluth, Joseph, 115
Rosenbluth, Marcus, xi
Rosenbluth Everywhere, 174–75

Rosenbluth International:
    accessibility in, 204–6, 224
    associates' drawings of, 7–8
    client-driven growth of, 123–24,
        150
    client support in, 199
    culture of, see corporate culture
    founding of, xi
    going public, 17
    independence of, 151–53, 168
    leadership in, see leaders
    neat offices in, 200–201
    officers of, see officers
    organizational chart of, 18
    people-first philosophy of, 9–10,
        36, 97, 179–80
    as privately held company, xvi
    redesign of, 133
    reservation center of, 149
    and September 11, see September
        11 attacks
    Service Company of the Year, 113
    turning points in, xiv–xv, 150,
        264
    Volunteer Days, 110
    who we are, xv–xvi
    world headquarters of, 106,
        201–2, 205
    world presence of, 155
Rosenbluth International Alliance
    (RIA), 153, 154, 155
Rosenbluth Mobile, 175
Rosenbluth reserve corps, 123–24
Rosenbluth University on-line, 68
rural communities, 223
    alternative labor sources in, 212
    customer care centers in, 120,
        209–11, 219
    farming and business in, 212–13
    fence-building in, 49–50, 217
    financial benefits of offices in, 211
    human resources in, 212
    international, 216–17
    invitations from, 218–19

meeting facilities in, 217–18
opportunities in, 218–19
permanent roots in, 213–15
satellite locations in, 215
summary, 220
terrific people in, 215–16
24/7 environments in, 214
Russell, Frances, 78–80

SAFE, Operation, 19–20
Saint-Exupéry, Antoine de, 132
sales:
    business development, 204, 205
    openness in process of, 196
    and productivity, 141–42
salmon (corporate mascot), 98,
    104–5
salmon pins, 109
Santa Claus management style,
    130–31
scavenger hunts, 107
scrapbooks, company, 22
seasonal staffing demands, 123
security, 91, 249, 261
selection, 31–36
self-improvement, 121
September 11 attacks, 225–64
    author's Washington lobbying
        following, 248–49, 250–53,
        256, 258, 259
    Biztravel closed as result of, 92
    client support after, 243–44,
        245–46
    company response to, 226–27,
        229–30
    fear, 228, 230, 232, 238, 251,
        261
    fighting back, 246–50
    furloughs rescinded after, 249,
        258, 262, 263
    furloughs resulting from, 20,
        237–46
    and Global Security Suite,
        175–76, 261
    initial cutbacks following,
        232–36
    initial letter following, 227–31
    perspective letter, 260–61
    recovery from, 250–64
    reprisals to, 228–29
    silent heroes of, 230
    travel curtailed after, 230, 232,
        240
    welcome back letter, 258
serendipity, 209
service, 73–96, 222
    art of, 74, 78–82
    aspiring to perfection in, 94
    attitude in, 74, 75–78
    automation, 205
    award-winning, 189
    communicating, 102
    to community, 120
    critical components of, 155
    deregulation as opportunity for,
        148
    elegant, 5–6, 99, 157
    enhancers of, 160–62
    exceeding expectations in, 99
    formula for, 74
    guarantees of, 92–94
    heroes of, 78–80
    implementation of, 205
    incentive program for, 88–89
    infinity of, 95
    intangibles of, 55
    measures of, 89–91
    mental safety net, 75–76
    philosophy of, 55–56
    process of, 74, 82–95
    quality in, 82–88, 196
    remaining busied in, 76–78
    summary, 95–96
    teamwork in, 78
    technology for, see technology
Service Company of the Year,
    113
Service Day, 113

shadowing, "Walk in My Shoes,"
119
short-term assignments, 112
sincerity, 100, 103–4
"Site Visits of Terror," 108
social responsibility, innovation in,
120
software:
    build or buy?, 166–68
    proprietary, 151, 157, 162
software design, 121
Source, The, 204–6
sports, teamwork in, 78
standardization, global, 155
Stanley, Sir Henry Morgan, 194
storytelling competition, 107–8
Strategic Markets group, 155
stress busters, 160–72
stress management programs,
57–58
success, fun as measure of, 106–8
suggestions, 16
summaries:
    corporate culture, 113–14
    critical decisions (future), 156
    cultivating happiness, 26–27,
    113–14
    encouraging ideas, 126–27
    finding the right people, 51–52
    gardening process, 143–44
    looking around you and ahead,
    192–93
    open partnerships, 206–8
    rural route, 220
    service, 95–96
    starting out right (orientation), 6
    technology tips, 181–83
    training tips, 70–72
Sun Also Rises, The (Hemingway),
117
Sun Solaris hardware, 176
supplier relationships, 196,
197–98
swimming upstream, 104–5

synergy, 49
system design, creativity in, 121

talent contests, 107
team building, 41
    busied in/busied out, 76–78
    code of ethics in, 103–4
    and performance appraisal, 131
    in sports, 78
    synergy in, 49
    through farm work, 213
team leaders (TLs), 60–61
Team Leader Training, 60–61
technical training, 64–65
technology, 157–83, 223
    automated quality assurance,
    166–68
    back-room systems, 168–81
    build or buy?, 166–68
    as company hero, 180–81
    corporate marriage in, 170–71
    creativity and, 176–77
    customization of, 159
    DACODA, 177–78
    data warehouse, 169–70
    delivering value in, 160
    development delays in, 180
    eCLIPSE, 178–79
    end-to-end package of, 179, 189
    front-room systems, 159–66
    happiness and, 179–80
    in the knowledge economy, 165
    middle-room systems, 166–68
    portal, 176
    positive impact of, 172–73
    power of information, 172–73
    progress and, 174–76
    "push," 163
    research and development lab,
    174
    service enhancers, 160–62
    sharing capabilities in, 171–72
    summary, 181–83
    translations, 173–74

as two-way street, 166
updates in, 162–64
VISION, 169–70
web collaboration, 164
wireless, 175
telecommuting, 118
telephone:
  answering, 99
  caller ID, 103
  "smiling" while using, 108
  voicemail, 15, 204–5
temporary help:
  need for, 123–24
  work done by, 210
Thales, 191
30-60-90 day reviews, 44, 45–46
third-party audits, 91
"thought centers," 106
Thought Theatre, 227
Three R's, foundation of, 206
three-way partnerships, 152–53,
  197–98
Town Hall Meetings, 16–17
trainers, promotion from within,
  68–69
training:
  by challenge, 66–68
  coaching, 65–66
  costs of, 25, 69–70
  cross-pollination, 139–40,
    142
  follow-up, 102
  Individual Development Plans
    for, 56–57
  as long-term investment, 69
  necessity of, 55
  on-line, 68
  perpetual, 222
  philosophical programs of,
    55–56
  Pre-Leadership, 60
  program sampler, 59–64
  for quality, 86
  summary, 70–72

technical, 64–65
see also learning
Transitional Learning Center (TLC),
  66
transition plan, 185
translation, 173–74
travel, as end product, 196
travel agency commissions,
  197
traveler satisfaction, measurement
  of, 90–91
travel management, pre-trip,
  167
travel vertical, 190
trends, forecasting, 187–88
trust, 195, 202, 218, 232
turnover:
  economic impact of, 101–2,
    179–80
  employee, 42

unemployment, 42
unhappiness:
  error rate as sign of, 24
  uprooting, 23–25
  see also happiness
United Airlines, UAL.com, 190,
  214
Up-Stream, 188–90, 198, 214, 215,
  260–61, 263
US Airways Cargo service, 190,
  214

value-adding activities, 130–31
values, corporate, 98
video-wall, quality statistics on, 106
"Virtual Golf," 108
VISION, 169–70, 172–73
VISION @Rosenbluth, 170
VISION Consolidator, 170, 172
voicemail:
  Ask Us Anything, 15–17
  frustration of, 204–5
voice over IP, 164

voluntary time off, 143
Volunteer Days, 110

"Walk in My Shoes," 119
web accessibility, 205
web collaboration, 164
web supersite, 174–75
weekend thinking, 126
Williston, North Dakota, 214
wireless travel solution, 175
work ethic, 103

Working Woman, 10
work-life rhythm, 18–19
work-life station, 105
World Trade Center, New York, 226, 230, 231
WorldWide Leaders Meeting, 13

your turn, 223–24
Yusuf Bin Ahmed Kanoo group, 81

zero-based business, 132–33